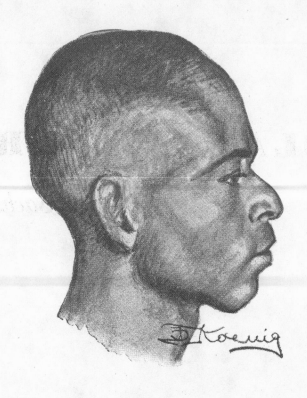

John Chavafambira, *nganga*

BLACK ANGER

by Wulf Sachs

GREENWOOD PRESS, PUBLISHERS
NEW YORK   1968

For

BRENDA

and

MARTIN

CONTENTS

PART ONE

Memories of the Past

I

HE HAD LIVED in South Africa all his life. "So," he said to me, "you are going to settle in Johannesburg. Well — here's the best advice I can give you. Leave your ideas in Europe. You're going among blacks — gentle, happy savages — children, children who never grow beyond the age of ten or twelve. So, if you have any notion of treating them as equals, forget about it."

The Johannesburgers talked in a similar vein. Their attitude toward the blacks was as irrational, fraught with such blind fear and hostility that argument was useless. I saw I would get nowhere with the whites. There was only one other way. I would get to know the blacks, not as blacks but as human beings. I first began to study them seriously in connection with my work at a mental hospital for blacks. I discovered that insanity in its form, content and causation is identical in both blacks and whites.

This discovery made me eager to investigate the inner workings of the black man's mind in its normal state, to learn whether the emotional undercurrents and overtones of his thinking and feeling were not also identical with the white man's.

I had difficulties in approaching this problem, for many reasons. To begin with, it was not easy to find a native who would be willing to become the object of a deep and pro-

3

tracted psychoanalytical study. Africans could be found who were willing to subject themselves to various psychological experiments such as mental tests; but examinations such as these have been carried out many times, without, in my opinion, leading to any appreciable understanding of the black man. Every psychologist knows now that a mere collecting of answers to questions submitted does not give an insight into the mind. I believe that under no circumstances can a knowledge of human beings be obtained merely from a superficial observation of a limited number of people. Only a probing into the depths of the human mind, into the wide range of desires, conflicts, strivings, contradictory and confusing, can give understanding. And if this applies to the study of those whose language, habits, and daily life are identical with ours, how much more careful must we be in dealing with those who live in entirely different surroundings, who are strangers to us, and whom we approach usually with either masked hostility or unconscious aversion, or with sentimental idealization and studied friendliness.

What I sought, therefore, was a native who would speak to me freely, as if he were thinking aloud, and so enable me to watch the building up of free associations and his reactions to them. By a fortunate chance, I got in touch with an ordinary African, a witch doctor, whom I shall call John Chavafambira, who had lived for a number of years in Johannesburg.

The fact that John was a witch doctor added interest to my study. At that time a witch doctor was to me a romantically mysterious figure. I thought of witches, witchcraft, and witch doctors in the confused manner of many white people, who imagine them to possess supernatural powers over good and evil. But actually, this was by no means the

4

case, as will be apparent from the story of this man's life. John was an ordinary medicine man, known among his people as a *nganga;* in our terms, a diviner and herbalist. He told fortunes, gave medicines to guard against diseases and to counteract bad luck; he inherited his profession from his forefathers, and his sole ambition was to devote his life to helping other people. As he would often tell me: "There is such a lot of trouble among our people; such a lot of jealousy and poisoning. They need therefore help from a good doctor. And this cleverness in medicine can only come from the father. All my fathers [forefathers] were very clever *ngangas.*"

My introduction to him came through a woman anthropologist who for months had been collecting sociological information in Swartyard, where John lived. She had discovered that John's wife was suffering excruciating pain in her legs, and I was called in to help. John, rather shyly, and speaking hesitatingly and apologetically, remarked that his own medicines did not appear to help her and suggested that some powerful poisoner must be working against him, or else that her disease was the result of living among white people, in which case his medicines would be of no avail. "I hear that you are a famous doctor," he added. "Please help my wife. She suffers so much."

As luck had it, I was successful; and one day when she was a good deal better I remained longer than usual in their tiny room and began a conversation with him on diseases, their causes and treatment, speaking to him as one doctor to another. He was obviously flattered. And when I expressed my willingness to explain the white man's methods of treatment, his interest grew.

"In order to become a good doctor," I told him finally, "one must have a good understanding of people. One must

5

know what they think, what they wish to do, why they are unhappy . . ." He nodded in agreement. Encouraged, I continued: "But to know others, you must first know something of yourself." And I explained to him, in a simple way, the essence of the unconscious. He was, no less than white people, surprised by the possibility that there were things in him of which he himself was not aware. "We doctors," he said, "can know everything through the bones, or through talking with our *midzimu* [ancestral spirits]. But it is true that I cannot throw the bones for myself." I seized this opportunity to elaborate upon the subject; and when I offered to help him discover this hidden part of himself, he accepted willingly.

I found out later, however, that he did not believe in my ability to do this, and that what really prompted him to come to me was his desire to learn the white man's medicine, so that he could best his professional competitors, Uncle Charlie and Cousin Nathan, on his return to the kraal.

I arranged for him to come early in the morning to my consulting room in town, within ten minutes' walking distance of Swartyard. This was an important and favorable point, avoiding the necessity of his taking the native bus, which would have meant my giving him money for fares. Giving him money had, above all, in the beginning to be avoided. I knew that the majority of informants were paid by the research workers, and I always doubted the value of material thus obtained. In my case, it would have been disastrous to introduce money into our relationship. Our work had to be carried out in an atmosphere of friendliness and mutual interest: a kind of interchange of medical knowledge. For the final success of my studies, it was essential that John

6

should become so attached to me that he would be willing to give me information, not sell it. And even when he fell into bad times later on, I never gave him money directly, but through a third person.

I carried out my studies of him chiefly by the classical method of free associations. He came every day for an hour at a time, lay down on the sofa, and was asked to say whatever came into his mind. Contrary to the usual analytical practice, I wrote down whatever he said in his actual phrases and in their actual sequences. I was surprised at his quick grasp of what was wanted of him, and how freely he would talk to me. These talks lasted, with a few interruptions, over a period of two and a half years. During that time I went out with him to practically every place he spoke of and talked to most of the persons he mentioned. I even went out as far as his kraal in Southern Rhodesia, where I met his family.

I am telling John's story in normal English, as opposed to the broken though fluent speech in which it was told to me. Nevertheless, it is John's story, unaltered in its essence. The reader may doubt the truth of some of the events related: I often doubted it myself; but a fantasy of the human mind is just as interesting to us as the realities of life, for it gives perhaps even more insight into the nature of the man than actual events for which he may not even be responsible. For example, the fact that a man talks continually of flying is obviously more important than the fact that he has once or twice flown in an aeroplane. John was also telling deliberate lies (and quite a number of them), especially during the first two or three months of our association. For instance, he denied that he was practising as a doctor, and that he threw bones. The reason for this was simply that he was afraid of

7

me. In other instances, he lied for reasons common to all of us — to boast and to impress.

But in fairness to John I must add that when I visited the kraals and various other places he had described to me, I was astonished at how accurate were his memories of the past.

8

II

JOHN arrived punctually on the morning of the first day. I shook hands with him, and inquired about his and his wife's health. This extraordinary concession made him at once uncomfortable. He quickly withdrew his hand with an apologetic glance. I was uncomfortable, too. For the first time in my life, I had to treat a black man as my equal, and my greeting was obviously artificial.

I let him settle down. He looked around the room. The laboratory table in the far corner attracted most of his attention. Then he went over to the case of medical instruments. He passed over the shelves of books and the desk with its litter of papers, for these were familiar to him from his work as a domestic servant in European houses. The sofa was in one corner and screened off from the rest of the room, and presently I asked him to lie down on this. My chair was just behind it. Needless to say, the room was not darkened, nor did I use any other hypnotic tricks of persuasion. From the beginning it was clear to me that John was not a patient to be treated for some mental disturbance, but a subject for study. I was eager to discover just what was going on in John's mind, and therefore it was important that I should remain in the shadow, for I knew from experience how easy it is to influence a person's mind into giving the answer expected. To begin with, I asked him as few questions as possible, and then merely when it was essential for the understanding of what he told me. But for the most part I preferred to wait until the truth emerged from among confused or contradictory statements. On the whole, I succeeded in making him take the initiative himself in the choice of material.

On this first day he began his story at the point where he had left his native kraal — his village near Rusapi, in Manyikaland, Southern Rhodesia — for the Union of South Africa. The choice of this beginning was significant, for it was a turning-point in his life. It had occurred ten years previously. He was a young man of about twenty (he could not definitely state his age) when he left the kraal to seek a new life among new people. "Not that it was bad in Manyikaland," he told me; but he wished to cut himself adrift from Charlie, his uncle and present father, who was greedy and selfish.

His real father, Chavafambira, had died when John was a baby, and his mother, Nesta, had married the husband's younger brother, Charlie, as was the tradition of the tribe.

John had no money for train fares, and so he walked the 700 miles from Manyikaland to the borders of the Union. There his bad luck began. He was certain that it was his meeting with a strange old man that was responsible for his future misfortunes.

"It was very hot, and dusty, and I was so tired when I came to the police station in the Union. I walked already for seven days on this hard dry earth, the burning sun always on my head. Have you been in those parts, Doctor?" He turned to me. I nodded. "Then you know how hot it is. I couldn't find any shadow. I couldn't see a tree. Only a long road without an end in front of me. And when I turned one side or another there was nothing but dry veld. Like dead.

10

Then I suddenly noticed a body lying at the side of the road. I quickly went towards it and saw that a man was dying. I got a fright. What shall I do with an old dying man? But I was a doctor. I must help. But Charlie told me not to practise the medicine. So I was kneeling beside the man thinking, what shall I do? At last I opened his mouth and pushed in some medicine which I had on me. The Rhodesian medicines are very strong. At once the old man opened his eyes and looked at me. He whispered: 'I am dying. I am old. I wish to die. But not here so far away from my kraal, or my spirit will wander forever.'"

In answer to my question, John explained that when a man dies his spirit passes from his body, through his mouth, and straightway makes for the place wherein it existed during the man's lifetime. But if a man dies unburied, in the bush, in the water, or in the enemy's camp, the spirit wanders about, lost and forever doomed to wander. Such a possibility is dreaded by every African.

John consoled the man, telling him that he was a *nganga,* son of the famous Chavafambira, the son of Gwerere, the family of famous doctors. "My father's father was a chief and made guns. He was the *nganga* of our big chief Mutassa," he proudly told me.

It seemed to John that the old man must have been feigning illness before, so rapidly did this statement revive his strength and hopes, and he begged John now to save the people in his kraal.

2

FOR days afterwards, John continued with this story, telling it with full detail and amazing description. I listened, astonished at hearing such a strange tale from an ordinary African native; and even now I cannot help wondering how much of it was fiction.

He had regretted his conversation with the old man, for it had placed him in a dilemma, since he had already given a vow to Charlie that he would not practise medicine until he had reached a more mature age. But the old man's story was so pitiful. There had been no rain for three years in his kraal, the people were starving, the cattle dying. . . . Three years without rain! John thought — Three years with spring days as hot as this! . . . Gradually the old man regained his strength sufficiently to stand erect, and then, with John's assistance, he led him to the kraal.

The place made an unfavorable impression on John.

"The huts stood dirty and disorderly. They looked peculiar, they gave me a pain in the heart. Were they so old; or did the people make them such funny shapes? The little children were few, and they looked so dirty and without life. It was unusual," John emphasized; "our kraals are always buzzing with babies. I stood for a time with the old man, when people began to crawl out. And they looked at me . . . like man-eaters. I stood and looked at these poor, ill, unfortunate men and women, and I wondered if their troubles were due entirely to drought and starvation. Perhaps they prayed to the wrong god, maybe they were Christians and forgot their dead people. Were they at peace with their *midzimu?* Had they killed the goats to them? I wanted to ask them this, but I couldn't."

Involuntarily, I studied John's well-nourished body as he told me this, and visualized the contrast he must have presented to the physical degradation of those people. John is nearly six feet tall, with well-formed muscles rippling under the firm texture of his smooth purple-black skin; the modeling of his head strong to the point of grimness; the nose like the flattened beak of a hawk, and the mouth, thick and sensual, typical of his race.

The old man explained to the people that the Manyika doctor would smell out the evil one who had bewitched the kraal. At this, the crowd stared suspiciously at John. He felt uneasy. He was again tortured with indecision. Why had he let this stranger divert him from his original plan? An old man crept towards him and feebly patted his foot, stretching out an appealing hand to him. Everybody waited, hushed and still. John felt that he had never been in such a difficult position before. His heart was heavy within him. "I was sure that it was bad luck that had brought me to this bewitched kraal. Was I also in danger of being bewitched? But I had medicine in my calabash to protect me. I was thinking, Should I disobey my father and help these unfortunate people? It was difficult to decide, Doctor," he exclaimed, getting up from the sofa. I agreed that it must have been, but said no more.

He felt that he had no right to break the tradition of his fathers. He made up his mind. He was too young to practise, his father had said; for in the young the lust of the body made the calling dangerous. The sweet firm outline of a young girl's breast might cause him to betray his trust. A young man, in anger, might use his medicines to kill and not to cure. He remembered clearly his father's words: "For the young to learn; for the mature to practise."

13

But the sight of these people, standing in expectance, starved, emaciated, and the children apathetic and on the verge of collapse, made a stronger appeal to him than that of professional tradition. He agreed to do the smoking-out.

3

LATE that night he performed the first part of the ritual. He went down to the thin trickle of water that in the rainy season would be a river and washed from head to foot, as the law of his profession demanded. He was unable to explain to me the reason for this cleansing; as so many other rites connected with his profession, he did this unquestioningly, simply because it was prescribed by his ancestors.

It was a pitch-dark night. The kraal was deserted, its people huddled in the huts. They dared not come out; a witch, an evil spirit, had poisoned the kraal. John tried to convey to me the tragedy of bewitched people. They are suspicious of their very selves. The witch could be one's daughter, wife, or concubine. She might be lying with one in the same blanket. The feeling of doubt and suspicion gnaws at everybody's mind. They want to find out who the witch may be, and yet at the same time they fear to know who is the woman who has poisoned the children, dried the rains, and killed the cattle. John was sure that these people disliked him because he was a Manyika doctor, a foreigner who would make them his debtors.

Outside, he carried on his work. He had with him a clean child, a six-year-old boy. "It must be a young child," he asserted; "one who has not yet sinned against Mwari, our god."

14

Both John and the child were naked. They paced to and fro around the kraal, softly and secretly so that the witch should not be aware of their activities. (Even after my comment, John could not see the contradiction between this secrecy and the belief that the witch is omniscient.) John carried a small bag of rock rabbit skin, very smooth to the touch. In this lay the horn containing the medicines: the roots carefully dug, the powdered leaves sedulously prepared, the skillfully mixed fats of animals. First, John put a little of the oil from the horn on his forehead, and then put some on the boy. The oil was to make them immune from the *murowi*, the *umthakathi*, as the people of the Transvaal call the witch. Next, he took his buffalo-tail and splashed the oil on his foot and on the foot of the child. Should the *umthakathi* come in the form of a cat or a baboon, he and the child would be able to stand their ground, secure in this protection.

The child then sprinkled water round the huts. John stood still. He was talking inwardly to his family *midzimu*, to his father's, Chavafambira's, spirit. "You cannot talk to spirits in the ordinary way," he explained to me. "You just talk in a hum, with your lips hardly moving, so that no one can notice your talk." And the father soon spoke to him from within himself. (John feels his father right inside himself when he talks to him.) John turned to the boy. "You mustn't be afraid. The *umthakathi* cannot hurt you because you have done nothing wrong against the dead people. So my father told me. Now I will give you the medicines. They will be very strong, because you are clean and fresh. You are lucky, and so will the medicines from your clean hands be lucky and strong."

They both bent and touched the earth.

The child dug the first hole. He made it with a small

15

sharp stick, whimpering a little as he worked. John opened the bag of soft brown rabbit skin — the bag that his father had used — and drew out the horn. The child put his forefinger and thumb into the mouth of the horn. Only in such a way must the medicine be touched. (I have seen this medicine. It is a soft, fatty, pastelike substance of a grayish-brown color, with a sour smell.) The child thrust this into the hole, filled in the hole again, and smoothed it with his feet. John hovered beside him, watching, like a bird of prey on still wing.

They moved on, repeating the performance, ringing the kraal in an encompassing circle. The little boy filled thirty or forty holes, each hole the size of a man's thumb. Then John was sure that the poisoner had been leashed. He put the medicine horn reverently back in his father's bag and sent the child back to his hut.

He gathered up his blanket and wrapped himself in it. He was afraid to sleep with the strangers. I asked him whether he was afraid of the witch, but he made no reply. He preferred to sleep under the black sky. For some time he stood staring into the darkness; then a feeling of deep inner satisfaction began to come upon him. He felt the presence of his father, his protector and guide, whose life and spirit he was destined to perpetuate.

John told me that his father would often come back from the dead to speak with him. For John, as for all Africans, there is no rigid dividing line between the living and the dead: he has no conception of a hereafter. The dead continue to exist in this world in the form of *midzimu*, the spirits of the ancestors; and John believes implicitly that the *midzimu* come and speak to him, giving him advice and help. This is an interesting form of what psychologists call total introjection of an object. This enabled John to retain

16

his lost father and mother who were so dear and important to him.

"I stood very still, listening attentively to my father's voice that was so pleasing to my heart. My father was pleased with me. He said that rain would come. And the same night, Doctor, I was awakened from a dream by lightning and thunder. The lightning was so strong, it looked to me like a black ox in the sky flicking his white tufted tail. And in no time the strong rain came."

4

WHEN John came to see me next morning, he began of his own accord to tell me of the dream from which the lightning had awakened him that night. In the dream he and the little boy were collecting eggs. They went here and there, gathering up the eggs from nests in the grass. There were so many eggs that they filled four baskets. Then they sat down. All around them were hens, scores and scores of black hens. John was just telling the little boy that they must sell the eggs, when the lightning awoke him. Then, sheltering under the lee of a rock, he had pondered over the dream.

I asked him how it was that he could remember this dream after so many years. "Oh, it was such a good dream," he said. "To dream of eggs and the number four is so lucky. Besides, I often have such dreams." And then he went on, pondering the dream, confusing past and present.

"Plenty of fowls . . . that means plenty of patients. I shall be a famous doctor and have plenty of patients and cattle, and plenty of children. I shall be rich. Richer than Charlie and Nathan. Nathan is my cousin who, I was afraid, was trying to kill me. Charlie doesn't like me. Will he try to kill me? He is not a good doctor. But to dream of eggs was lucky. I knew I would get a letter that would bring me luck. I shall get a child. If a girl, I shall get back my mother. If a boy, my father will come back. The little boy in the dream meant luck, too. It was a lucky dream. Next morning I had to kill a black chicken to my mother and father's *midzimu* because I had seen in the dream so many black hens. I felt very happy when I woke up, for I had my father's bag and my father's horn with me. I wished I had my father's stick. . . ."

He described the stick. "It was a thick, short piece of wood, carved in the likeness of a woman: the face, stomach, thighs, and legs of a woman; even . . . you know . . ." He referred to the genitals that were quite clearly defined, as I had seen quite recently on my visit to his kraal. Inside the stick was a hole in which his father put medicines, oil, and all kinds of fat. The stick talked to his father. "I am not talking of Charlie, but of my real father, Chavafambira. Nobody else could hear it. The stick explained everything to my father." John himself had never heard it speak because only his father knew what medicines to put inside. If a thief came by day or by night, the stick told his father. "When Father died, Charlie would talk to it. And when Charlie dies, the stick will come to me."

"What about Nathan?" I asked.

"No. My father, when he died, said I should take his place when I am old enough." He had wanted to touch the fascinating stick when he was a child, but children had no right to touch it. The thought of the stick, always feared and coveted, even now threw John into a state of anxiety. He remained silent for some time and then returned to the story of the bewitched kraal.

18

5

THE rain had ceased as abruptly as it had begun. In the Transvaal rain always comes in brief showers. John drew his blanket more closely around him and rose to his feet. The huts stood near him, shadowy in the half-light of dawn. A goat came from behind the rock and stood regarding him with malevolent eyes. It brought a sharp smell, stinging his nostrils. The world grew brighter. The people came out of their huts. Rain had come, and there had been no new death. But they showed no gratitude towards John. They looked at him out of pinched eyes filled with fear and hatred, like the eyes of jackals. He felt hurt, and a great homesickness came over him. He ate a little of his food and then went away from the people, out into the fields. There he stayed till the coming of darkness, when he returned to repeat the ritual of the night before.

He was still some little distance from the huts when he became aware of a woman standing in the narrow path, with her hands clasped tightly together and her head bent. John greeted her involuntarily in the Manyika tongue. She raised her head, keeping her eyes averted, and then, to his surprise, returned his greeting in the same language.

John felt awkward in her presence. This seemed strange to me, for normally he appeared quite at ease among members of the opposite sex. But with this woman he seems to have spoken abruptly, in obvious confusion.

"She looked at me funnily, pointing her shaking finger at the buffalo-tail which I carried. 'That,' she said in fear, 'that will strike my mouth when you throw the bones, *nganga.*' I shuddered. I told her to be quiet. 'The grass and the trees whisper.' But she didn't listen to me. 'I know

I'm finished,' she said. 'You are a Manyika *nganga*, of my own people, and the bones will not deceive you. I am the *murowi* who brought death and destruction to these people. But they are not my people. And I hate them.' I looked at her and didn't believe. How could she say such a thing, for this meant death! And I told her, 'You are telling a lie. You are so young and beautiful, you cannot be a witch.' But in my heart I knew she didn't tell me a lie. And I felt sorry for her. But she laughed at me. 'What is the matter with you, *nganga*?' she said mockingly. 'You look like an empty egg that the black snake has sucked. Why should I not confess to you? You can see how it is among the people. Everything is bad and out of order.' I said to her, 'Your blood must be very bad against these people.'"

At this she had angrily turned upon John. She told him that her mother and father had trekked here from their kraal near Umtali while she was a little child. They lived here for many years, but the people did not like them. They hated her father. He was killed one night in a quarrel. It was over her. An old man of the kraal wanted to take her as his third wife, but her father wanted her to marry a Manyika, so they fought with him and killed him. Then they poisoned her mother and her brothers, and she was left on her own. In time she was chosen by her dead people to be the instrument of their revenge. In dreams, they taught her how to stop the rain, and how to destroy the people and cattle.

John was astounded by her story, frightened and fascinated. "Why is it," he asked me, "always a nice young woman becomes a witch?" And, not waiting for my reply, he continued: "A young girl gets easier hold of people, as this one got hold of me. She — a witch! It was terrible." Better than most men, John knew the ghastliness used by

20

the *murowi* in her work of evil and destruction. John was so appalled at the thought of her being a witch that, deep in his heart, he called to his mother for help; and, as always, she came to his aid.

I was struck by the fact of how little John, throughout his life, gave himself a chance of thinking out a problem for himself and making his own decision. Always his mother or his father came to his help. In this direction he remained an infant throughout life. Usually, during the psychological development, an identification with the parents takes place: that is, a part of the parents becomes internalized into the mind of the individual, in the fashion of an unconscious moulding, with the result that the internalized characteristics become an integral part of the individual. People talk and act, like and dislike, in common with their parents' ideals and tastes without themselves being aware of it. In John's case it was different. Father and mother, though dead, remained accessible to him whenever he was in need of them. They were as omniscient as God, but in a concrete and tangible form. The *midzimu* even lived in their former huts in the kraal, according to John's conception.

In this case, his mother came to his aid. "My son," she said from within him, "why distress yourself? This Manyika girl is no evildoer. Rather does she take into her hands what her family spirit has done. Why do you blame her?" (It is remarkable how John invariably made his mother or father say whatever he wished!)

The words eased his heart. He took the woman's hand in his and told her to have no fear since she was merely doing what her *midzimu* had told her. He promised to arrange it with the dead that no harm befell her.

She bent her head at his word of reassurance, clapped

her hands softly together to show her thanks, then, turning, went swiftly and silently to the kraal.

6

HE performed the ritual again that night with the little boy, as before. When they had done, rain came again: a steady downpour this time, that lasted till well after dawn.

I was naturally skeptical of such a prompt response on the part of Nature to a witch doctor's ritual, but I dared not inquire for fear of arousing John's suspicion. Rain might have come that morning, as on the previous night, simply because it was the end of spring and the beginning of the rainy season in the Transvaal. I have found out from other witch doctors that they give careful study indeed to the realities of life. None of them would undertake to make rain in the Transvaal in July, for there is not the slightest chance of it in midwinter.

The people of the kraal were more friendly towards him that day. So promptly had the spirits answered him that he seemed too great a doctor for their jealousy. A sense of awe took hold of them. Only one more night for the "fencing" of the kraal, and on the third morning there would be a general assembly in front of which John would throw the bones.

With a great effort John concentrated on the ritual of the third night, when for the last time the little boy ringed the kraal with the protection of John's medicine. But when it was done, and the child had scampered off to his hut, John felt like a pricked bladder, so weak was he. Wearily he put away the medicine horn. The skin of his father's

22

bag under his tired fingers seemed to him as soft as the smooth thighs of the girl. Tomorrow he must throw the bones. He knew, with complete inner conviction, that they would condemn her.

Meanwhile, the rain had come again. A storm this time. Lightning flicked across the sky; thunder muttered, crackled like thorns under a pot. John sat on his haunches and watched the sky ripped from horizon to zenith. And in his agony the sweat rolled down his face as if he were working hard in the heat of noon. At last relief came. Between the harsh rumblings of the storm his father's voice came to him. John clapped his hands softly in the prescribed greeting and listened to the *mrem-mrem* sound of the *midzimu:* —

"Listen, my son: your blood is too hot; it mixes with your brain; it confuses your thoughts. Gather together my bag and horn that I have given you, your buffalo-tail, and all that you have brought to this strange kraal. Do not wait to say good-by to the people. Do not wait to collect the cattle that have been promised. Set out now and go swiftly from here. I, your father, tell you so. Look not back at these huts, but walk steadily till I tell you to stop. Up now, and go on with your journey. Further, do not practise medicine until I tell you to do so. I am not angry with you for what you have done, because you have helped the people."

Joyfully, John arose. Yet his heart was not free of pain. His father's censorious words were still ripe in his ears: *Your blood is too hot; your brain is not ripe to be a doctor.* But he must obey his dead father, Chavafambira. The dead would exonerate him for leaving the kraal without throwing the bones. He would sacrifice a goat and a white chicken to them.

III

IT WAS difficult to tell truth from fiction in this romantic story. But for the understanding of John, it mattered little if the greater part of the story was fictitious. A psychological reality, as I have stated — an event which we imagine to have happened, emotions which we believe we have experienced — influences our minds and our lives just as much as actual facts. A child who sees a bogey-man in a dark room may not be able, even in adult life, to free himself from his fears, even though he knows logically that there are no bogey-men in this world.

What impressed me most in the whole story, which took John about two weeks to tell, was the fact that this ordinary, so-called primitive African had been influenced by a woman in his early youth, in the same way that we are: the image of the first love remained in him, as in us, for life, consciously or unconsciously playing a role in his destiny.

2

FOR days after this he talked of his daily life, with his wife and children. I will relate this in due course, but rather than confuse the reader I prefer to give the story

24

of his life in chronological order instead of in the disconnected manner in which I encouraged him to talk to me.

Late in the evening, after leaving the bewitched kraal, he reached the town of Pietersburg. He had intended going to Johannesburg, but he was tired; also, he liked the town. So his father's spirit conveniently came to him the same night and bade him stay for some time in this town. He rested there the night, and in the morning set out to find work, going from house to house uttering the natives' password: "Work, missis?" Mostly he was met by abrupt, discourteous refusals, but eventually he found a position in the kitchen of a hotel; his pay, the big sum of one pound a month.

He washed dishes, prepared vegetables, cleaned floors, and did such other odd jobs as needed to be done during the course of the day. His hours were long, from five in the morning till late at night, but he did not mind. He was eager for experience of this new world; and being quick-witted he soon worked deftly and well, and was courteous in manner, so that after a month the proprietor promoted him to the position of waiter. Now he wore a white twill suit, a red sash, and a black fez. On his sturdy, muscular frame these clothes must have hung well, giving him an air of dignity.

Yet, although the outward events of his new life had begun so auspiciously, inwardly he felt lonely and depressed. The incident of the bewitched kraal was fresh in his mind, and his failure there wounded his pride. Again and again his father's censuring words recurred to him: "Too young to practise!"

The native servants slept in ramshackle sheds in the back yard of the hotel, the men quartered together in one room; and night after night, when their work was done,

25

they would sit drinking and discussing the events of the day. They talked chiefly of evildoers, misfortune and sufferings of the black people, and the strange ways of the white man.

"You know, Doctor, there is plenty to talk about; for misfortune and suffering is everywhere for the natives. I was frightened to hear that the story of the bewitched kraal and a foreign *nganga* had already reached the town. Native news travels from man to man quickly. And the people in the hotel talked and talked about this affair. Night after night they would tell the story, but it wasn't true what they were talking. They say that I have betrayed the people, though I brought the rain. But I didn't discover the witch. I told so the people, and I was very sorry I said it because I was very much afraid that they would find out who I was."

Indeed, he held himself aloof from his companions, lest a chance word should betray him; for he had told no one that he was a *nganga*. He drew the blankets over his head as he listened to their talk. The latest version was that the young *nganga* had refused to find the evildoer. This had annoyed the *midzimu*, who had killed him by thunder. A young woman had disappeared from the kraal on the same night. . . .

Too young to practise! Too young . . . too unwise . . . too ignorant! . . . At night, exhausted though he was after the long day's work, he could not sleep. For hours he would lie wakeful on the hard floor, thinking of the Manyika *murowi* woman. The images of the witch, of his dead father and mother, and of the people in the kraal, intermingled with the figures of the people he had seen during the day. The images crossed and recrossed his mind like ants scurrying busily about their nests. He realized that his ambition

26

to follow his father's footsteps must be abandoned for many years to come. First, he must live and gain experience. Only then could he practise his traditional profession.

The realization must have been very painful to him, for anything connected with medicine was dear to his heart. He was what is called "a born doctor." He had a compassion for all who suffered, a desire to help and cure them. He came, further, of a family of great "doctors." His grandfather, Gwerere, had been a renowned practitioner in an art handed down to him from his own father and grandfather. John's father, Chavafambira, had been a famous doctor, rich also in cattle and goats and land. John's paternal aunt, his father's only sister, had followed the same profession, and was hailed as a *ngoma*. His own mother, Nesta, was also famous far beyond the borders of her kraal.

She was chosen by the ancestral spirits as their intermediary with the living. She would get periodical fits (obviously epileptic), which were vividly engraved upon John's memory. He remembered well how irritable, quarrelsome, she would be with him and his sister Junia, on the morning of the eventful day. Her body would stiffen, her limbs twitch, her eyes open wide, and with immobile pupils stare into space. White foam would bubble from her mouth, and a few drops of blood trickle down her chin. The people knew that the dead, the *midzimu*, came down to talk to her on such occasions, and, through her, to deliver a message. When the fits were over (a sign that the spirits had finally settled in her body) Nesta, faint and sleepy, would begin to talk to the crowd that had gathered in the small hut.

She did not talk directly to them. Her husband, Charlie, the *nganga*, stood by her, and through him she would deliver the message, answer questions, detect crime, and foretell the future.

Having to hide from his fellow workers the fact that he was a *nganga* was frustrating to John. He was especially proud of his profession because Chavafambira had selected him as the future doctor, passing over his two elder sons, Patrick and Amos. No wonder he held himself aloof and went among these people as a stranger!

This aloofness provoked much discussion among the natives in the hotel, who, like all oppressed people, keep in close contact with one another. The men openly resented his apparently snobbish reserve.

The women were more friendly, some of them clearly showing their admiration for him. But even with his admirers he maintained a detached bearing. He knew his attraction for women, and enjoyed in full the admiration he evoked, yet remained entirely unperturbed. Now and then passion troubled him.

I made no further inquiries, for it was not easy at this stage to talk to John of sexual matters. He said that he had succumbed to temptation only once, with a young Basuto woman. But she was married, and the role of a back-door husband did not appeal to him. The affair fizzled out in a few weeks.

There was, however, a native woman in the hotel, a chambermaid named Maggie, with whom he would pass his leisure minutes. Maggie was a cripple, and made no pretensions to good looks. John's interest in her was provoked by his profession. He questioned her about her lameness. She told him shyly she had had it since childhood.

"Since I was very little, about two years old." She was not much younger than John, but his superior manner and his bearing made her seem a child beside him. He nodded encouragingly to her, and under the warm glow of his sympathy she became more communicative. "They dropped me on the ground. The trouble is here." She indicated her left hip, and John noted that her left leg was in fact shorter than the right.

"That is very bad luck. You get tired from your work, I suppose?"

"Yes," she replied; "especially when I have to stand for a long time. My feet ache in the evenings so much."

John looked at her intently, a professional trick he had learned from his father, Charlie. The African medicine man is no less adept at the bedside manner than the European medical man. He might have said more to her, but there was no time. He had stopped in the middle of work to ask even these few questions, and now he continued on his way, down the corridor, a loaded tray in his hands.

3

TO Maggie, life tasted sweeter from the moment of her first meeting John. She guessed that the handsome Manyika talked to her only because he pitied her lameness, but what mattered the reason? His sympathy was pleasing; she felt that they could become friends. Indeed, an even more alluring dream than friendship came to her mind, for she dreaded the possibility of not being able to marry; not merely because she wanted children, not merely for personal pride, nor because she was unhappy at home, but above all because she was tired of working for the white people. The sharp-tongued, eagle-eyed Scottish housekeeper, who insisted on bedrooms that shone with cleanliness, caused Maggie the blackest despair. She was forever redusting furniture, remaking beds, repolishing tooth-glasses that the housekeeper refused to pass as satisfactory. "Ye lazy slovenly lump!" she would fling at Maggie a dozen times a day.

At home, in her kraal, it was no better. Her Zulu mother was as exacting in her own way as this white "missis" at the hotel. There was only one escape from this unintelligible passion for cleanliness and order — a home of her own, a home where she could lie abed as late as she liked and sleep in the afternoons; where no old spinster could nag at her to put this away or sweep that away. A gloriously lazy existence would be Maggie's in her own home. And, in this connection, John seemed a godsend. She must not lose him. She guessed the reason for his interest, and she played upon it. As some women exploit a fine complexion or a dimple, Maggie exploited her lameness. And, much to the indignation of more attractive young women in the hotel, the friendship between John and the crippled Maggie grew.

It became their habit to spend their free time together. On Sunday afternoons Maggie accompanied John to church. Maggie was not a Christian, none of her family belonged to the church, but she liked the service and the choir. To John, although he belonged to the Anglican Church, religion was a holdover from the missionary school that the Reverend Robert had run in John's native village.

On the way to and from the church, Maggie would tell him about herself, deliberately exaggerating her "bad luck!" Her abominable stepfather had made life at home utterly miserable. Her parents were Zulus; their kraal was in the Drakensburg Mountains, in the famous Valley of the Thousand Hills; there she and her sister Mary were born. Her father, a policeman, had been sent to the Northern Transvaal. He had been killed by native hooligans, members of

30

the Amaleita Gang, and her mother had been left stranded
and penniless with four children. The government paid her
no compensation, and gave her no assistance when she expressed a desire to return to Zululand. Since the widow was
so far away from home, her husband's brother did not
marry her according to the tradition. So she had worked
for a living as a washerwoman to support herself and the
children, and eventually she had married the middle-aged
Shangaan whom Maggie hated so much.

John fully understood her tragedy; as a good medicine
man he loved to listen to Maggie's sad story. He liked being
with her; she fed the flame of his muscular self-assurance
so wholeheartedly. John was a good speaker and Maggie
often gaped in wonder at his descriptions of his home, the
beauty of Junia, his sister, the rank and riches of his fathers.
When once he told her impulsively, "Maggie, you are as
short and fat as my mother Nesta was," Maggie was flattered and encouraged. She asked him to tell her more about
his mother, how she had died, and John, carried away more
perhaps by his memories than by Maggie's interest, told her
that it had happened five years ago.

A terrible disease had fallen upon the land. (It was the
influenza epidemic of 1918.) Kraal after kraal was invaded
by the pestilence. People died like flies and their bodies
were hurriedly buried outside the kraal, Christian and pa-
gan alike. There was no time for ritual. The disease raged
so fiercely that at the end there were not enough men in
the kraal to dig even the shallowest grave. Outside the kraal,
vultures dropped silently from the sky, questing tirelessly
for corpses. Everyone was haunted by the fear of death.

"At first the people appealed to my father, Charlie, for
help; but neither he nor any of the other *ngangas* could do
anything. They told the people that the disease came from

31

the white folk. It was not sent by the *midzimu,* or by the Mwari, but by the white people. So many were killed in the great war of the white people that the blood of the dead had caused this great sickness."

I asked John if they had any help from the white people, and if there were any white doctors. "Not in our place," he told me. "Only the white-haired missionary from the school tried to help us. He rushed from kraal to kraal in his motor-car, giving medicines. Nathan helped in this work. One day they stopped the car as usual beside a body lying by the path. Nathan reported that it was not a patient, but a corpse; and then he saw the white man himself struggling for breath. He died before they reached the mission. The same night, Nathan took ill. I was afraid that I should get the sickness, too. But it was my mother who got it next. She became very ill. In the end she died. Only my sister, Junia, and I were with her when she died. Junia was a very small girl then. She whimpered helplessly by the wall, watching her mother die. I tried to lift Mother in my arms, to help her, but it was no use. She died; she seemed burnt up with fire, so black did she become. Yes, Charlie was right. Only the white man's poison could burn a person like that. I was so terrified. I screamed aloud, wild and frenzied. Nathan's mother and Charlie rushed into the hut. That is all I can remember."

He himself had sickened after that. A high fever raged within him; he lay ill for nearly a year, and all thought that he would die. But finally he recovered. Nathan, he found, was very ill, but he too had recovered. Of their family, only his mother had died.

4

THE friendship between John and Maggie developed along the usual lines. I understood that there was no direct physical element in their relationship. I suppose Maggie, crippled and plain-featured, could not compete with John's memory of the Manyika witch. I learned many years later that in any case Maggie was frigid.

Yet Maggie was not without her attractions. Sometimes, as he looked at her, John wondered what her hips were like without the disguise of clothes, and such thoughts brought desire in their train. John was no novice in love-making; he had had a woman "properly," as he put it, when he was only twelve years old. But, in Maggie's case, he lacked the impulse to make further advances. Maggie was disappointed and annoyed: she guessed his lack of affection for her.

John himself was not easy about the whole affair. He grew attached to her; she made a stronger appeal to him than he wished. What she did, he found, concerned him more than he had thought. This he came to realize when another waiter in the hotel, Gideon by name, began paying marked attention to her.

Maggie, perceiving instantly the strategical use to which she might put Gideon, responded to his advances. There was a sly, devilish look in her eyes when she told me how she had played off one man against the other. She made Gideon believe that she was actually the unwilling object of John's devotion. Gideon and Maggie suddenly became friends. Gideon even began accompanying her and John to church on Sunday, and assumed a distinctly proprietary air in regard to her. The folk at the hotel began to talk

33

about it, throwing out veiled hints to John that Gideon was running ahead of him.

John was annoyed. The business had reached a stage that he by no means welcomed. He had either to retire or to vanquish Gideon. He was young, arrogant, impulsive, and naïve. The thought of yielding place to Gideon was repugnant to him. Yet some part of him, I have the impression now, was reluctant to have the matter settled definitely. He felt dimly that he did not want a more intimate relationship with Maggie, and certainly did not want to marry her.

Maggie, for her part, continued to play the game well. Not until years later, and only after he had threshed out the whole affair with me, did John realize how cunningly she had contrived to stir up his jealousy and make him resent more and more the intrusion of the would-be lover. (I was often sorry for having made John understand Maggie's game. He would taunt her with it when they quarreled, and back his argument with my authority.) Nevertheless she went to a Zulu medicine man to throw the bones for her that would reveal what the future held in store. He told her that she would marry soon, a foreigner from a far country. The foreigner, she decided, could only be John. The doctor gave her a love potion, which he declared to be infallible. John smiled as he told me this. Neither she nor the Zulu doctor realized that he, by virtue of his profession, was immune to magic and medicine charms: his own medicine in his calabash protected him against them.

The rivalry between John and Gideon resolved itself eventually through a fight. It occurred one Saturday night when they were all at a dance in the Pietersburg location. Each had been drinking heavily; each was in a quarrelsome mood; they found fault with each other's words, and a heated, abusive altercation took place. Both carried sticks, and they brought them into play. The sticks, however, soon broke, and they threw them aside and closed with each other, wrestling, pummeling, rolling over. Everyone in the hall stood and looked on. At last, after a grueling struggle, John threw Gideon so that his head struck the hard floor heavily, and he lay inert, his face bruised and bleeding.

John did not realize that his victory over Gideon was not achieved without Maggie's help. She had seen to it that Gideon had been served with an extra-strong concoction of Kaffir beer. A black woman is just as determined in her fight for a man as a white, except that her methods are less sophisticated.

Thus John's claim upon Maggie was proved. However, he was not happy in his victory. His relationship with her was changed; there was no need for others to make veiled hints about it; he saw it instantly himself; she had a more possessive air towards him now; and she had it by right, for had he not himself laid open claim to her through the fight?

John thought the matter over moodily night after night. He was caught, like a man in a swamp whose every movement makes him sink deeper. He realized now that their relationship could have only one result: marriage. But he did not want to marry Maggie. He did not want to marry a stranger. If marry he must, let his wife at least be a Manyika woman. . . .

Yes — the Manyika woman. . . . She was beautiful; she knew witchcraft; she could teach him the secrets of her magical powers. Yes, he told himself vehemently, rather the beautiful Manyika *murowi* than any other woman. But then a thought occurred to him: would the *midzimu* permit such a marriage? For marriage in John's society was governed by endless taboos.

He began studiously avoiding Maggie. He stopped going to church. He busied himself about the hotel so that he should have little occasion and hardly any time to talk to her during the day. He tired more easily and more frequently than ever before, using this as an excuse to see less of Maggie; it gave him a feeling of relief.

But Maggie was the cleverer of the two. Intuitively she understood John's tactics. But she was now less than ever prepared to give him up. She again decided to appeal to his pity and sympathy. One day, as he was mooning about the yard, he heard the sound of weeping. He found Maggie in tears on the floor of her room. What had happened? he asked her apprehensively. Sobbing, she told him that Gideon had threatened to poison him. John smiled. It was true, she assured him. She had warned Gideon that she would tell John, but he had laughed at her and knocked her down. She was afraid of Gideon, he was so jealous. She was sick and tired of the work here and the nagging Scotswoman. She yearned to be home again. Her kraal was only three or four hours' walk from the hotel. Wouldn't John take her home?

He made no reply, but he was deeply moved. How could he refuse her, a cripple? Compassion stirred in him again, and with it a feeling of shame for having purposely avoided her lately. He didn't want to marry her; still, he would take her to the kraal. She, a cripple . . . of course he must take her.

And so Maggie obtained three weeks' leave for John and herself and they went to her kraal, which was only about fifteen or twenty miles from town.

5

THEY were welcomed by Mawa, Maggie's mother, a tall, well-built Zulu woman. Her husband, George, was not in the hut at the time. He was with his second wife in a hut some yards away, working off the effects of a drinking bout.

Mawa made a favorable impression upon John. I met her myself, years after, and can realize how enchanted he must have been with her. She was a tall, grayish woman, spotlessly clean; but what most impressed me were her hands: black outside, the palms nearly white, slender and with tapering fingers; it was difficult to associate them with an ordinary kraal woman. She possessed, further, a reserved graciousness and quiet voice. "She was like my mother," John concluded his first description of her; "and her hut was as clean as my mother's hut."

After the evening meal, Mawa's husband returned. He was still drunk but was partially sobered by the presence of John, whom he guessed to be a suitor for Maggie's hand. "He didn't care for Maggie," John remarked bitterly to me; "he must have been thinking of the cattle he would receive if I married her." John spoke very contemptuously of George, who impressed him as a gross and stupid fellow. He disliked him instantly, and my own opinion of George agreed with John's. His eyes were small, mean, greedy, shifty; they never met the look of another man. His gray hair and long drooping mustache appeared to John unusual and unnatural. And even next day, when George had sobered, John found him still stupid and unpleasant. The old man retained enough manners to talk about recent births and deaths among friends in Pietersburg, the condition of the veld, the dipping of the cattle; but when he reached the business of Maggie's marriage and *lobola*, which would go to him, he was touchy, obstinate, and cantankerous. Finally, after hours of circumlocution, the *lobola* was fixed at four cows and eight goats.

When this had been decided, John explained that his animals were in Rhodesia, that it would be difficult to get them. Marriage, therefore, must wait a while. George could do no more, and John prepared to return to Pietersburg.

At this point in his narrative, John suddenly began talking about Maggie's sister, Nellie. Such a diversion made me suspicious, and I asked him directly to tell me more about her. After telling me of her marriage, how many children she had, and where she lived, he remained obstinately silent, and ignored the subject of Maggie and Nellie altogether, until I made it quite clear to him that I was very interested in the whole affair, and that, if it were not unpleasant to him, I would like to hear the whole story. This is what he told me:—

Maggie was very depressed when she heard of John's intention to leave the kraal and return to Pietersburg. She sensed danger. Once away from the kraal, John would not return. He was obviously trying to get out of things. She consulted her mother, who suggested that John might like to marry Nellie.

Maggie understood. Nellie was her younger sister, and a pretty girl. If John married Maggie, it should be a condition that Nellie should be kept for him as a second wife. Such arrangements, John remarked to me, were quite common, though the Church was very much against them. In any case, Maggie and her people were not Christians. Maggie told me herself that she thought this idea an excellent one. Nellie should be the bait. There was no jealous passion in her attitude towards a second wife, although she later, in married life, was troublesome about nonexistent love affairs of John's. I suppose custom and tradition change the emotional attitude of people, as with a lover's not minding when his mistress sleeps with her husband, but objecting bitterly to another lover.

So Maggie did not mind sharing John with Nellie. It was better than losing him altogether. There was even something pleasing in this scheme: after marriage, Nellie should look after their home. Nellie, like her mother, was crazy about housework. The arrangement would be ideal.

John met Nellie the same day at a party celebrating the birth of a first-born. Nellie wore a bright blue dress, a blue *doek*, and blue earrings of glass. John found her young and pretty. Mawa contrived that Nellie should be beside him most of the day.

John and Nellie went out into the late afternoon and sauntered over to the shade of a small group of trees near by. A cool breeze came and soothed his hot temples, drove away the sick feeling within him. He lay down beside Nellie, on the grass. He stroked her hand. He cupped her firm little girlish breast and moved his hands caressingly over her well-formed buttocks. Teasingly she rolled away from him in the grass. He laughed softly and followed her, seeing in the warmth in her eyes that she was his for the asking.

I could never discover whether John actually had any intimacy with her that afternoon. He stubbornly refused to talk about the incident and at that time I had no means of breaking his resistance.

6

NEXT day, John came to my consulting room with
the story of a dream. He was fishing in a big river with many
other men, one of whom was a Manyika. They found three
sticks which they put into the water, bound together with
one rope. Then they all waited, expecting to catch fish.
The men called to John to help them because the stick
was too heavy for them. John jumped into the water and
got hold of it. They pulled it out, but there was no fish
and no water, only a hole. All the water had disappeared.
The others began to quarrel with John. Why did he
deceive them, they said. "We are wasting our time for
nothing."

John attributed great value to this dream. As a witch
doctor he was always having to interpret his patients'
dreams, mostly prophetically. "Water . . . three sticks . . .
What does it mean, Doctor?"

"What do you think?" I said.

"Three sticks are me and my two brothers. Water is a
woman. Charlie always used to say so. Looking for fish, but
could find none . . . bad luck. Does it mean quarreling?
Or perhaps I will sleep with an unclean woman? But I
mustn't sleep with a woman except in marriage. Because
my medicines will be no good, and the people will be quarreling with me. The patients were quarreling in the dream.
I am sure bad luck will come."

Past and present were intermingled in this dream. The
dream had certainly some relationship to the incident with
Nellie and the marriage to Maggie, about which he had
been telling me the previous day. But at the same time, I

discovered that on the previous afternoon he had been approached by a woman in Swartyard to sleep with her, and he had refused, not without regret. His further associations with this dream were very interesting. "The Zulu they don't eat fish. But they go out fishing."

"You were out fishing too," I interrupted, "and you are still ashamed of it and therefore won't talk about it."

I explained briefly to him the meaning of his failure dream. He reached for the forbidden, and therefore the expedition was unsuccessful at the end. I added that failure dreams were common to all peoples. But John, ignoring my comments, changed the subject.

"Nathan was going to marry" — he was obviously referring to an event many years previous — "he had enough to marry. Patrick thought I should also marry. And why should I? Well, of course, some day I must; but only when I will be a doctor, because a doctor must have a wife. Charlie told me so. If a doctor is not married, then he went about with other women and his medicines were spoiled."

Three things were forbidden him: one, to sleep with any woman but his wife; two, to eat a sheep, because it is not a clever animal; three, to touch a pig with his hands when it was dead, or to eat its flesh, because pig-meat spoils medicines.

And then he remembered last of all that he must not marry or sleep with a girl who had the same *mutupo*. "*Mutupo*," he explained, "is the animal who protects the man." Every man has his own special *mutupo*, which he inherits from his father. John's own *mutupo* was *soko*, the monkey. "It is like sleeping with your own sister," he went on. He remembered the warning of the elders: "When you meet a girl, ask first of all what is her *mutupo*. If she is *soko*, your own *mutupo*, don't make love to her, but be to her like

41

a brother or a father." Maggie had no *mutupo*: she was a Zulu.

"What was the *murowi's mutupo?*" I asked him.

He was nonplused. How clever it was of me to ask him such a question, he said, confused; but he didn't know her *mutupo!* How could he have forgotten to ask her such an important question? He didn't even know her name!

7

DURING the next few days he told me of the final development of his marriage affair. When he returned to the hotel in Pietersburg, he found a letter from his brother Patrick, asking when he intended returning home. His cousin Nathan was doing well; he had a teaching post in a recently opened native school, and had set up a business in native medicines as well, so that he had been able to marry a girl of their kraal. (It was to this that he had referred during his interpretation of his dream of fishing in the river.) Patrick's wife and son were well, and so were their brother Amos and their sister, Junia.

So Nathan was married ... he would have a son. John was certain of this. He would have a son and so perpetuate his *midzimu*. Patrick had a big son. Their *midzimu* were safe. He, too, wanted a son. Every African wanted a son. How does a man live except through a son? And then the thought came: why not marry Maggie and get his son?

For days he thought it over, and then at last he gathered up his things, left the hotel, and went back to Maggie's kraal.

She was very happy to see him. Nellie was working in a near-by town. George again asked John some pertinent

42

questions in regard to *lobola,* to which John repeated his old arguments. George agreed that to get cattle, to get stock, from Manyikaland was very difficult. But the white people used money. Why should the *lobola* not be turned into and paid in money?

John was dismayed at the suggestion. Something in his nature revolted at the idea. *Lobola* was not the purchase-price of a woman. In his tribe the cattle were never delivered in full at marriage; a portion would be delivered some time — it might be years — afterwards, when children had been born. He tried to explain to George that *lobola* was not necessary for a marriage to be valid. It meant only that the father had the custody and rights of the children born in marriage when the *lobola* had been paid. If he did not pay the *lobola,* the children belonged to the wife's parents. Surely Maggie's dead people would not approve! For cattle are cattle; but money . . . what had money to do with *lobola* and the ancestral spirits?

Lobola, as John had rightly put it, is not in the nature of a dowry, but rather a means of strengthening family ties. Unless the parents ensure the good behavior and chastity of their daughter, they are in danger of having to return the *lobola.*

But George remained deaf to all his pleading, and in the end John gave in. It was agreed that when he paid George twelve pounds he would marry Maggie. Furthermore, George insisted that he should build a hut and settle down. This, too, John promised to do, with mental reservations that never in his life would he live in that anomalous kraal. It was not for this that he had left his own kraal and the detestable Charlie!

That night he took his blankets and slept under the trees where he and Nellie had lain. He felt lonely, heartsore, and

43

undecided. He wished for a companion, a mate. And as he wished he heard Maggie's uneven footfall on the twigs. She came and lay down beside him, talking tenderly, as soothing as a mother. He caressed and fondled her. He was at peace.

At the end of a month's stay he married her. Of the money for *lobola*, he was able to produce only four pounds. The marriage was not solemnized in church, neither was it registered in court. The chief sent to their hut two messengers, to whom, in the presence of John and Maggie, George declared the fact and conditions of the marriage. John confirmed his debt in regard to the *lobola*.

In years to come, that debt was to be the least of his regrets in connection with the whole affair.

IV

THE "ceremony" over, John prepared to return to his work in Pietersburg. He again met stubborn opposition from George. The old man grew furious at the prospect of John again becoming a waiter. "How can a doctor wish to forsake his profession for menial work?" he demanded.

"He went on asking me, threatening me, and accusing me of all kinds of things, but I made no reply. I stiffened, for I was afraid, really afraid that he might hit me; and I hate very much the business of fighting. Luckily George only spoke in anger, and my heart felt very sore while he was talking. I didn't listen to him. I was thinking in my heart about all the things that had brought me to his kraal; if only I had not met that dying man there would have been no trouble. But what is the good of talking this way?" he suddenly exclaimed to me. "It was all bad luck. My *midzimu* were against me."

Gloom, thick and heavy, oppressed his soul; like a sinner, he yearned for someone to whom he could confess, someone who would understand and advise him. I asked him why he did not talk to Mawa. He could not say precisely. He felt he could not tell her then that he did not love her daughter, disliked her kraal, detested her husband. And, in any case, since he had made up his mind to go back to Pietersburg, he kept silent.

45

George, meanwhile, boasted to everyone that the famous Manyika doctor was going to settle in the kraal and practise in association with him. Soon this news reached the woman chief, and a message was sent to George that the presence of his whole family was required at the chief's hut at noon next day.

"George, when he wants something, will do anything to get it. You will meet him. You will see he is not a clever man, but very strong."

John was right. When, on my visits to the kraal, George wished to get something out of me, he nagged relentlessly until he succeeded. He wanted John's friendship, or at least no hostility from him, and so, that same night, when John was under the blanket, he came and called him in a voice as kind and sympathetic as he could make it. John wondered what the man could possibly want with him at such a late hour, and asked him suspiciously what was the matter. George said he had come to tell him a few things he might like to know before he made up his mind to leave the kraal. He was, he said, the official circumciser for the whole district, and, as luck would have it, he was at the moment carrying out this ritual.

John knew that circumcision rites were practised by many African tribes, but he had never witnessed them himself. Neither did he know, even from description, the details; in his native Manyikaland they had no such rites. George proposed walking down to the circumcision lodge, or *murunda* as he, a Shangaan, called it, and John hastily accepted his offer, fearful lest George should change his mind. For he knew that a stranger might not approach the place by himself; punishment and disgrace awaited such curiosity and presumption.

"We walked slowly along the narrow path towards the

white, stony hills and then took a short cut through the fields beyond the palisade and out into the open veld. George talked incessantly about the white people, but I was interested to hear about the circumcision, about the *murunda*. I stopped him and asked him to tell me something about it because it was all new to me. He was surprised that our nation, the Manyikas, didn't cut our sons when they became men. The Shangaans, he told me, are all cut, sick or healthy, weak or strong. George himself was only thirteen when his father brought him to the lodge. He was frightened and ran away at first, but they caught him and thrashed him with sticks for this. When they cut him, he said, it hurt so much that he nearly dropped dead. For three days they gave him no water; for three days they tortured him. I couldn't believe that this cruel, selfish man could have been tortured by others."

I explained to John that people become cruel when they experience cruelty from others in early childhood.

"No, you are wrong, Doctor," John emphatically disagreed. "Cruel people are born cruel. George is a bad man."

After about an hour's walk they finally reached the chief's kraal. George pointed to the chief's hut as they continued silently past to the foot of the mountain, advising John to be as quiet as possible because there were warders about. (I was given the same advice, although, on the day of my visit, there were no boys in the *murunda*. But even so, no one is supposed to inspect the place.) They climbed the hill, where they soon found an ideal place for observation. Their nook was, at the same time, well hidden from anyone below. George warned John that this hill was the lair of a terrible snake, but John need have no fears because George's magical powers would protect him.

The air was still and clear; the moon, full and bright, lit up the country for miles around. Squatting on his haunches, John gazed about him. Without difficulty he discerned the lodge: a shabby structure in a narrow cleft between the hills, with a low wall of stones around it. The building itself was roofless and without proper walls. There were two entrances, one facing him and the other to his right, and George explained that the first entrance was for the initiates and the other for the warders and elders.

The circumcision school, John told me, was held in the winter, every third or fourth year, provided they had had enough rain and a good crop of mealies. For it was a big feast as well, with plenty of beer. It lasted three months or more. Usually, the *murunda* is situated in an isolated spot, in a valley between hills, hidden away from the people; but this was not the case in George's kraal, and when John commented upon this, George shrugged his shoulders and asked: "What can one expect from a woman chief?" For it was the chief who decided the place and time of the *murunda;* it was the chief, also, who sent the messages to the various headmen of the district.

When George was a boy, only fully adolescent youths were sent to the *murunda.* "But now," he told John, "they bring boys of seven or eight years. In such cases, the parents send an ox to the chief to make the little boy big." (An excellent form of bribery without the taint of crime — a practical example of successful magic.) The circumcision was carried out with a special knife made by a native blacksmith. Under no circumstances must it be a white man's knife. George took it out from the little bag that he was carrying and handed it to John, emphasizing that it was a great honor and privilege to inspect it, for no one but the circumciser should have access to it. "The knife,"

John told me, "was so long and sharp that if you just touch it, it cuts right through" — though when I saw it, it was merely a rusty piece of fairly sharp steel; with our present-day conception of aseptics, I wondered that so many people escaped infection from it. I suppose this applies equally to all cases of ritual circumcision.

During the actual operation, the circumciser sat outside the lodge, the center of a large gathering of initiates. He had jugs of water and various medicines about him and special leaves which were applied to the wounds after the operation. George did not wear the usual mask. He maintained that he had no reason to be afraid of recognition by the boys, since he cut them for their own good; before they were cut, they were not yet men, and many of them cried for fear. Therefore, when a boy is brought forward to him the other boys shout noisily, trying to drown the cries of the coward. When George was cut, he said, there was no such nonsense. As soon as the cutting is finished, the boy spits on the ground and shouts: *"Mafehfeh!"* which means that he has been cut.

When all the boys had been circumcised their faces were painted with white stripes, and they were allowed to rest until evening. Then they were led into the enclosure, the *murunda* proper, for the first time. Next day, the training and teaching began.

The *murunda* was not only a place for circumcision but also a school for boys. They were given various duties to perform, and were not allowed to be lazy or idle; they were starved and trained to stand suffering; they had to eat quantities of dry cold porridge with no water to drink and were flogged if they did not. The porridge was brought twice a day by their mothers, who deposited the food at a place away from, and hidden from, the *murunda*. The women approached the school shouting obscene remarks, making vile references to the boys' sexual organs, the boys replying with equal obscenity, boasting, to thereby show the women they were already men.

A fire, called the "elephant's fire," burned near the low stone wall as John watched, its ruddy light falling upon the bodies of youths lying next to one another, head to head, shoulder to shoulder. In the silence, John could hear their breathing and every now and then a low moan of pain. He thought he heard someone crying but George denied such a possibility. These boys, he said, having been circumcised, were now men, and would not dare to cry.

"But why torture them so much?" I asked John.

"George said, 'We cut them, starve them, beat them, to make men out of them. Their way is too easy. They do nothing but sing and jump and dance and play and make love to the girls. Now they must suffer and become men. Let them suffer,' he said; 'let them feel pain!' His voice became funny. His breath was heavy. I saw him turn the knife in his hand and I moved away, fearing that he would cut me. I was sure, Doctor, that he wished to cut me, to make a proper Shangaan out of me. I got a fright and quickly turned back home."

It was after midnight when they returned, and John's sleep that night was uneasy. He dreamed he saw people dancing: men, women, girls, and boys — mostly boys; many boys — they were all dancing. During the dance, one boy fell dead. Then another. Then a third. And more. They were taken home for burial. Then they all arose and said: "We were not dead. We were only sleeping."

John awoke in fright. The old people were jealous of the young boys; they wanted to kill them, and that was why they cut them. Did George want to cut him, too? Maybe

50

that was why he had taken him to that place! He must get away from here as soon as possible.

George's diplomacy had been in vain. . . .

2

JOHN'S fear of George was definitely exaggerated. Many years later, when John was undergoing further analysis, I discovered an interesting variation of the Œdipus triangle which clarified this irrational fear of George and generally of every man, black or white, in authority.

Normally, in a boy, the love for the mother brings out a resentment and hostility against the father, a feeling from which the child frees himself later by the process of identification — becoming like the father himself. But John could not find this outlet, because he knew little of Chavafambira, whom he could not remember, though he must have been six years old when his father died.

John, like other African children, was breasted until the age of four, and during these years was literally in perpetual contact with his mother, either at her breast or at her back. Even at night, he, not his father, shared the hut with her. Sexual relations between husband and wife are forbidden during the breast-feeding period. And then suddenly the breast was taken away, he was sent away to another hut, and his father appeared out of the blue to usurp his place by the mother's side.

The Œdipus drama was, thus, more severe for John than for the average white boy, who gets to know his father and to love him. This peculiar father-son relationship created in John the image of a great, godlike Chavafambira. The sudden intrusion of a big stranger increased the grief and

51

resentment over the loss of mother love. Luckily for John, he found in Charlie, his stepfather, a good substitute for his hostile emotions. This dramatic childhood experience had a retarding effect on John, and on every African child in his fight for independence — though today this important psychological factor counts little compared with the poverty and starvation, the economic exploitation, and the severe racial discrimination to which black people are subjected in South Africa.

V

BACK in Pietersburg with Maggie, John managed to get his old job at the hotel, and for a time he was content. But very soon restlessness began again to gnaw him. His persistent dislike of foreigners cut him off from the other natives, and being the only Manyika in the town, he found himself thrown more and more on his own resources, till this very loneliness began to pall upon him. Nor was he compensated in his domestic life for his isolation from the outside world. Safely married to John, Maggie surrendered completely to her natural indolence. She became lazier, more feckless, and more talkative every day, and John withdrew himself slowly from her. Maggie quickly sensed this reaction and resented it; she could not bear what she considered to be an arrogant superiority. She began talking openly to her friends about it, complaining of his grumbling. She could never live as she wanted to; nobody left her in peace. She was willing to work, she said; but someone must have bewitched her. Other women had better luck: they got through their work quickly and easily; with her it was not like that.

John remarked dryly that other women were up at dawn, cleaning their rooms, washing, doing their work, while Maggie lay abed till noon. But she continued to blame her ill luck for everything, resenting and upbraiding him. A fine doctor, he was — who could not even give her medicine to change her luck!

Yes, everything was due to bad luck: that John was dissatisfied, that she was getting so fat, and above all that she had been married a year and had no child. This was the worst luck of all. Barrenness — what a dreadful disgrace! A childless woman! A reproach both to herself and to her husband!

"A woman who has no children," John told me, "is like a cow that has no calf. What good is she to a man? Because it is good to have children; they help to work the land. And of course through them you continue to live."

When I asked what he would do if his wife had no children, he told me: "Then I would take another wife."

The scandal of Maggie's sterility was, in fact, a great grief to her mother. A year, and no sign of pregnancy . . . it was a calamity. So much so that the old Zulu woman paid a special visit to Pietersburg to discuss the matter with John.

She arrived during the day, when John was away at work. He found her when, tired and dispirited, he returned home in the evening. The night was dry, hot, airless, dusty. The heat oppressed him sorely, as on that memorable occasion when he had so wearily tramped the hot brown road with the stranger whom he had never ceased to blame for all his misfortunes. A feeling of apathy, almost of distaste for his present life, rose within him. Why was he oppressed like this? Why did he have to bear this burden of responsibility in this cheerless, inhospitable town?

The heavy scent of great white moonflowers weighted the hot air. A candle burning in his room made of the open door a pale yellow oblong flanked by blue shadows on the whitewashed walls. And he thought bitterly, how like a prison the place had become.

He came in slowly, with dragging, leaden steps. And then he saw Mawa. Instantly, almost involuntarily, he stood erect. He gave her half a crown — a symbolic act that signified the purchase of her benevolence and attention. Then he gave her the formal greeting for such an occasion, avoiding as etiquette and custom prescribed looking directly into her eyes.

This gave him an excellent opportunity for observing the room. It was a place transformed — bright, clean, and tidy. He guessed who was responsible for this transformation.

John was pleased to see his mother-in-law. He had always liked her, and now he was grateful, too. They sat down, Mawa, John, and Maggie, and when the rules of good manners had been satisfied, Mawa approached the subject of Maggie's sterility. It was a very serious matter, she said, and one that should receive careful attention. John agreed. But he felt he must first tell her about himself. Might it not be punishment by his *midzimu?* And, without looking at his mother-in-law, he narrated a dream that he had had the previous night — a dream the details of which he had forgotten, but which he remembered as indicating that his father might be cross with him. He wanted also to tell her next the whole story of the bewitched kraal and his omitting to kill a black hen to his parents' *midzimu*, as he had been told to do; but Mawa was more concerned with her own dead than with his.

She suggested that the young couple should come back to the kraal so that Maggie could go through the ritual which would bring a child. John agreed. Maggie was not asked her opinion or consent. And so they returned with Mawa.

AT the kraal John's wife was taken away from him, so that he was made to feel even more of a foreigner than ever. To him, their alien rite seemed stupid. Nevertheless, when his father-in-law, George Mashangaan, who conducted the operations, demanded an ox, John brought it.

Before the ox was killed, George rubbed medicine on its back and in its mouth. When it was dead, its blood was poured on Maggie's head. She shivered in fear and awe as the thick warm fluid crept down her body, enveloping her in a nauseous veil till she stood in a pool of blood.

She slept that day and that night with the blood upon her. Then, early next morning, before sunrise, they took her to the river and washed her. She returned to the kraal, clean and clothed. John, too, smeared medicine upon himself — his own medicine — and then washed in the river. This he did on his own initiative: it was not part of the tribal ceremony, in which he was not included.

Then they ate the flesh of the ox. Only the old people were given this privilege. Afterwards, the bones were burned in the fire and the ashes thrown into the river. John watched, alien and aloof, wondering at the significance of this strange ceremony. He asked them what it meant, and the old people shrugged their shoulders. "All do it," they answered. "Such an ox was killed to your wife's mother's brother, and to her granduncle, your wife's mother's mother's brother."

The ritual, ceremony, and feast lasted for three days, and then John and Maggie returned to Pietersburg. For two weeks now John slept in another room. During this time he was forbidden to have intercourse with his wife. Thereafter the married pair must come together again. "But I didn't rely on that only," he pointed out. "I drank medicine, herbs that I had collected myself, as my people had told me in the night when I was in Mawa's kraal."

Within a few months of resuming marital relations, Maggie informed John that she was "with a child."

John went out to the kraal of his parents-in-law to kill a goat to Mawa's dead brother and uncle. He did so out of respect for his mother-in-law, whose uncle, she told him, had been in his time a famous doctor in Zululand. Then Mawa visited Maggie and was closeted alone with her. Maggie told him afterwards: "My mother put water on my head. She did not talk properly, so that I could not understand."

Then Mawa came out and told John: "When your child is born, you shall swallow your spittle." So he knew that the child would be a boy. His *midzimu* would be perpetuated. He felt supremely satisfied.

I was often surprised at the way events in John's life occurred according to his prophecies; they cannot all have been mere coincidences. But the explanation lies in the way he told his story to me now. As in so many stories of telepathy and clairvoyance, it was unconsciously presented in a reconstructed form, in accordance with what had happened; and it must not be forgotten that John was describing events of ten years before. When, later in our association, I took to testing him in a discussion of current events, John proved to be a very poor fortuneteller indeed!

3

JOHN'S first sight of his tiny son roused strong emotion in his starved heart. He felt uplifted, fulfilled. But disappointment soon followed. The feeling of exaltation, of being *en rapport* with his dead people, dwindled, vanished, and Maggie again became a constant irritation. He had never loved her; pity alone had drawn him to her. Now her infirmity provoked pity no more.

As the months wore on, his feelings of depression deepened. He was worried by bad omens. A horse got into the yard one day and cropped the grass round John's room. This incident, a four-footed beast choosing his vicinity, made him uneasy. Someone wanted to poison him. A white horse, too! It was impossible to regard this omen with indifference; particularly as a black snake was seen to crawl over the steps of the room and disappear in the bushes near by. John expected trouble with the dead, probably with his parents.

Even his son gave him no lasting happiness. The baby was dirty and neglected, always crying, always crawling about in the filth and squalor of the room, unheeded by its slovenly mother.

Maggie was content to loll lazily in her tumbled bed for most of the day, and John felt that life could scarcely be more miserable. Yet there was one relief. Maggie was still feeding the baby and by the laws of the tribe intercourse with her was therefore forbidden. To have had to feign passion for her now would have been more than his nerves could have borne.

Now an almost irresistible desire for the company of his

own sex rose in John. He longed for his cousin, Nathan — above all for Samuel, who had been so understanding, so ready with sympathy. This man had been a friend of his schooldays. He was an adult, indeed a married man. He had come to the school to learn to read and write and a tender friendship had sprung up between the young precocious John and the quiet, determined man. For years John had almost forgotten him, but now he yearned for him again. His need for the companionship took him to dances.

These were held a short way from the town, in a native eating-house. Groups of men and women would gather on the rickety veranda, or under the trees, and drink and smoke and talk. Perhaps John reached nearest to happiness at these times. The vague sense of uneasiness that worried him when he was alone, or while he worked, at any time, in fact, when he had leisure to think, dropped from him. The men he met were foreigners; there were few Manyikas in Pietersburg. But they were men, and a few drinks made them friends. Many of them were more experienced than he, and he listened with rapt interest to their tales, tried to visualize a seaport, ships, the sea. . . . He learned about Johannesburg, most mysterious, most exciting city of the whole country. They stirred his imagination, these stories of gold mines and huge buildings and motor cars, of hordes of human beings, black and white, and of curious people, like the Chinese and Indians, who were white but not Europeans.

John never had enough of such company. Sooner or later some woman would induce him to dance. The stimulation, the proximity of the woman, her flattery and cajolery, often had their natural consequences. And then the old feeling of depression, futility, guilt, would wind about him like a fog.

It was after one such dance that something happened to convince him that his dead people were angry with him. He was walking home with some of the other men. There was no moon, and thick clouds obscured the stars. The gloom seemed almost tangible, and by instinct alone their feet kept to the path. Then suddenly, without any warning, a brilliant light appeared from nowhere, and blazed fiercely ahead of them.

So unexpected was the sight that the little company of men stiffened. No one spoke. Then the file moved slowly forward. It was as if this strange quivering light drew them on: a magnet of living fire.

And then — nothing. Nothing. The soft, thick blanket of night pressed against their wide eyes. Ahead, behind, and on either side of them, was the emptiness of complete darkness.

As they went on, they talked in subdued voices. They were profoundly disturbed by the apparition. What did it foretell? John felt sweat on the palms of his hands and drops of cold moisture on his forehead. His heart was heavy with sinister foreboding. Calamity awaited him, he felt sure. Sleep that night was impossible. During the few hours before it was time for him to rise again, his mind churned over the events of the past few years. The face of the Manyika witch came to him, her sad, sweet face, the softly moulded shoulders, the slim hips and the young firm body. Even now in vision she stirred him to passion, so that his questing hands moved uneasily as if for the excitement of her flesh. In the past, he had taken pleasure in his work, but now he became less and less interested. He began to feel irritation at his enforced servility. He grew less anxious to oblige, less prompt, less efficient. He had now an increasing hostility. Minor unpleasantness with visitors occurred.

60

He brought beef when mutton was ordered, grew careless about having the coffee properly hot. It seemed to him that there could be no pleasing visitors.

Even the proprietor he found exasperating. This man, a simple Russian Jew, seemed to John to be very rich — did he not own a hotel, a big house, a motor car? Actually, the poor soul, whom I happened to know, was on the verge of bankruptcy, his house in the hands of the bondholder. Worried out of his senses over money, he was rabid about little economies, small meannesses. To John, this economy was incomprehensible, and annoying.

One night, about ten o'clock, a tired commercial traveler came into the hotel, flung down his hat, and ordered a cup of coffee. He found the coffee tepid. Shouting for John he angrily demanded coffee that was hot. John's civil manner deserted him. He took the cup insolently, and went back to the kitchen. He put down the fresh cup of coffee, boiling hot, so carelessly that it turned, soaking the man's trousers. He sprang to his feet, shaking his trouser-leg and cursing John savagely: "Blasted nigger! Bloody Kaffir!"

The proprietor appeared, adding his revilements. John was infuriated. His first impulse was to run to his medicines and poison this insulting man. But he knew that the native poisons did not affect the white men. How he hated these two white people; how he longed for revenge; yet what could he do?

He felt more than humiliation; it was deeper than that: a feeling of imminent disaster.

The hotel was built like so many South African hotels, with the bar, lounge, and dining room facing the street, and, at the back, a grass quadrangle onto which opened bedrooms and bathrooms. To save money only a few, and scattered, lights were on the passage along which John was returning from the *débâcle* in the dining room. A middle-aged spinster, who lived in the hotel, chanced at just that moment to come out of the bathroom. What happened afterwards appeared to him even now, ten years later, quite incomprehensible.

As John drew near her, her robe, thrown carelessly over her nightgown, slipped to the floor. Automatically, John stooped to pick it up. Only then did the woman become aware of his presence. Immediately she imagined that what she had always feared was happening; she was being attacked by a black. She began screaming, utterly hysterical and uncontrolled. Doors were flung open; people ran to her. John stood in his tracks, the silk robe in his hands, dumbfounded by the sudden pandemonium. The woman was sobbing out a story of assault. She was sure that John had been stealthily following her, she had felt his hands on her; he was trying to drag her into the room. Loudly she shrieked for the police.

The proprietor hastily pushed John into the kitchen, assuring the onlookers that the case would be carefully gone into in the morning. His wife took the tearful "victim" to her own bedroom, volubly comforting and calming her. Those hotel guests who were permanent residents knew that the fear of being raped by a black man was an obsession with this spinster. They considered John quiet, respectful, and were prepared to accept the possibility that there was some mistake. Newcomers, however, including the commercial traveler, took a more sinister view. An assault on a white woman called for quick justice. The proprietor, sweating profusely, succeeded at last in getting them all back to their rooms. Returning to the kitchen, he told John to clear out to his quarters. He was quite certain that John was innocent, but realized that things looked ugly. In

South Africa, he knew, all white women had a mania about being raped by blacks. This particular spinster made such a nuisance of herself, complaining groundlessly of imagined advances by the hotel servants, that he often told his wife that he would celebrate the coming of better times by throwing her out.

John found the story was all over the native quarters before he got there. All the hotel servants were assembled in the room at the end of the yard. The atmosphere was tense with apprehension. Candles stuck in the necks of bottles illuminated the room, throwing grotesque shadows on the men talking in low excited voices. John went in and sat down calmly on his bed. The headwaiter, an old Sotho named Joseph, who had worked for twenty years in the hotel, questioned him.

"This is a bad thing," he said. "It is a great trouble." The others agreed. John said nothing. Joseph leaned forward. "Did you ever touch the white woman?" he asked. John shook his head. "I don't know," he said. "Perhaps I did. Perhaps I did not. I don't know."

John was numbed by the swiftness of events. He had been angry with the whites. He had wanted revenge. Now he wondered. Had he really touched the woman? He did not think so, but he was not sure. Anyway, he did not particularly care. His luck was bad; he was in trouble. He had felt it coming.

"If you knew the law of the white people," said Joseph grimly, "you would not sit and say 'I don't know.' The white people are very cruel with us about the white women. Tomorrow the police will come. They will take you to jail. They will hit you while asking questions. When you come to the court the white woman will say you tried to rape her."

John said impatiently: "You talk nonsense. What do I want with that old woman? She is like a hen that is past laying. She is old and she is a European. Don't I know the law of the country? This is children's talk." It seemed ridiculous to him that he, who avoided even black women, should be accused of assault on an old white woman.

Joseph cut in: "You are too young to know that the hen that cannot lay cackles the loudest. Thus the kraal thinks she has cleverly hidden her nest, and her reproach is taken away."

Still John paid no special heed. If it gratified the sickly white woman to scream and imagine things, what did it matter to him? It was his luck that was bad. He had got into trouble over the coffee, and then over the woman.

"Joseph is right," another waiter put in. "The white woman will say you tried to rape her."

"And I will tell them that it is all a lie," said John. Joseph laughed sardonically. The others drew in their breath, whistling their derision. "In the court, the woman, not you, will be believed. The white, not the black. Besides, the white woman will have a man to talk for her. You will not have a speaker for you."

"What will they do?" John inquired. There was a significant pause. "Perhaps prison." Joseph hesitated. "Perhaps hard labor." Joseph's dry old voice croaked. "Perhaps lashes."

Lashes! John knew about lashes. That was how the chief Mutassa used to punish delinquents. By lashing. So the white people did it, too! . . .

"Lashes?" he said. He knew them. They were terrible. He was afraid. Better to be dead than beaten. He must run away, the people advised him, before the police were called in. This friendly advice pleased him. He must run away.

An excellent plan. Yes, run away from the hotel, from the insolent guests, from the stingy proprietor, and, of course, from Maggie. She could go back to her parents, and he would send for her later. He must run away. He could run away — to Johannesburg! Almost triumphantly, he felt his original destination to be within his reach now.

4

EARLY next morning he searched out the proprietor. The little man was sitting in his office, not pleased to see John. He had hoped that John would have already run away, disappeared, thus settling matters simply and satisfactorily.

"You see, Doctor," the proprietor told me later, "times were very bad. A drought for three years. All the farmers insolvent. And at such a time — this affair! I would have had to call the police, and this would have given the hotel a bad name. A court case would have ruined the business. I looked at John. I felt sorry for the Kaffir. You know — he is also a human being. He was a decent boy. He had never even been drunk. 'How do you know a good boy from a bad boy?' my wife would say to me. You know, I discuss everything with my wife. 'They are all savages,' she would say. 'For a time they are good; then suddenly, like wolfhounds, they will break out.' 'Well,' I said to her, 'guilty or not guilty, there must be no court case. You must pacify the old bitch. Tell her they will put her age in the paper.' When John came to me, I didn't know what to say to him. What a fool to come back to me! Could there be better proof of his innocence? But, go on! Tell that to the magistrate! I wished John had run away, but to tell him directly to go would be to help a criminal. I tried to talk to him, I began hinting at the cruel methods of the police. And, not looking at him, I murmured: 'It will be safer to go to the kraal for a while.' John replied bluntly: 'Baas, I want to go away from here. I want to go to Johannesburg. I am going straight now.' 'Excellent!' I thought. 'The very thing!' I explained to the guests that the whole thing had really been a misunderstanding and that, in any case, John wouldn't be employed in the hotel any longer. The rest I left to my wife. I said nothing to John. I certainly refused him a reference. A funny world, Doctor . . . a man was innocent; and there I was, afraid to say a good word for him!"

So John went to Maggie and told her the whole story, stressing the need of his going away. Maggie did not understand what he was saying and maintained that they couldn't imprison an innocent man on account of a silly old woman. But she quickly grasped the fact that he intended going away and sending her back to her parents, and she flatly refused to comply with his plans. She began berating him, accusing him of every crime imaginable, of cruelty, of disloyalty. She talked for hours. . . .

Maggie and the child boarded the train with him.

PART TWO

White and Black Medicine

I

NOW that I come to the story of John's life in
Johannesburg, I find I cannot tell it as he told it to me.
For he would invariably confuse past and present events;
often he would begin to tell me about his difficulties during his early days in the city, and then suddenly switch
over to his present life in the Swartyard. The connecting
link between past and present was always the same — oppression by the white people. There was another important
difficulty, and that was his mistrust of me. He mistrusted
every white man, for he fully realized that a white man
always wanted to get something out of a black. He asked
me once quite frankly, why should he expect that the
woman anthropologist and I should be any different?

The truth is, he was quite right in that respect; for a long
time John was to me merely an object for psychological
study.

2

I CAN clearly visualize John's arrival at Johannesburg Station, hundreds of men and women, excitedly
gesticulating, pushing backwards and forwards, shouting
and cursing, chattering and squabbling, jabbing one an-

other with the sharp corners of their wooden boxes as they fought for the exit. There is only a small portion of the long platform for non-Europeans, so that they are all crushed together, jostled down a paved incline "like cattle into a dip," as John himself complained.

John was tired out by the time the train pulled slowly into the station. No sooner had it stopped than a flood of people crushed, carrying John and his family along in the rush. But Maggie's lameness held them back, giving John a chance to observe the people around him. A small, wizened, yellow-skinned Hottentot, clad in a ragged miscellany, clutched his tall shepherd's staff, swearing softly, but competently, in Afrikaans. A huge, copper-skinned Zulu, his crimson and black blanket worn with an insolent air, forced his way through the mob. John attempted to follow him, but was held up by a tight-pocketed group of half-a-dozen women, their hair dressed fantastically, their bodies draped in brown woolen garments, bead-embroidered, a dozen copper necklets sheathing their throats, and bracelets of copper and beads round their legs and arms. A black policeman, in navy-blue uniform and hat turned up at the side, did his best to push through a dozen Shangaans, their loins girt with bright-patterned cotton cloths, the torso nude or covered by a discarded waistcoat. A disgruntled Indian hawker tried to keep abreast of an African who carried his wooden box by a leather strap thrown over his shoulder. There was a medley of tongues — Sotho, Zulu, Xosa, Afrikaans, English. Well-educated Africans from Johannesburg pressed along the narrow passage, cheek by jowl with men and women from East Africa, country-folk dazed and bewildered by the strangers and the throng and the magnitude of their surroundings.

At last John succeeded in disentangling his family from

70

the crowd. It was late morning; dusty, windy, and bitterly cold. Maggie, holding the child, stood uncertainly beside her husband as he scanned the unfriendly, self-absorbed people and the tall buildings all about them. Of what consequence were they to anyone in this teeming mass? And then three native men walked down the pavement. As they passed, John heard his own tongue; not pure Manyika, but a Mashona dialect. The home language fell so pleasantly upon his bewildered senses that for a moment he stood uncertainly watching them. They had gone a dozen paces before he strode quickly after them and hailed them. They exchanged greetings, shook hands, asked and answered questions; and then the Rhodesians agreed to pilot the newcomers to the native buses that plied between the town and Pimville location where they lived. They had to walk quite a distance. John was bitterly disappointed, Maggie tired and frightened, and the baby wailing fretfully till a kindly old woman took it in her arms and gave it some toffee to suck.

They had scarcely gone a hundred yards from the station, when there occurred an incident that left a lasting impression on John. At the intersection of two streets, they were suddenly stopped by a policeman on point-duty. They stood still, waiting. And then from round the corner came a mass of Africans, black and colored, old and young, handcuffed in two's and escorted by white and black policemen. They walked in silence, wretched-looking. The policemen in their uniforms, and with their guns ostentatiously displayed, plagued them continuously, pushing them into line, barking orders at them, forcing them to go ahead in the narrowest spaces between the press of traffic.

The prisoners were being led from the court to the jail. John did not yet know that, every morning and afternoon, one could see such gangs of natives. Nowadays he no longer pays attention to them unless he spots a friend or acquaintance among them; but at the time he was terribly impressed. Why was it, he asked me, that white people were never treated like that? For them, there was a closed motor van. Only the blacks had to walk through the streets, in rain, hail, dust, and bitter cold, like oxen driven to the slaughter. Could the white people not get a motor van for the black people? "They have motor cars to catch us in the streets," he pointed out.

As he watched the procession, he remembered the warning of the other waiters in Pietersburg: "They will put you in chains and take you to prison." Arrest, police, jail, chains, suffering — endless suffering for his fellow men! Till now they had been mere words, constantly heard, but no more than words. Now they became a ghastly reality. And the sight bred in him an anxiety and fear that were to overshadow his life for years to come.

They took the bus — a dirty, ramshackle, creaking contrivance that was soon packed with a crowd of people sitting almost on top of one another. Outside, the wind and dust increased, and intensified his misery. Pimville itself appeared to him inexpressibly dreary. It was a slum of the worst type. In it were people herded together from the four corners of the Union, thousands and thousands from every tribe and bastards of no particular tribe. The streets were tracks with great ruts and *dongas* in them, filled with refuse in which dogs busily scratched. The houses were filthy hovels built of stray materials gathered from rubbish heaps; rusty corrugated iron, old wood, green brick; and the resultant habitation was fenced around with beaten-out paraffin tins, odd bits of wire netting and rope.

This appalling poverty had been accentuated by the

bewildering richness of the white man's town through which John had just passed. He strode behind his friends, his face drawn and grim with disillusion. Behind him, with the child in her arms, limped Maggie.

His friends offered him the instant and generous hospitality of fellow countrymen, in spite of the fact that there were already six people in the room they occupied. However, two more and a child would not make much difference. But when, within a week of his arrival, his friends found him a job as waiter in a boardinghouse, Maggie refused to remain at Pimville, which was five or six miles from the town, and John protestingly got her accommodation in Swartyard in Doornfontein. Here they shared a room with an old Pondo woman — an *isanussi*, woman doctor — and two other women who also had children. The overwhelming squalor in which she lived did not distress her; she was pregnant again, and lazier than ever.

John visited her only occasionally. He was earning good money and gave her half, and she was satisfied. She had enough to eat and no work to do, no one worried her, and most of the day she spent in bed. Soon, halfheartedly, John drifted into living with Edith, one of the housemaids at the boardinghouse where he worked.

3

THIS affair was of questionable value to both of them: Edith did not receive from him the attention that her romantic and jealous nature expected, and John derived little pleasure from it. It was not enough to compensate for the aimless, stale life with Maggie.

There was, in his relationship with Edith, none of that

sensation of fulfillment that gives a man so much more than mere temporary gratification of physical need. In common with so many other men in this world, John, when the intimacies with Edith were over, experienced disgust, resolving never again to go back to her. But unlike the Don Juans and Casanovas, he felt no inclination to compensate for the poverty of his own sexual emotions by the number of love affairs. He became neither promiscuous nor revengeful. His difficulties expressed themselves in homesickness; he longed for the women and girls of his childhood, for contact with his living relations and for the proximity of the dead, who, to him, had never really been dead. Above all, he yearned for his mother, Nesta; for her protection and support and love. Of all the women he had met since leaving home, one, and one only, had he really loved. Witch or no witch, she alone, it seemed to him, could satisfy his every need. There was little wonder that life in Johannesburg seemed to him as flat and stale as it had been. The only relieving feature was Maggie's absence.

There were, however, compensations. The big city fascinated him. When he was free, he would often walk down the hill into the town where trams and buses clanged and snorted past him, and the big shops filled his eyes with longing, and the kaleidoscopic electric lights amazed him anew at night. Sometimes Edith would take him visiting to a friend of hers who was a maid in a flat near Nazareth House, an orphanage. He had never seen an orphanage before, nor could he understand the need of one. Children were an asset: if the parents died, someone was always keen to adopt them into a family.

Being a black, he was not allowed on the trams, and only on very few of the buses, so he saw the town as the black man invariably sees it; he walked. He walked everywhere, through the business center, motor-town, away to the west through Fordsburg Dip near the Chinese quarter; further still, through a suburb that begins with solid artisan houses and peters out in wretchedness and poverty till poverty gives way to the veld. And the veld springs to life again where mines scatter themselves along the main reef road.

John explored it all, watching with curious and envious eyes the activities of the people, black and white and mixed, whose ways, speech, and manner of life were so foreign to him and accentuated his solitude.

On the rare afternoons that he was free, he would go out to the great mine compounds at the time when they sent out their thousands of black laborers across the white reef road. He would watch the stream of people and listen to their talk, and if at first it was only the sight of a Rhodesian face and the sound of a Manyika's voice that cheered him, gradually he became friendlier to all that were black.

From the comfortable, middle-class suburb where he worked, he could easily walk down Jan Smuts Avenue and on to the Zoo, or further still to Parktown or Houghton: expensive suburbs where the big houses of the rich lie separated from one another by spacious gardens and lawns. The enormous wealth of the Europeans bewildered him. He would wonder about the lives of the lucky people who lived so luxuriously. He was curious, and yet he was afraid to investigate. What little he had learned of the white man's law filled him with fear. The stories of life told to him by the old residents in the town instilled in him fear and terror of the white man's way of treating the black. Occasionally he would remember the kindly missionary who had taught him, and the hotel proprietor in Pietersburg who had never really ill-treated him, and the mistress in

Salisbury for whom he had worked and the lovely children he had looked after there; and at such moments he would be skeptical of these tales of the white man's cruelty. But then, at times, when he was tired, angry, or disappointed, bitter with the burden of life, different images would present themselves — the residents in the boarding-house who never addressed a black save as "dirty Kaffir" or "bastard nigger"; some unpleasant incident in the streets, such as when he had seen a young native boy beaten by his employer, a garage foreman, or a native woman thrown off the pavements because she did not give way quickly enough to a European, the continuous interference of the police, and the prisoners who were escorted daily from the court to the jail.

He was in a quandary, for he could not make up his mind about the white people. He knew that they were clever, otherwise they could not have built all these big houses, these shops with all the wonderful things in them, the perfect roads, gardens, the motor cars, gramophones . . . but was this cleverness good or evil? He discovered that the black people in Johannesburg were also clever, much cleverer than his people in the kraal; yet, for all their cleverness, their life was hard. Work, work, work . . . always work, and always for white people.

He wondered why his own people were not so clever as the whites. Why did Mwari create such differences between them? He feared the white people, feared their might and the evil they could do. The white people were clever, but bad. They had no heart. They came from the sea, and, like the fish, they had no heart. . . .

It was while telling me of his disappointment in Johannesburg that he recalled an incident of his early childhood. His cousin, Nathan, had set out for Umtali to seek work,

76

and John had run after him. For the first time he had seen a town. A native was riding a bicycle. He was so terrified that he had burst into tears. And then, for the first time, he had seen people with white skin. They frightened him still more. Now, as he told me this, he laughed at these naïve childish fears; but I am not so sure that he is free of them even now.

He wanted to know so much during these early days in Johannesburg, but there was no one for him to question. His fellow waiters were ignorant and stupid in their explanations. So he turned to Edith. She made a boast of having been to school, of being able to read and write. He questioned her about the African people in Johannesburg, but she also did not know. Many thousands lived in and around the city; no one, she said, knew just how many there were, for they were ceaselessly coming and going, going and coming. They stayed in the city a year, two years, three, and then went back to the kraal. He remarked to me that Edith, not being a pure black ("colored" as they are called in South Africa), did not understand that natives must go back to visit the place of the *midzimu*. But when I reminded him that he himself had not been home for ten years, he at first kept silent and then explained that he had no money. "Besides," he added, "Maggie won't go to my kraal."

I gathered from him that Edith had talked to him of the evil of the transition from the kraal to the town, of the de-tribalization, the breaking-down of custom, religion, and traditional morality, and the consequent confusion; but even now I am certain that he does not fully understand this side of his fellow man's tragedy. He remembered clearly her mentioning the question of the color bar. She dilated upon it, telling him how it was applied not only in respect

77

to work, but even in pleasure. One who was not white could not ride in a tram, nor enter a tearoom or restaurant, nor travel in a decent coach in the train, nor visit the theater or movies — save for the few dirty, tumbledown movies, vermin-infested and uncomfortable, that were open "for natives only."

To Edith, the color bar in the movies was the sorest point of all, he smilingly told me. He himself had never yet seen a film, but Edith was crazy about them; and since she was not allowed to visit the resplendent movies in the city, nor see the films till six or seven years after their release, she regularly bought such popular magazines as she could afford, often showing them to John and explaining their contents.

He felt sorry for her as he listened to this tale of woe. He looked with sympathy at her thin body, her flat breasts, her pinched face. She was not beautiful. She was not even pretty. Her skin, neither black nor white, but a kind of dirty khaki, was displeasing to him. And she was so thin. He wondered why most colored people were so thin. But she was clever. She knew a lot. And this aroused in him admiration and a kind of respect. On the nights when she had been imparting all her information he was more loving towards her; on such nights he would remain with her till morning.

Gradually life became brighter for him. He liked Edith, and her knowledge of things fascinated him. She tried to persuade him to read some of the Bantu newspapers, but he was too lazy to read; the words formed themselves so slowly that by the time he reached the end of a sentence he had forgotten the beginning. He much preferred Edith's clever talk. Also, she would tell fortunes, not like a *ngoma* or an *isanussi*, out of her head or by throwing bones, but with playing cards. He was very skeptical of her fortune-

78

telling, for he was certain that the future could only be told through the medium of the ancestral spirits. Nevertheless, he was very upset when she told him one night that the cards showed trouble, that a woman would come between them and that he was going on a long journey. As the weeks passed by he gradually forgot her prophecy, and then one evening a woman did come between them, in the person of Maggie herself.

During these happy days he had practically forgotten Maggie, and now she had trudged up the steep hill of Harrow Road to discover the reason for his neglect. She found him in Edith's company, but luckily there were other girls in the room. The sudden sight of her, stout and ugly in her sixth month of pregnancy, angered him at first, but he calmed down quickly and received her in a friendly manner. Edith, too, welcomed her warmly. Tea and sweets were offered. Maggie was given a comfortable chair and soon found the company so congenial that she forgot her quarrel. The women remarked upon her condition, guesses were made as to the sex of the future child, and finally arrangements for the confinement were discussed. Edith gave expert advice, recounting her own experiences.

Such topics of conversation never embarrassed John. He had none of the white man's attitude towards illegitimate children. To him, a child was an asset, so why worry about its paternity? In his kraal, an impotent husband provided his wife with a more fortunate man, the resultant children, however, belonging to the legal husband. But for all that, he once told me, not without irony, that he knew a man who was proud of possessing six children, the youngest aged three, in spite of not having visited his wife in the kraal for twelve years!

At the end of her visit, Edith won Maggie's heart completely by offering to see her home, and while they were gone John went for a stroll. He returned to find Edith sitting on the edge of the bed, in her petticoat, reading her film papers. He sprawled down beside her, idly looking at the photographs. The handsome actors, the beautiful, half-dressed women with their perfect bodies, prominent breasts and buttocks, and amazingly long and graceful legs, usually intrigued him greatly and aroused him sexually; but tonight he felt too restless, too bored. Then, suddenly, his attention was arrested. He sat staring at a picture. Then he turned to Edith.

"Look!" he exclaimed in wonderment. "Here is a Bantu man among all the white men!"

Edith glanced at the photograph. "Oh, that's Paul Robeson," she said. "He is an American; didn't you know?"

She told him all she knew about him, and John was amazed. He knew vaguely that there were American Negroes who were African Bantu by origin; he had heard of the better opportunities they had in America; but of fame and wealth, of acceptance by Europeans, he had never dreamed. This was a revelation to him.

4

FOR days afterwards, he lived in a world of fantasy. He would go to America. He would sing the Manyika songs. His voice was good, and he could master the language. He would acquire great wealth, open a shop. He would buy a gramophone, a house, furniture, a motorcycle. No — a car! He would send his people money. Patrick and Amos asked for money whenever they wrote to him.

He was so full of the idea that he began talking about going to America. But the reaction soon came. The journey would probably cost a lot of money, and he had nothing; in fact, a waiter, newer in service than he, had had a raise and was already ten shillings ahead of him in monthly wages. He had no luck. His *midzimu* must be cross with him. And rightly, too. He had not killed a goat for over two years. . . .

He knew men who put money on the races. One night he dreamed of the number four, and decided that he must back a horse, number four. "You know, Doctor," he explained, "number four is always lucky." So he took his last ten shillings with the idea of making his fare to America. But on his way to the bookmaker he came across a party of blacks on the pavement who were listening to a gramophone playing in the doorway of a little shop. He stood and listened.

The record begins with a mine boy asking his boss, a European miner, for a special pass. His companions sing a chorus explaining the purpose for which he wants the pass. John listened, fascinated; and even now, when I play the record to him, he is enchanted with it. The gramophone cost fifty shillings, and each record three-and-sixpence. He put down his ten shillings as deposit, gave his name and address, showed his pass, from which details were taken, and returned home with an antique gramophone and two records that scarcely reproduced a sound. He was pledged to the storekeeper for months to come. The gramophone still lies, broken and useless, in a corner of his room.

The American dream faded, but the desire for money, quick money, grew. He heard stories of the big wages earned underground and flirted with the idea of mining. He began going out to a mine on the outskirts of the town.

The gaunt headgear of the men, the huge circular cyanide tanks, the dumps of gleaming white sand that are the ghost of tons of quartz, the slime dams banked by terraces and walls of solidified slime, pink and yellow and white, caused him to stand gazing in wonder. He saw the little cocopans, trucks worked on a cable, busily shuffling along their rails. The hoarse voice of the hooter that marks each shift became a commonplace. He watched the skip, loaded with rock, hauled out of the shaft and tipped. Often he would sit on the long wooden benches in the eating-house, or loiter outside the store, asking questions of the Africans who had on them the fine yellow dust and the strange smell of the mine.

But what they told him was discouraging — about the miners' phthisis, when the lungs become so hard, as one of the black assistants in the mine hospital told him, that a knife blade snaps when it is thrust in. They described the darkness, the wet walls of rock down the shaft, the narrow *stoeps*, the intense heat of the earth's bowels. He had frequently felt earth tremors in the town, and now he learned that these were caused by the collapse of tons of rock. They told him how falls of rock, pressure bursts, entomb men beneath unthinkable masses of rock; when all about them the rock creaks and groans and one false move may bring down more; how the alarm-signal rings three times. They described the pitch-darkness at such a time, the confined space in the *stoep*, and the intense heat that leaves men gasping after a few minutes' work. He saw for himself the ambulance and rescue apparatus, the hospital; he watched the injured being carried out on stretchers.

In the compounds, too, he found men of different tribes often engaged in inter-tribal fights, and the thought of such an experience appalled him. Besides, the mine laborers

82

did long hours of sustained manual work, under strict supervision and discipline, and that was distasteful to him. He
was told by an educated man how the raw native succumbs
to the enticements of the store, the prostitute, the illicit
liquor seller, how the chief of the kraal takes away part of
his earnings and how seldom the miner retains any of the
remainder.

He realized that there was no short cut to wealth. No
wonder, he remembered, the Manyika chiefs forbade them
to work in the mines. His interest in the prospect faded, and
soon he ceased spending his free time in the blue shadow
of the dazzling white dump.

II

FOR nearly a week after relating the events of the last chapter, John talked very little. At first, I was not disturbed by this, for I knew that many unpleasant things had recently occurred in the yard (events which I will record in due course), and I was not surprised that he bore a grudge against me — the white man — on account of whose caprices and ill-will he and his fellows suffered so much. But soon I realized that it was dangerous to leave him in this resistant mood, and I tried to induce him to talk about the white man in general, and about the woman anthropologist and myself in particular, in the hope of thereby giving him emotional relief. But the fear of the white man was too strong, and he remained silent.

I then began telling him about my patients, and inquired about his practice, how it was progressing and what type of patients he had. Then I offered him medicine for various illnesses — stock medicines such as cough-mixtures, laxatives, and aspirin — and this re-established, for a time at any rate, our friendly relationship, so that one day he even invited me to go out with him to the veld to collect the roots and herbs for his own medicines.

So one Sunday morning the anthropologist, John, and I went outside the town, and there he initiated us into the sacred art of his medical dispensing. And it was that same afternoon, which is still very vivid in my memory, that, after a good meal with me, talking to me for a few hours at a stretch in the homely, peaceful surroundings of my private house, he told me the story of how he began to practise in Johannesburg.

For some time he had been neglecting Edith, but one day he went with her to visit her sick mother. They found the old Xosa woman in a pitiful state of anxiety and physical distress. Both her legs were badly swollen and she could scarcely walk. She believed that one of the servants in the house had poisoned her, maintaining that he had taken one of her stockings and had used it for making poison, that he had called her names, and that this painful swelling was the result. She clamored for a witch doctor, and refused to attend the non-European hospital for treatment, as her mistress tried to persuade her to do.

A sudden desire to help her came to John. He yearned to treat the swollen legs. He knew exactly what root to burn, so that the smoke would go round the limb. He knew the medicine to take, how to grind it and mix it with animal fat into an ointment, how to put it on the foot and rub it in. She should sleep with it on, that night, and next morning he would take his horn and with a razor make a number of cuts in each leg. Into the cuts he would put certain medicines. But he had turned his back upon his profession after that terrible affair in the bewitched kraal, and so he said nothing.

Nevertheless, the case preyed on his mind so much that, that night, he could not sleep, and decided instead to visit some friends not far from the boardinghouse. There it was that he met a practising *nganga* named Ephraim, and soon he was telling him of Lizzie, Edith's mother.

Ephraim, a pock-marked, saturnine old Basuto, listened,

and finally John persuaded him to visit Lizzie and treat the swollen legs. John accompanied him and eagerly watched the diagnosis and treatment. "But how careless he was!" John told me; "it was not in such a slipshod manner that attention was given by Charlie. Ephraim was entirely unworthy of respect. I questioned him about the case, and asked if he thought Lizzie had been poisoned, and if he would throw the bones. 'What do you know about these things, to talk to me in such a way?' he flung at me. 'This makes my heart very cross!' he threatened me. 'My father was a doctor,' I answered, but Ephraim cut in before I could finish: 'Your Rhodesian doctors! They know nothing. They are swindlers, rogues. All they want is money. I suppose one day even you will claim to be a doctor, as so many of you fellows do. You swine! You only poison people. And why the hell our people let you come near them, I don't know!'" And while his patient moaned with pain, Ephraim went on sneering and using obscene language that made John tremble with indignation. He was glad that Edith had not come with them.

At last Ephraim calmed down and began to treat the case. John considered his manner of talking to the patient entirely lacking in professional etiquette. He was slap-dash, obviously inefficient. Indeed, his main interest seemed to be his fee. I asked John whether it was wrong for a doctor to ask for money. "No," he replied; "a doctor should not give medicine or throw bones without being paid. Charlie even said that if a patient did not pay the cattle he had promised, the doctor should talk to his medicines so that they would not help. But there was no excuse for Ephraim's coarse remarks to Lizzie. He actually swore at her, demanding the two pounds he wanted for curing her!"

While he waited at breakfast next morning, John upbraided himself for not taking Lizzie's case himself, and all day long the affair was in his mind. When he went home that night, he reverently went through his medicines. He drew out the soft skin bag containing the bones. These he took out, handling them, examining each one. Here was a branch of his art that he knew to perfection, for he had learned the throwing of bones from a famous specialist, a Ba-Venda doctor in Pietersburg. He spread the bones out on the floor, touching now one, now another, with reminiscent finger-tips. He felt sure of himself when he handled them. The image of the suffering Lizzie came before his eyes; he could see the swollen legs, the distorted face, the pleading eyes. He thought, too, of Edith's anxiety. And he threw the bones for Lizzie, concentrating on the patient as he did so; for John believes sincerely that good or evil can be done to people at a distance, without the necessity of actual contact with them.

The bones confirmed Lizzie's suspicion, and next morning he told Edith that her mother was right. "She was poisoned through the legs," he said. "But I have put medicines that will cure her."

Edith was sarcastic. Since when had he become a *nganga?* What did he know about treating legs and finding out poisons? He was taken aback by the rebuke. He explained that as the son of a medicine man he had always been interested in medicines, and professed to have studied with a doctor in Sophiatown and that he had often gone with him to patients to see how he cured. He was sure that Ephraim was a bad *nganga.*

Edith, who had faith in white doctors alone, in "real doctors," as she put it, showed no interest in John's studies. She merely remarked that she would take her mother to the hospital whether she liked it or not.

87

But that same evening, when John went to inquire after her mother's health, Edith casually told him, avoiding his eye, "Yes, she is better; and she is not going to the hospital. You must have bewitched her."

He protested that he did not bewitch people, he was not a poisoner, but only a medicine man: she should know the difference. For a moment he was sorry to have admitted his profession, but it was too late, and finally he was glad to confess to her that he was already a *nganga* and had been lying when he told her that he was merely studying to become one. And from that time he began to feel that he must definitely leave the boardinghouse, give up menial work, and resume his profession.

But what of the necessary drugs? Where could he dig the roots? Would the local roots be the same as at home? At that time he was sure that Transvaal roots would not be so effective. But there was no use worrying about that: without his father's help he would not know what drugs to use or what to do in difficult cases — and his father sent no word yet.

Nevertheless, he now found himself mentally diagnosing the cases of the other waiters when they complained of illness, or told incidents of bad luck. He even gave them occasional advice. And now, at night when his work was done, he was always busy with his medicine store: his horns, roots, and powders, the shriveled head of a cock, purple, red, and yellow coloring matter, and calabashes of various sizes and colors, chiefly yellow. His friends, when they came in, would find him thus engaged, and in imagination he began to lead the life of a doctor even while, in the world of fact, he set and cleared tables, polished spoons and forks, and presented the bill of fare.

At last a particular friend of his, Simon by name, who had

heard hints from other waiters, put the question to him point-blank. For an instant John hesitated, and then told him the truth. He was a *nganga*, son and grandson of famous doctors. And when he had confessed he was glad. It was not surprising; for it was obvious that the desire to give up his job was growing stronger every day; indeed, I believe that he deliberately displayed his drugs to the other boys so that he would be discovered and forced to retire from his work. The slip of his tongue with Edith was undoubtedly of the same nature and significance. For he craved to become a doctor again. Though he did not fully realize it, his pity and compassion had been stirred very often during the past few months. Everyone to whom he spoke seemed ill or miserable. Stronger than ever he felt the urge of his hereditary calling, the desire to help and to cure. The incident of Edith's mother was the culminating point of a psychological situation that had slowly been coming to a head.

The meeting with the distressed stranger on his first journey on the road from Manyikaland, the encounter with the Manyika girl in the bewitched kraal, had diverted him from the normal path of his life for years. Now Edith seemed to be taking him back to his destiny, to the life of an *nganga*, decreed by his father. All this stretch of long eventful years between the two steppingstones, the bewitched kraal and the sickness of Lizzie, seemed to have been a dream from which he was slowly awakening.

This, John did not understand. But he was well aware of the mental conflict, of the struggle between desire and fear, the common companions of all human beings. There was his desire to practise: for this his whole being craved. But there was also the fear of disobeying his father, whose censoring words he had never forgotten. This conflict led to inner anxiety and had intensified the external dissatisfaction. Nor did his relationship with Edith give him any longer what little satisfaction he had formerly enjoyed. In his work, though he was an excellent waiter, he became more and more apathetic.

External events seemed to have played into his hands, for at this time the boardinghouse changed hands. John felt apprehensive about the new proprietress, and, in fact, found her, as he had expected (and very likely wished), rather insolent. At the end of her first three months every one of the old waiters save John had left.

In spite of his proficiency, he did not seek another job. Edith, to whom his behavior was inexplicable, vainly sought to reawaken his ambitions, and even went so far as to put him in the way of a better job. But it so happened that by the time he got to the hotel, the place had been filled. It was a pleasant building, the wages were better, the mistress seemed kind. But John had unfortunately missed his opportunity.

We can understand that his "bad luck" was subconsciously intentional; he was too concerned with the lure of medicine; as a deeply religious man regards this life only as a temporary existence, so John endured his work as a waiter for the sake of his future life as a *nganga*. His status as a waiter mattered little to him; indeed, he might have welcomed the insolence of the new proprietress as supplying a valid excuse for his giving up his job.

At the boardinghouse things went from bad to worse. There was grumbling among the servants, and the new owner nagged them continuously. "This white devil; what does she want?" they would ask themselves. Then one evening, a waiter who had answered her less civilly than she expected was dismissed with shrill vituperation. John en-

90

tered the kitchen as she shouted: "Go away at once! Money? You won't get any money! Go before I call the police."

The word "police" struck a chill into John's heart. He felt sorry for the man. There was so much suffering for the Africans. How unlucky they were! There was a new waiter from Natal who wanted to kill himself, his luck was so bad; no girl would love him. John's heart ached for him. If he had been practising medicine he could have helped the poor fellow, who had obviously been bewitched. Yes — there was trouble, bad luck, all round. A man whose wife had run away with his money and children; a woman's husband when drunk had struck her on the head so that it bled profusely; a woman, of whom Maggie had told him, who had come from the kraal with five children, all of whom had died in one year — "she sits the whole day crying"; a waiter who complained that his brother had spoiled two girls, they had babies by him, and now their father was demanding ten pounds, otherwise he would put him in jail; an unfortunate girl who came to ask for love potions; a young Manyika who came for luck-medicines because he lost job after job — so the long tale of woe unfolded itself before his eyes.

So much misery! His heart was heavy with the pain of all the world. Unhappy loves, broken marriages, sick babies, sudden deaths. In one week John lost two friends, one killed in a car accident, the other dying of a sickness of the lungs.

Such a harvest of sick bodies, tortured minds, broken hearts. And the very men who should devote themselves to healing and protection were nothing but a pack of charlatans and money-grubbers, incompetent, unprofessional, like Ephraim. Some native doctors, he found, actually went in search of patients, going from house to house, offering their medicines and services. What would be the end of a profession that had forgotten heredity and tradition in the scramble for mere money?

As for the white man — clever as he was, he failed even to cure the ills of the body. Of poisoning and witchcraft, of course he knew nothing.

One day John went with Simon to the native hospital, as the latter wanted to see his sister, who, with her two little children, had been seriously burnt. A candle had set fire to the curtains of a wooden room. At the hospital they were told, very casually, that the woman and both children had died. The man who spoke did not even say a word of sympathy to the unfortunate Simon.

"How can such people cure when their hearts know no sorrow for the sick?" John demanded of me. "A fire means that someone has sent poison through thunder. What do the white people know of medicines against thunder?"

Some days later, a fellow waiter was taken off in an ambulance. "The old devil did not even ask the man's consent." Driven by his curiosity, always strong, and in medical matters uncontrollable, John went again to the hospital. He wanted to convince himself of the white man's impotence in healing. He also wanted to see how they practised. As he walked to the entrance, he saw some women patients on the balcony. All were dressed alike, lying in narrow beds, all very clean and neat. He found the same in the men's wards; all the same. He had great difficulty in finding his friend; they sent him from place to place. Didn't these people know their own patients? His father, Charlie, had a large number of patients, yet he could remember all of them without difficulty.

John stood beside the bed, looking down on the dying man. A native nurse came in, moving from bed to bed.

92

She was a good-looking girl, had a fine figure, but he could not catch her eye. She looked at nobody, did not open her mouth. It seemed to John that she would put the glass tube into the mouth of a dead man and not notice it. It was appalling in its inhumanity. How could a man be treated by a doctor who did not know his name or the name of his father? He thought of the intimate contact, obtained by an African doctor as he throws the bones, when he finds out the luck of the patient, which is the final deciding-point in the treatment. And then, how can one help a patient if one does not know his enemies, against whom one must protect him first of all? John thought, further, how every detail of the patient's family life and past history is shared by the doctor before diagnosis is made.

No wonder every patient they brought here died — as an old man outside the hospital had assured John was the case. What was the use of futile child's-play like the little white pills and the medicines in bottles? And, finally, medicines were powerless. And what did the white people know of the *midzimu*? It seemed dreadful to him that these clever white people should be so blinded by their own conceit that his countrymen could die like this, with no practical assistance.

Surely, surely it was his duty to help his people? Yes — his people. For, more and more, he regarded himself as a Bantu, not merely as a Manyika, as he had done when first he arrived in Johannesburg. But his father had made no sign, and until he told John to practise he must not take a single case. "For the mature to practise; for the young to study."

In the meantime he devoted himself in such time as he could to the study of drugs, roots, poisons, illnesses. He made several acquaintances among *ngangas, ngomas, isanus-*

93

sis, and all the other numerous folk, men and women, who were dealing with the sick and suffering.

One day Ephraim took him to Mai-mai, an open-air bazaar, with a number of stalls where one can purchase roots, powders, skins, tails, bones, love potions, luck medicines, amulets, and the like — all the necessities for medicine-making. To John, the sight was an outrage. That doctors should sink so low as to prostitute their profession thus! How did the *midzimu* fit into such a scheme? The whole basis of the practice of medicine was shattered unless identification, feeling of oneness with the father, with the ancestral spirits, were preserved. And there was, further, the ritual of digging, preparing, and mixing. Sick at heart, incredibly disillusioned, John saw the cynical Ephraim purchasing for money that which careful labor should produce under the direction of the revered dead.

Profanation! Chicanery! John felt like a man in quicksands. The solid earth of tradition gave way beneath his feet. He felt bewildered, lost. Shocked by the living, ignored and abandoned by the dead . . .

2

AS if life were not troubling him enough, Maggie now added to his difficulties. She had moved from Doornfontein and had taken a room in Pretoria Street to be as near as possible to him. He was like a trapped animal. No longer was he free to spend his time with Simon and Ephraim and the other boys and girls. Constantly he would find Maggie waiting for him after work. In any case, he had to go to her, or she would not hesitate to make a scene in front of the other waiters. Sullenly he realized that this would always be the case when he had a job. As a doctor, he would be away all day; if necessary, all night. His professional duties would free him of her constant supervision, worse even than that of his employer. Besides, though frigid, she would make sexual demands which irritated him. Her proximity annoyed him. And yet he would do nothing directly; he always fought shy of decisive action; always went the way of least resistance. It was hard for him to say: "Go away; I do not want you"; but how easy to evade with: "I cannot sleep with you tonight. I will spoil my medicines. The medicines will not be strong unless I stay alone."

At this time, too, an even deeper dislike of Europeans came to him. Terms of opprobrium, which formerly he would have passed over with a shrug, now filled him with shameful humiliation. When he was pushed off the pavement by a bumptious white youth, burning resentment flared up in his heart. A choleric old man, with a liver pickled in alcohol, cursed him as a bastard, not a nigger, and John felt suddenly cold and physically sick. One day he was so tired that he risked entering a tram, hoping to fool the conductor by saying that his missis was downstairs — for in such cases Africans are allowed to use the trams — but the lie was discovered, the tram stopped, and he was pushed out on to the street, not without physical violence. Stage by stage there was born in him a grim determination one day to revenge himself for such degradation.

And then there were the eternal pass questions and "specials." On one occasion, he was stopped in the street by a man, quite possibly not even a detective, who declared that his pass was not in order. He was searched, and all his money was taken from him.

Every African man must be in possession of a pass. Without it he cannot look for work, travel, move from kraal to town or appear on the streets between the hours of 9 P.M. and 6 A.M. The police have the right to demand a pass from any African and it is an offense to refuse to produce it. In Transvaal an African man must on various occasions carry, in all, eleven passes issued by the authorities, who have discretionary powers to refuse an African the required pass.

The eleven passes are: A pass that entitles the African to travel, enter, or live in the province. A pass from the employer that has to be registered with the police every month. A pass from the owner of his kraal-land. A permit to enter an urban area. A permit to seek work. A service contract. A permit for one's wife to live in the town with him. A permit to live in specific parts of the town. A visitor's permit, if the African is on a visit to his parents or relatives. A lodger's permit if he hires a room. And, finally, the curfew pass, given by the employer, that entitles the African to appear on the streets between 9 P.M. and 6 A.M.

Of these pass-laws the Chief Justice, Dr. Krause, has said: "Every raw unsophisticated and honest African entering an urban area would, generally within twenty-four hours, find himself in prison."

He longed to get away from white people, to be free of their employment, free of their rigid time-tables. "One night while I was talking to Maggie, she told me about a man who had committed suicide. He hanged himself in the next-door garage. I also thought how nice it would be to die." Then, suddenly serious, he told Maggie: "Once, once before, I really wanted to die. It was when my mother died." Maggie was obviously startled by his tone of voice, but she said nothing, and he sat musing over the past. Suddenly he sat up abruptly, a smothered ejaculation breaking from him: "My age!" he said, his voice hoarse with emotion. "I must be nearly thirty!"

He felt a curious thrill. For between thirty and forty is the ideal age to practise as a doctor. And his wish was finally fulfilled, for that night he dreamed that he was back in Rhodesia.

"My mother's hut was burning, was still burning when I arrived. After a few minutes, the hut was burnt. I rebuilt it in a couple of minutes. From the hut I went to a big river. My son Daniel was there. I took the child over the river on a small stick. Beyond the river I saw my mother."

On waking he remembered that his mother's hut was once burnt. He was very small then, and his mother had cried bitterly. He understood now that the burning of the hut in the dream meant that his mother wanted him to help in building her home, to do what the father would have done on such an occasion; that is, to help all women: to build up their homes for them and help them in their bad luck.

When he told the dream to Maggie she grasped instantly that it meant that he was now mature enough to replace his father and build up a home. She told him so, and this, and the dream, cheered him considerably. The dead had not forgotten. Now, he was sure, things would move more swiftly towards the fulfillment of his desire.

And so, that night, it was with reverent anticipation that he settled himself to sleep. Nor was he disappointed. His father came to him to teach him how to be a doctor. He took John to the top of a mountain and showed him medicine roots which he had dug out. He showed him a number of goats, telling John to count them. He counted them, but when he had reached about thirty, he woke up shivering with excitement. At last! Here was the message, obvious enough for a son — go dig your roots, practise as a doctor, for now you are thirty, the prescribed age. . . .

Again he dreamed. There was a very big snake in the room. He tried to kill it, but could not. It had a big head and four teeth. He was not afraid. He called another boy to assist him. They left the snake and went outside. After a long time they returned. But the snake was gone. He awoke. He could hear Maggie's breathing: she had a heavy cold. It was time for him to get up.

He told me these three dreams in one afternoon, so vividly that, rereading the verbatim reports I have of them, I have some doubt as to their authenticity. The only explanation that I can bring in his favor is that such dreams usually impressed him tremendously, and as a *nganga* he paid considerable attention to them, pondering what his father might say about them. It is also true that, on looking through about two hundred dreams that I collected during the two-and-a-half years, I find in them a constant repetition of the same theme whenever his father or mother is concerned.

A snake! When a doctor dreams of snakes it means that his medicine is finished and he must dig it again. He must kill another snake, kill it himself, not obtain it from someone else. To kill a snake means also to kill all temptations of youth or bodily pleasure. So John knew that he must go and dig. He remembered how his father used to take the snake poison out of people. He had seen him do it for three people. He would take medicine, put it in his mouth, and draw out four small teeth from the arm. Charlie had explained to him that when a snake bites the small teeth come out; then the teeth travel right up the arm. After he had taken out the teeth, he put in medicine. He had told John

98

that one must never cut in a case of snakebite. (This treatment, as it happens, is not empirically wrong, and is practised by all nations. The fanciful explanation about the four small teeth, however, John could not explain to me.)

These dreams brought a strange new peace to his heart. He was once more in contact with the *midzimu*. His dead people were his friends again.

3

NOW small ailments began to keep him from work. He had toothache, stomach-ache, headaches. The missis expressed her annoyance freely. John felt that she disliked him, but he did not care. On the contrary, he seemed to go out of his way to annoy her; so much so that the other waiters were surprised that he was not dismissed.

One day some people came to find him. They waited with Maggie until he came home, and then told him they wanted him to visit a patient. The old man said: "She is my daughter. She is very sick. Her skin is hot like fire. We have had many doctors, none has helped her."

John's heart began to beat excitedly. He remembered very clearly how he had gone with Charlie to one girl patient. He had been very young when he had held the black horns and the golden calabashes, bringing up the rear as they jog-trotted through the night till they came in sight of the red-gold of the kraal fire. They had found a young girl wrapped in a brilliant striped blanket, lying on a reed mat. The light of a small candle shone on her frightened face and wide eyes. Charlie told him to put the palm of his hand on her body, just below the heart. He could hear the hurried breathing of the parents, and the girl's labored intake of breath as his cold, damp palm touched her scorched body.

Sitting on the floor beside the girl, Charlie began the divining by the horns. The sick girl stared at him. On her forehead Charlie made a sign like a cross, and then upon his own. Then he rolled the horns in the palms of his hands and put the male horn in the calabash. He seemed to be holding the calabash rigid, but, as he explained later to John, the wrist must be loose and vibrating. A bat flew in on velvet wings and beat about the hut. The girl moaned in terror, but Charlie did not move his eyes from the horn, and as he began to speak the bat dived into the night. Clearly, as though it had happened yesterday, John remembered Charlie's words: "The male horn says the old woman is jealous about the girl's father. She took the earth from the girl's feet and mixed it with medicine, burnt the earth with the poisons, and put it on the girl."

A large goat was brought into the hut. Very far away a jackal howled. Charlie, still on his haunches, leaned forward and smeared oil from the big horn on the goat. Then he made a humming noise and spoke to the goat. "You poisoner. You poisoned the girl. This sickness from the daughter must go to you, and you must die. . . ."

Charlie had approached the girl, drawing in his breath with a loud sibilant *tsss*, which puts terror into the evil-doer. A sudden draft from the door set the candle flickering and a huge distorted shadow of the goat leaping up the wall. He was given a long knife, as long as his forearm, and he had to plunge it into the hairy throat of the goat. . . .

The memory was so vivid that even now the sharp smell of ammonia and the detestable odor of the goat twitched in John's nostrils. . . .

The father of the patient began to describe the symptoms

and now John had no doubt that this case was exactly the same. There was no detail that he did not know. He knew the sickness and the treatment; he knew how he could cure the girl, gain fame, independence.

A small crowd of his friends began to gather, all interested in the case. They urged him to go, turning to one another and telling of prophecies come true till John tired of their flattery. One incident after another was recalled, and even Maggie roused herself in the general admiration of her husband and added her quota. And at last he agreed.

The soft clapping of their hands was balm to his heart. It was late at night. He went back to the boardinghouse and demanded to see the missis. He told her of an urgent message from his wife's kraal near Pietersburg, and said that he must go at once. Reluctantly she paid him the three pounds due to him, which, after three years' work, were all that he had to show.

4

THUS it was that John set out on his medical mission, so rudely interrupted at the doomed kraal of the beautiful Manyika witch. It was as if he were going home after a long, dreary absence, he thought, as he entered the patient's room. A lonely, frightened little boy feels just this sense of security, haven after a storm, when his mother's warm and loving arms enfold him, against her protecting breast.

As he handled the case, with a sureness of technique that brought immediate comfort to the agonized parents, he felt a great tenderness for the sick girl; a tenderness that surged up in his heart, engulfing the whole suffering world; tenderness that included even himself, John Chavafambira, who had been so lonely, so miserable, so insignificant. Indeed when, in silence with lip-speech alone, he addressed the scrawny scapegoat provided by the parents, "You must die. The sickness from the daughter must go to you," it was as if the fever, the dryness, and lassitude from which he himself had suffered so long were being loaded on to the beast about to die. So that there was a double healing performed. The girl quickly recovered, and John, his reputation enhanced, seemed like a man raised from the dead.

III

AFTER telling me about his taking up the art of a *nganga* John narrated this dream: —

"I was in a big mountain with my first father. I don't know his face. I was too small when he died. But I told myself that it was my father. He showed me a hole in a big stone. He told me I should go inside this stone. I was afraid to go inside this hole, although I wanted to very much. Then he went in first and I followed. I was not afraid then. It was very dark. There was a horn of medicine. There were plenty of horns. There was also a big black snake. He again told me not to be afraid. The snake looks after the horns. I told my father, 'I know that you are dead. How is it you are with me?' He answered, 'I am dead, but I walk, and you don't see me.' I felt in the dream a bad smell coming from my father. I thought it was his body. Then we came out, Father first and I after him. We went up to the mountain. He told me to go on my own. He will look after the medicine. And I went up and up. Then I woke up.

"When I started the practice of medicine, after I have come from the sick girl I told you of yesterday, I dreamed three times the same dream. It means my father wants me to be a doctor and likes the way I am doing it. Natives say it is not good to dream of dead people. It means they want you to follow them, to be dead. But I think different."

103

These dreams, and his remarkable success with the sick girl, decided him definitely to begin his practice as a *nganga*. He established himself in a room in Jeppe, a suburb of Johannesburg, and brought Maggie and the children to live with him. Maggie even now talks of those times as the happiest. John's practice grew; new patients came daily to consult him; he became once more kind to his wife as in the old days in the Pietersburg hotel, remembering with solicitude her illness and lameness. As a doctor, he was glad of his marriage, for no doctor should be without a wife. Again, as of old, they slept together, and it was not long before Maggie told him that she was once more pregnant. He was not displeased. His heart craved children, children through whom he would be perpetuated, and it pleased him, now that life was running more smoothly, to think that there was another child coming.

Many people sought his advice and assistance. "A man came from my wife's place and told us all the cattle died. The white doctors say it is only because there is not enough grass, but this, Doctor, is not true. The cattle were poisoned, and my medicine helped them. Then a boy, Dunde, was brought by his father. He slept with his mother as a man with a woman. It was true, because the mother confessed," he insisted, sensing my disbelief. "I didn't know what to do for the man. I heard afterwards that the father killed the son. We used to sleep with sisters, but not properly; and not with Junia; she was too young."

Most of the cases concerned love — lost love or unrequited love, impotence, sterility. Few came with bodily ills, in suffering and anguish. He confessed that he had great difficulty in treating many of the people in the town. "I know everything about thunder," he said. "When a person or a house is hit by thunder, the people must throw away the

104

meat, or put medicine on it. Then one could eat the meat without sickness. But when a house is hit by thunder, it must be burned. How could I burn a house in Johannesburg?"

The room in which he and Maggie lived soon became quite a social center. A diversity of folk was attracted by its hospitality; in the evenings they would come and listen to the gramophone or take part in endless discussions about life, especially about the difficulties of life imposed on them in the towns. They discussed religions, their own and Christianity.

"My wife dreamed of angels," he told me once. "She saw them coming from heaven. One had a long, big knife and was going to attack her. She stretched herself on her stomach and called for help, but nobody came. My wife believes in angels, although she is not a Christian. I am a Christian; I go to church every Sunday. My wife doesn't want to go; she always says by-and-by. I pray in the church; I sing. Angel means somebody wants to kill my wife. She asked another old woman in the yard about the dream, and she told her that the angels mean that she will soon be quite well. But knife is a bad thing in a dream. One can kill with it: it means danger. It means I shall sleep with my wife very soon."

"Why?" I asked.

"Because a knife came into the dream and means we are near to sleep together. I can feel that my wife wants to sleep with a man."

As always, it amazed me how identical much of the primitive symbolism is with Freudian dream symbols, how universal are the representations in the unconscious mind of sexual activities, in this instance the representation of the male organ by a knife.

And then, straight away, John went on to talk about religion.

"We used to talk a lot about Christians. Even now we do. We don't think a lot of Christians. We don't believe in Jesus. We used to pray in olden times to our native god, Mwari, and to the *midzimu*, for rain. It always helped. Now we pray to Jesus and rain never comes. We have no corn, no land, nothing. We all hate the Christians; they talk, talk, and nothing comes to us from it. I am only waiting to go home and learn how to pray to our god and will never pray to Jesus, and won't be a Christian any more. I became a Christian when I was quite small. I was still stupid. My mother was a Christian and also my second father, and all the children were baptized. My children were not baptized and never will be. My father also does not believe any more in Christianity. He became a native doctor. The Christian priests are even so bad [he probably meant stupid] that they are against native doctors and native medicines. When a missionary comes to our houses at home, they chase him away. Nobody wants to talk to them. In the kraals nobody wants to be a Christian any more. Why should they be? [And here he became rather agitated.] The white people came to our country, it is the natives' country [he was emphatic about it], took everything away from us — the land, the cattle — and made us work. We cannot move without a pass, have to pay taxes; and they have given us Jesus. We don't want him. I read in the Bible that the Jews also refused to have Jesus, and believe in God. We are also the same; I won't send my children to church, but I will send them to school to learn native and English."

One day, he said, a strange man came and joined the circle. He was a silent, taciturn man, who listened to their

106

talk but said nothing. He came often, although he was not a patient. He eventually broke his silence with a bitter attack upon Christianity, remarking, at the end, that the missionaries were no longer popular among the kraal-folk, who were turning away from the churches.

"That is true," a chorus of voices attested, though the majority of those present were Christians belonging to various denominations.

"I am also a Christian," the stranger said. "I belong to the Apostolic Church. But my *midzimu* are angry with me because I don't kill any goats to them, and the minister talks of hell where I will go if I remain a heathen. I want so much to know what is this heaven and this hell."

"Yes, and they also tell us that *lobola* is a sin," someone put in. "To have more than one wife is a sin. How can one marry without *lobola*? And how can one wife work the land?"

"They say if you make a sin you go to hell," the stranger interrupted again. "I would like to know what it is, hell." His face was stubborn and dull. Fear of hell seemed to have drained all life out of him.

Tentatively, someone tried to explain. But he failed. For the conception of hell is utterly foreign to the African mind. When people die, they become *midzimu*, and continue to live in the places where they lived in the flesh. They actually continue to live, only in a different way, and are in constant and intimate contact with the living. The dead and the living form a chain that must not be broken. There is no division of the worlds between them; the idea of hell, of "the other world," is utterly incomprehensible to them.

"And why do they want us not to talk to our *midzimu*? You are a *nganga*," they said to John; "why don't you ask

107

them?" "When I go to church," another said, "it is the Catholic Church. I look at all the statues. I like to look at them and think they might be my *midzimu*."

"Yes, that is right," John remarked. "The same happens to me in my church. I pray, I think of my *midzimu*, and the faces change even if I don't close my eyes. The woman with the child turns into my mother, Nesta."

John sat silently pondering this thought, till Maggie broke in loudly: "Well, I don't want any other *midzimu*, and I don't like the priests. I won't be a Christian."

But John loved the statue of Christ. He even referred to him as the Great Healer. Was he perhaps, he wondered, the great-great-great-grandfather of all the *ngangas*? He knew that Christ was born in Africa, and wished that he could have proved that Christ was a real African, black as all Africans. But he knew from the Bible that Christ was a Jew, and he had not seen a black Jew.

Strangely enough, John never commented upon the multiplicity of denominations. He did not understand the differences between them, but assumed that, as there were many tribes, so there were many *midzimu*, all representing their various people in the One Supreme Being that all acknowledged. Just as in the kraals each *midzimu* had to have a man or woman through whom one could communicate with the ancestors, so the ministers and pastors and priests were people who talked to the *midzimu*, to Christ, or the Trinity.

So John had his simple solution to the problem of the many denominations: a problem that the missionaries feared would prove a stumbling-block to their converts. Paradoxically, the diversity of Churches was to the latter a natural and normal thing.

John returned again and again to the subject of the

strange man, who must have made a tremendous impression upon him. This man seemed to have been determined to thrash out the problem to the bitter end. Turning to John, he would say: "Your wife is right. She has her *midzimu*. Why should she look for others, for new ones? I was a fool, and now I suffer. Because the priests are white people, and when they talk to Christ they must take the white people's part."

"Just as the magistrates in the court take the white man's part," John said to me. "In some country place, I forget the name, a magistrate sentenced four natives to two weeks' hard labor for talking too loudly in the streets of the village; while a white man who admitted that he had knocked a girl of thirteen unconscious for no reason whatever was allowed to go free."

John's statement was correct. Only a few weeks earlier I had read the account in the papers. Also, the authorities had erected a fence around the township, with sharp edges on the top. They proudly told the natives that they had found fingers on the top — left there of course by unwelcome intruders: people who had no permission to see their friends and sweethearts. . . . "Yes," he admitted, "some of the policemen and magistrates are not good to us. We are in very bad luck with the Europeans."

John asked me why Christ did not come in dreams like the *midzimu,* to help and advise him. He said that he had never been helped in his practice by the Church. On the contrary, his priest, an Anglican, forbade his people to consult witch doctors, telling them not to believe in the bones, but to go to the hospital for treatment. Speaking of these matters always excited him.

"Why," he expostulated, "does the priest speak against us native doctors, and leave the people unprotected against

109

evildoers, *abathakathis, ticoloshes,* and all the other bad luck?"

Then he remembered another man joining their circle. In appearance he was an ordinary African, but in manner and bearing he was different from the rest. His handshake, firm and strong, surprised John. The newcomer spoke with quiet confidence. There was no chair for him, and his hesitation before sitting down on the floor with the others was obvious. He introduced himself, a Xosa named Tembu.

"And by what name do your employers know you?"

"Tembu. I don't change my name to please others. I am an African, and I stick to the name my parents gave me."

"But when you were baptized," someone said, taking for granted that the newcomer was a Christian, "didn't they call you John, or George, or something?"

"Yes, they did, but my parents never called me by that name; and the teachers in the school hated to call us by foreign names. I hope none of you are called Threepence or April or other foolish names."

Meanwhile, John's practice flourished and his fame spread. People began to talk of the marvelous Rhodesian *nganga,* of his potent medicines, and, above all, of his genius in throwing the bones and telling fortunes. It was well known that he possessed the gift of settling disputes, of bringing together husband and wife; he was, in fact, known as "the peacemaker." He achieved much merely by talking, for he had a persuasive tongue, though in the case of unhappy love he gave love philters, Rhodesian potions that were far more efficacious than those of the Zulu and Sotho.

"Are only the Rhodesians good doctors?" I asked him.

"There are good doctors from other nations, too," he conceded. "I think in Transvaal the best doctors are the

110

Ba-Venda, the second the Shangaan; the Zulus are the best poisoners; of the born fortunetellers, Sotho and Shangaan are the best. But Manyikas have the strongest medicines. In Rhodesia are the best medicines. Many native doctors come to Rhodesia from other places, just to get the best medicines. My real father was the very best doctor in Rhodesia. I agree that the white people are also good, but they don't know about *abathakathis;* they can't make thunder; they don't know how to protect people. I cannot operate, but what is the good of cutting? The white people cut the woman if the baby goes the wrong way. My father would put his hands on the stomach with some medicine, and then the baby would come!"

IV

JOHN was often called away from Johannesburg to attend a patient. Once he was gone for three months in Kroonstad. For the whole time Maggie heard no word from him, nor did she receive any money from him. During the first few weeks she managed to collect a few shillings from his patients, but it was not very long before she was driven to the same expedient as so many other women in similar circumstances: she took a lover who was able to provide her what she needed.

"It was not the first time," John told me, "that my wife was not true to me. In 1927 I was working in Berea. She asked me for some money. I gave her five pounds. She said she needed it to go to her mother. But she didn't go to her mother. She went to another town to meet her old sweetheart. A friend wrote to me about it. But what could I do to her? Give her a hiding? But I hate so much the business of fighting."

Maggie spoke to me also quite frankly about this present affair. It was not carefully planned by her, but happened quite by chance. One evening a young miner came to consult John. He found her miserable and lonely and tried to comfort her. This led to friendliness, and ultimately to intimacy.

At first Maggie found the new experience exciting: she

112

forgot John and was careless of the possible consequences of the affair. Most of her neighbors had lovers, and there seemed to be a tacit agreement between them not to betray one another.

But the initial thrill soon passed. The thought came to her quite suddenly that the bones might reveal her infidelity to the absent John. She became nervous and restless. A terrifying possibility occurred to her: on his return, John might put her through the ordeal of chastity; the frightful test her mother had told her about, which was practised by witch doctors of all tribes. Her restlessness grew to irritation and affected her sleep, hitherto blissfully calm. Now she lay awake far into the night, imagining the various tortures John might inflict on her. And even when sleep came, it was disturbed by nightmares from which she would awaken in a cold sweat of terror, not daring to go to sleep again.

One dream was especially vivid. She was out in the open veld, in a part of the country strange to her. She heard footsteps. She ran hard, wild with panic. Her lover was suddenly standing in front of her. Half dead with fear, he called out: "They are going to poison me!" Then she found herself in the kraal; in a strange kraal. She was surrounded by hundreds of angry eyes, all accusing her of being the cause of their misery. An owl hooted, spelling magic and witchcraft. She protested her innocence, but the people laughed.

The scene changed again, and she was with John in a chief's hut. John was pouring medicine into a big pot full of boiling red liquid. "Put in more . . . more!" the chief shouted. "Let her drink it while it is boiling hot. If she is not guilty, she will vomit the medicine. If she is guilty, let her die." Maggie screamed and pleaded for mercy, but the people laughed. Then her lover was dragged in, stark naked. They were both taken together. It was late afternoon. Two men caught her with strong hands and tied her to the naked man. They were tied to pegs driven into the ground. Everyone disappeared. Then somebody came and covered her head with a thick blanket. Almost suffocated, she tore off the blanket and threw it away.

All day the memory of the dream haunted her. That evening she told her lover about it. He took a serious view, and questioned her closely about a witch doctor's methods of testing his wife's fidelity. She had great difficulty in remembering anything.

"Yes," she said slowly; "John told me I must not sleep with another man, especially if there were medicines in the room. I would die, or the *nyatsi* [back-door husband] would fall dead."

From John I later had a full account of the various taboos in this connection. "Nobody must sleep with a woman in the house of a *nganga*, for it will spoil his medicine. The medicines will be sleeping with each other and they will not be lucky. When I want to sleep with my wife, I must put a *chinameta* on the floor. She must not touch the medicine. I touch it. My own wife mustn't sleep with another man in the room when there are medicines. He will die, or she, if he remains alive. And Maggie knew before I left for Kroonstad I had medicines somewhere. That's why she was so frightened. She also knew that I can find out if my wife sleeps with another man. She goes home. I see her. I take a coin from my pocket and a little bit from the male horn, and put it in the fireplace. Then I go straight to her. If she is guilty, she will fall down, cry, and her whole body will tremble. If she didn't sleep she will greet me. Then I look at her for half an hour. The way she talks, looks at me. And if nothing happens, then she is clean. Then I take a special root and talk to her. If she is guilty she will run the whole day like mad. Then the Rhodesian doctors make medicines which they put into the wife's tea or food. We both drink it. Then I sleep with her. Then I take out a new knife and put medicine on it, and the closed knife I keep in my pocket. When I go away I have the knife with me. If another man sleeps with my wife, then they cannot be separated because the knife is closed. I learned this medicine from a Mutuko, and Maggie knew all about it because I talk to her about my medicines. I want her to be afraid of me."

And Maggie, indeed, talked far into the night with her lover, telling him everything she knew about John's powers over her, till the man must have regretted having had an affair with a doctor's wife!

The outlook for both of them was extremely gloomy. The fear of John, present and absent, became unbearable, and they agreed that the affair must end and that Maggie must leave Johannesburg. He advanced her the railway fare and, a few days later, having sold up her furniture and belongings, she departed with her two children for her mother's kraal. The decision to return to her mother is indicative of her state of depression, for she had never been anxious to go to George's home, and in these circumstances the prospect was detestable.

Meanwhile, John had been working on a difficult case in Kroonstad. His task was to change what a seer declared to be a snake in the womb of a pregnant woman into a normal human child. He used the rites prescribed by his father. A boy-child, strong and healthy, was born to the parents. John was acclaimed throughout the neighborhood, and many people came from afar to consult him.

When John returned to Johannesburg he found his room locked, empty. Maggie was nowhere to be found. No one knew where she had gone. Shortly after her departure, the African tenants in that particular area had been turned out by the municipal authorities who, in pursuance of a policy of the segregation of blacks, had prohibited the letting of premises in the area to Africans. It seemed to John a cruel blow. So many had made their homes there and were, within the limits open to them, comfortably settled.

But it was not long before he learned the full details of Maggie's love affair. He related it to me now as though the whole story were undisputed fact, but at the time he disbelieved it, for he said he well knew what women's gossip was. My own belief was that he was indifferent to his wife's morals, and to give credence to such a story was too much trouble. He decided to trust his bones and ignore gossip. And the bones obligingly showed Maggie to be innocent.

2

WITH an easy mind he began to look for a room. This was more difficult than he had anticipated, for hundreds and hundreds of natives were being expelled each month from one or other urban locality, and none wanted to go to the townships and locations outside the town. After much difficulty he managed to get a room in Swartyard, a native tenement known among the initiates as "*skokiaan* yard." This nickname came from the fact that in Swartyard *skokiaan*, Kaffir beer, and other intoxicating liquor, was illegally made and sold.

The yard was near the center of the town. When natives

were expelled from other central urban areas, Swartyard somehow remained; some said by accident, others said by careful bribery of the authorities. Whatever the reason, it remained.

Swartyard was a triangular area of about a thousand square yards where stood a hundred or more ramshackle rooms, built of corrugated iron and thin wooden planks. The rooms were built in three or four rows, with very little space between, and intersected by three narrow alleyways. Two huge garbage bins, serving the whole yard and constantly overflowing, flanked the narrow entrance. From them an unbearable stench permeated the whole place. There were six latrines, in a shocking state of neglect and disrepair, and totally inadequate for the five hundred souls that used them. The children did not bother to use them, as the alleyways inside and the pavement outside showed. In dry weather the yard was littered with refuse; in the rains the place was a quagmire. Repeated requests by the inhabitants themselves, and by the health inspector, that the area be cemented remained unheeded. In the whole yard there was one solitary tap of running water.

The rooms themselves were a striking contrast to this unsavory mess: clean, neat, even decorated with curtains, pictures, and shining brassware.

In this yard John rented a room. He did not stay alone for long. Maggie soon heard of his return, and hurried back, leaving the children with her mother.

Maggie had changed. She feared the bones and the ordeal of chastity; she was afraid that her unfaithfulness might have harmed John's medicines. John noticed the change in her, but made no reference to it. The gossip he had heard occasionally crossed his mind, but he ignored it. But he showed his dislike for her more openly than before. She reverted to her usual lazy, slovenly, inactive existence. She gossiped with the women, neglected the room. She loved Swartyard; it suited her ideally.

Their room faced the street, a small room in the center of a row of similar hovels. It had no ceiling, and the roof leaked; the floor was bare earth; the tiny window had six little panes, half of them covered with tin, the rest dirty glass. In spite of the brilliant South African sun, the room was plunged into semidarkness whenever the narrow, low, tight door was shut.

Day and night there was continual noise. The partition between John's room and the one behind it was made of thin planks, badly put together and not even reaching the roof.

John paid thirty shillings a month for this room and was lucky to get it. The furnishing was simple: one bed, one chair, a table in which stood a tin basin, always full of dirty water, and a primus stove, surrounded by some kitchen utensils and chipped crockery. A draggled curtain dropped over the window. A couple of clotheslines from which dangled garments and blankets stretched across the room. In a far corner John kept his bag, his calabashes, and medicines.

Day and night the yard buzzed with life. Every afternoon between five and six the place was crowded with strangers; a continuous stream of people came to buy beer. On Saturdays and Sundays one could hardly move along the narrow alleyways, cluttered up with packing-cases, tins, cooking braziers, and crowded now with hosts, guests, and strangers.

Practically every woman in the yard made beer, except Maggie, and newcomers were still intimidated by the constant police raids. Maggie flatly refused to make it, to John's great annoyance.

118

"It is as much a wife's duty to make beer in the town," he would say, "as at home in the kraal. A man needs beer, for he likes to drink and entertain his friends."

Finally, on rare social occasions, Maggie agreed to make beer, but never as a commercial enterprise. She was too ill, too lame, to move quickly in a police raid. In reality she was afraid of work, for those women who took part in the industry displayed immense energy and alertness of mind. John implored, threatened, but nothing could change Maggie. Friends mocked him for his weakness; indeed, the whole population of the yard was incensed at her behavior.

"Maggie is not a good woman," he would often remark to me. "Other women make beer; they make two shillings a day, if they do washing for the white people. If I have no money, it is finish with me. No help from anybody. I must cook for her, I must clean the child; if I talk to her she says, 'You worry me.' I don't know, should I hit her? Or swear at her? I talk to her quietly, try to explain. It doesn't help. I always think I must go home and marry somebody at home."

"Very few women have anything to do with you because you are not like the rest," John would often tell her, to which she would derisively answer: "I should mix with all these women? Women who spend much of their time in prison? No, my mother Mawa would be against it. Besides, I hate the beer." This was not true, for John, on his return home, would often find her drunk.

I understood from him that other people tried to interfere on his behalf. On one occasion a woman patient of his, who came from Maggie's kraal, said: "But you know what beer means to your husband." At this a man sitting on the floor remarked: —

"Funny people, these whites. They let us drink beer in the kraal, because they know very well we drink beer when one dies, when a child is born, when we pray for rain, when a fortune is told, when a chief is welcomed. Why do they not allow us to have beer for these same occasions in town?"

A young Xosa patient, undergoing a prolonged treatment for "sickness of the bladder," said in a tone of bitter hatred: "We work hard all the week. Can't we drink beer when we finish work, in our leisure time? The white people only wish us to suffer. Why has God created such people?"

"But when we drink too much we make such a noise," John concluded this discussion with me. "We kill each other, we hit our wives, we become cheeky to the white people. Yes, we make too much noise and trouble. The white people don't like it."

Next day he returned to the subject; less timidly now, for there had been a raid in the yard only the previous night. What right had they, these whites, who deprived the African of everything, to forbid the ritual of beer drinking, the traditional drink of their ancestors before ever a white man set foot in Africa? Thousands and thousands of natives and colored people went to prison each year because of this law of the Europeans.

"If strong drink is so bad," he said, "why do white people drink it? And why do they sell all these drinks to the blacks? Money is what they want; to take from us our last penny. The same detectives sell to the natives the beer they take from us. Any woman in the yard can tell you about it. Yesterday, a woman worked the whole day making beer. Along came a black detective — dirty swine, they are worse than the whites — and found beer hidden in the ground. He smelt it with his dirty nose. And now her customers will come for beer, and she has nothing for them. Her husband earns fifteen shillings a week, and there are seven of them to buy bread and meat for, besides paying the rent for her room. How can she do it now?"

"Did they arrest her?" I asked.

"Cha! Cha! They are clever, the swines of police, but the women are cleverer. You see, they in the yard stick together; like the white people do. They make the beer in the middle of the yard; they keep it in the ground. When the police find the beer, whose beer is it? Nobody will tell. It is not in a room; it belongs to nobody. So they spoil the good beer; but they don't catch anybody. But not all women are so lucky."

He became excited and sat up on the sofa, continuing angrily, almost outraged: "Yes, not all women are so lucky. Once a friend of mine had a new customer come to her. He paid half a crown for beer. I have seen it myself. I told her to be careful, but two-and-six is a lot of money, so she gave him the beer. Before she had even put the coin in her pocket, they had arrested her. The man was a trap," he explained to me, "and the police had marked the coin he gave her."

No detectives came to John's room at any time. Maggie naturally used this fact as an additional argument for keeping away from beer. She made what John considered impertinent remarks about the foolishness of women who did not come for medicine to protect them against white people, but rather for medicine for more customers. John said wearily: "There is no medicine that affects white people," and his old hatred of her seethed in him. He showed it now whenever there was an opportunity. He never slept with her, kept away from home for days, and made it no secret that he wished to be free of her.

New rumors of her misconduct reached him. He himself

could easily have found proof of it, for she was regularly drunk. Who gave her the drink? The women in the yard? They disliked her, and beer would be the last thing they would have supplied to her. Men gave it to her. And men never gave beer for nothing. What should he do? Give her a beating, throw her out of the room? But she would not go. And what of the children? When his son grew up, they would both return to Rhodesia and marry Manyika girls. Meanwhile, he must wait and suffer.

He threw the bones to discover the cause of his bad luck, but he could get no satisfaction. So he went to a famous Ba-Venda bone-diviner, an old man who knew John and Swartyard well.

Three times he threw the bones, and each time they showed the same: male and female bones of the lion and zebra, of the cat and of the ox, of birds and of men — all of them were thrown together, on top of one another, interlocked, and the meaning was obvious. The people among whom John lived were bad. They lived in shame and in sin.

The yard was bad, the people were bad, and so his medicines were spoiled. John was pleased with the explanation. The yard was full of prostitutes willing to sell themselves for a shilling or two.

He kept silent for a long time, and then I tried to lead him back to the subject of the bone-throwing. The old man had told him that he himself was in danger, and John admitted that the bones spoke the truth. He was daily approached by women; he even dreamed of them, though luckily in his dreams he was always too strong to succumb to temptation: he kept himself clean. It was not his fault, but his medicines must have been spoiled by the atmosphere of prostitution and adultery round about him. He often

122

wished now that he could live among men of Tembu's type. In such an atmosphere, he was sure, his luck would be better.

3

ACCORDING to him, bad luck seemed at that time to permeate the yard. Everyone was racking his brains to discover the cause of it. Never had so many died there as in the past few months; never had there been so much thieving, so many family tragedies. He told others of what the old man's bones had said, but the explanation was not accepted. The sinful atmosphere might have spoiled his medicines, too. The priest in the church also said the same. Sodom and Gomorrha. But that was all nonsense.

Then one of the men made a startling suggestion. John told me of it apologetically. "It is unpleasant for me to tell you this, Doctor," he said. "It is about the missis" — by which he meant the anthropologist who was making a socio-logical survey of the people in Swartyard — "please don't tell her." I promised, and he went on to say that the man's suggestion was that bad luck had come with this white woman. " 'No, not the shopkeeper's wife,' he said, 'but that rich young woman who comes here in her grand motor car and looks at you as if she didn't see you properly. They say she is a spy working for the police. They are all talking about it. She asks questions all the time; silly questions about what we eat, how many children we have, what money we earn, and so on.' "

Though he professed now to laugh at the idea, at the time he was pleased to be able to join the attack. "I was especially afraid of her," he excused himself, "because I didn't have my license." For a *nganga* has to have a general-trader's license, which, by the way, he never had even when he had money, unconsciously protesting against the imposition so that up to this day he has never taken one out.

Soon the white woman was the constant topic of conversation. The residents agreed that she treated them kindly. But why did she question them? How much money did they spend? Where did it come from? Why did she write down everything they said? "Surely her hand must be sore with all this writing," they remarked. Who was she? Why did she come every day to such a place as Swartyard? A place which white people avoided like the plague. It was most extraordinary. What was her business? Was she married? Had she children?

However farfetched and unjust these accusations were, there was a psychological basis for them, as it was true that although she was merely collecting sociological material for a book, the publication of the book could theoretically have led to the closing of the yard. She herself tried to pacify them and was extremely kind to them, but obviously could not give them information about her private life. She tried to explain her aims, but this did not remove the mistrust and suspicion. Unfortunately, too, police raids and the visits of health inspectors became more frequent at this time, and both unpleasantnesses were laid at her door.

One day, Tembu came to the yard, and soon heard all about the mysterious visitor. John set all the information and gossip before him and asked him what he thought. Tembu's explanation was that the woman was simply studying African life. "He told me, Doctor, that we are to the Europeans still a mysterious people, though they know us for hundreds of years. These students come to us not because they care for us, but because they want to

124

write books about us. In the Milner Park" — by which he referred to the Witwatersrand University — "the white young men and women study to be doctors, lawyers. They learn about nature, about butterflies and flowers and stones, and they also study us Africans. When they want something from us, they are kind, speak to us nicely. But in their own houses they treat the blacks like slaves, not better than the others." But for all that, Tembu assured John, the woman was not a spy; she wouldn't betray him or any other African. She might even be of great help to them.

From that day the anthropologist noticed a change in John's attitude towards her. He became a supporter of hers, and made a point of being in the yard whenever she came, was friendly and obliging towards her and used all his influence to win over the other residents in the same direction. The anthropologist, for her part, very naturally relied more and more upon him in her difficult task of collecting information from the hostile women in the yard. She helped him financially, and he accepted her help freely, realizing very well what motives were behind her generosity. He told Maggie that she brought him luck with his patients.

But soon he knew that even better luck was coming, for he dreamed that King George came to Johannesburg.

"Plenty whites and natives met him," he described the dream, "the big man, the big King. All very friendly, natives and whites. I was very surprised. They all shouted, 'The King has come to help the people.' All sang, blacks and whites. After this, the King left us and went back to England."

Obviously help was coming, not only to him, but also to his fellow sufferers. For the King was the Chief of the World. He was coming to help the natives. Some white man would come and help would finally come through the white man. "So sure was I that a white man would come to my help," he told me, "that I was not at all surprised when one day the white woman came to the yard and brought you."

For it was on that day that I first came to treat Maggie's legs and for the first time met John.

PART THREE

Degradation

I

IN RECONSTRUCTING John's past I encountered the difficulty that he was frequently carried away by his fantasies and, more perhaps than the average white man, careless about the accuracy of his reminiscences. I would ask him: "Do Africans tell lies easily? Are they the same with their own people?" And his reply was invariably: "When you don't want to hurt, you tell a lie; but I don't mean anything wrong. Or when you are much afraid of people. We don't like the white people; they are always cross, cheeky with us. We don't know what they will do with us. Therefore I don't care what I say to a white man if only I won't be punished."

And when talking about the present there was the difficulty inherent in John's fear of the white man.

Now there were new difficulties. John was afraid to tell me everything, and for a long time would say nothing that had to do with me, or other white people. Any patient normally has inhibitions about saying anything personal to an analyst, especially if it is detrimental, and one can realize how much more difficult it was for John to talk about me and the white people he hated and feared. Luckily, I did not rely exclusively upon his conscious statements, for as an analyst I was used to reconstructing the truth from hints and indirect material. May I say *en passant* that,

129

contrary to the accepted belief, we do not jump to conclusions on the basis of a few facts, but pay attention to each word, to each action, so that, at the end, the sum total of the material permits of one conclusion which, sooner or later, is put to the subject of the analysis for his consideration. To a certain degree, the same process applied to John's analysis, with the difference, however, that there were no therapeutic aims, and no deep and farfetched explanations could be given to it. I have described already, during the first part of this book, John's behavior at the beginning of the analysis. A month later he described the impression he had had of me then: —

"When you came with the tall missis, I remembered Tembu's words. 'Another busybody who will write about me.' You shook hands with me and talked so that I felt funny in my heart. And then you were a doctor. I knew you European doctors have hundreds of medicines for all sicknesses, but what did the doctor want with me? Later, I talked about you to my friends. They suggested you were looking for patients. 'Didn't he offer to treat Maggie?' they said. But I said, 'He asked no money for it.' I remembered the dream of King George, and my heart felt at ease, for I was sure you would bring me luck."

One must realize that this was said when John was already quite attached to me, and one can reasonably doubt his sympathetic attitude towards me at the beginning. But it was no doubt true that the contact with two Europeans who were kind to him and apparently interested in him intrigued him very much. The mere fact that Europeans, and one of them a doctor, should sit with him for an hour at a stretch had a revolutionary effect upon his entire outlook.

Not that he trusted me. Maggie, I found out, often

130

reproached him for his lack of confidence. She was grateful to me because, indeed, I helped her considerably; but friends in the Swartyard and outside persistently warned John against me and the anthropologist. "No good will come of all these questions and talking," they said. Many in the yard went further, denouncing us as spies and declaring that we were responsible for the evil that was about to fall upon them. John, though not yet certain of our ultimate aim, was sure that we were, as he put it, honestly his friends. But still, watching the friendly and ingratiating manner of the Swartyard residents to white visitors, and remembering their bitter attacks during their absence, he decided that one must be very cautious in one's relations with the white. "Never trust a white man. We learn this in our cradle."

For a month he did not admit that he was already a practising doctor. Instead, he would complain: "If only I could become a doctor. My heart shivers when I think of it. I was a waiter, but I cannot be a waiter and a doctor at the same time." A few days later, not realizing that he was contradicting himself, he described how he had treated a girl for "sickness of the bladder." I did not draw his attention to these discrepancies. For nearly six months he denied that he threw bones, at the same time often mentioning that his medicines and bones were in a corner of the room and that nobody dared to touch them. As I found out later, he was originally coming to me not to please me, but to extract all he could get out of me concerning my medicines and Europeans in general. He was careful not to arouse my suspicions and copied me to an amazing degree. For example, he would ask a question and then let me talk without interruption even when I used words which he obviously could not understand. He confessed, during later stages, that he was carefully noting our speech, actions, dress, and especially anything connected with my medical work. "It seemed to me, Doctor, that I was again learning the medicine, as in my young days with my father Charlie. Only Charlie taught me better." Finally he persuaded me to give him pills, tablets, mixtures, and with these he decided to experiment.

His friend Simon sounded a grave warning. "You are a *nganga*: you must remain a *nganga* like your father and grandfather. Do not use the medicines the white doctor gives you." Others supported Simon. "No good will come of it," they prophesied. But John was already too much under my influence. Besides, unknown to himself, civilization had penetrated into his innermost being. He loved the town, its buildings and streets, he loved the suits and shirts and ties that he could buy in the shops; he would often speak of buying dozens of shirts and suits and ties, and it would have been difficult to find a European with a tie as neatly made as his. On the other hand, his friends continued to upbraid him for his friendship with the white man, so that he was involved in endless altercations and went through a period of severe inner conflict. His dreams were typical of this.

"I dreamed of a man in the yard who was fighting with me with a knife which he sticks in my elbow. I ran away. Then I stood up. I took my knife and stuck it right into his stomach. He ran away. I was after him. His friends gathered together and all of them liked to kill me with sticks. I ran till I reached a big house where I found white people digging the garden. Then my enemies ran away. I always dream the same dream of fighting with a knife. It doesn't mean me if I dream it. Charlie used to say it means two doctors are fighting each other and that my medicine is stronger than the other's."

On the same night he had another dream. "I am given four white pills. Very small and white. These pills are to clean my body and blood. White eggs and white pills always bring luck. Your medicine is wonderful medicine. All people now will be talking about me and I will get very rich. It's not lucky to see black in a dream, because black means dead people."

"If a black boy comes to your dream," he went on, "it means someone wants to poison you. In the yard there are plenty of boys who are poisoners; but I want to cure people, not to kill." As to the association of black chickens, he said: "If I would have dreamed the same dream at home, I would have had to kill a black chicken and give it to the dead. It must be a special kind of poison if you dream of a black chicken. What I think is that one of the men in the yard gave poison to the chicken and called my name. Yes, I remember. I have seen a chicken in our yard yesterday. The poisoner makes one chase the chicken the whole day, and when you come home you are mad. Some men, if they want to poison you, they put the medicine into a string which by itself changes into a snake. The snake bites you: you are dead. I don't go to study any more for a doctor, nor will I go. Your medicine is so much better. The coolies in our country can change a man into a dog, into any animal. They can change a shilling into a golden pound."

During this time he began to dream dreams in which I was directly concerned, and from which his ambivalent attitude towards me of love and hate was very apparent. "You, me, and another little native boy went to a mountain in your motor car. From there we went to another place of hills. When you were driving the car, you let it run alone. I was afraid. I told you the car would be smashed. We should go out of the car. I and the boy went out of the car

133

and we looked and saw the car running into a big house and smashing the house. We went and looked at the car underneath, when you came along. The car wasn't broken, so we went again. Now you started to drive again and let the car run alone again. I warned you that the car would be smashed but you didn't listen to me, and the car went behind some small hills and disappeared. We have seen big holes, but we couldn't find the car. So you cried and said, 'My strong car is broken,' and you sent me home to your missis that she should buy another car. I went along. I left you standing there. This dream made me very frightened because I thought you would meet with an accident in the street." (A suspicious anxiety over me, chiefly concealing unconscious death-wishes.)

Then, for twenty days, he did not visit me, and when he did come he began with the following words: "I was worrying all the time about you, Doctor. You must believe me that I was thinking about you all the time. I was all the time sitting and thinking about you. It was lonely. I was missing you. I hope you had a nice Christmas." This over-emphasized worry, and the fact that he nevertheless did not come to see me, confirmed my previous suspicions, and so did his remark as he left me. "Is the doctor cross with me? Does he think of me angry? I wondered very much about it. I'm so glad I came to see the doctor today."

And then I did not see him again for a long time, and again I suspected strong resistance to me, but this time I was wrong. I discovered him by accident in a native hospital. This is what had happened:—

One Saturday evening he left his room in the yard and went to walk the streets, away from the shabbiness and suspicions of Swartyard, the bad women, the gamblers and the drunkards, away from the continuous fighting. He

134

strode along, filled with conflicting thoughts. What did his *midzimu* think of it all? But it was so long since he had killed a goat to his *midzimu* that he knew there would be no reply from them. Up and down the street he went, vaguely aware of the blaze of lights from the cinemas. Why had God made such a difference between people? Why could all men who had white skin have dresses and money and go to the cinemas? Why all this suffering for the blacks? So preoccupied was he with his own suffering that he was like a man suddenly roused from sleep when his progress was rudely and roughly stopped.

He realized that he was in Eloff Street, the main artery of the town. Beside him was drawn up a yellow van, netted as if for the transport of poultry. Without ceremony or explanation, he was bustled into this dreaded "pick-up van," used for collecting Africans who were drunk or were without passes or specials that would entitle them to be in the streets after nine at night, or any undesirable Africans likely to be a menace to the white community.

Only at the police station did John realize his crime. He had been in the streets at eleven P.M. without a special pass; and for the next thirty-six hours he was imprisoned in a cell with many others as unfortunate as himself.

On Monday morning he was marched, handcuffed, through the streets to the magistrate's court: one of a similar gang to that which had affected him so deeply on his arrival in Johannesburg. In the courtroom he found a crowd of men and women — Indians, Africans, colored people — between whom there was one common tie: they were not white-skinned. One after another they were herded into the court, remained there a few minutes, and then were bustled back, having in the interim received trial and sentence: ten shillings or fourteen days, a pound or a month.

135

The magistrate, seated in his high chair away from all the other people, intrigued John. He compared him with the chief Mutassa who carried out justice in his kraal, and found him less imposing. He tried to catch his eye, but got only the merest glimpse of his face, so busy was he writing, writing. Although he knew English well, John was asked his name and occupation through an interpreter who spoke in a rough, abrupt manner. He mistrusted the man, and answered his questions unwillingly. The policeman who had arrested him stood in a box opposite him and talked to the magistrate and another white man. John hated them. He tried to listen to the proceedings. He heard that "the accused had no pass, had not paid his tax for years, had resisted arrest." "It is a lie!" he cried out, but the magistrate said something to the interpreter, who came over and asked John if he had a pound. The mere idea made John laugh. "Then you go to prison for a month," the interpreter laconically informed him.

Handcuffed to another native, in company with a large number of other "criminals," he was marched through the streets from the court to the Fort. He kept his head down. Almost every native he knew had been sent to prison; arrest by the police was regarded by all natives as more or less inevitable, like locusts, drought, and illness. But to John it seemed infinitely degrading for a professional man to be shackled to another man, publicly.

For two weeks after his disappearance Maggie could discover nothing at all. She went to the police station but could get no information there. She went to the white woman, but found her away on holiday. As for myself, I seldom visited the yard at that time, and as it happened I also went on holiday shortly afterwards. Maggie was left in utter ignorance of her husband's fate.

John in the meantime was spending his time working in a convict road-gang. The manual labor proved a severe ordeal for him, and on the day of his release he caught a chill. He complained of severe pain, but was disbelieved. He himself recognized his old complaint when he was seized by ague. His lung trouble, relic of the 1918 influenza, became active again, and he collapsed, lying for days in delirium in a ward in the non-European hospital where, quite by chance, I found him.

He was in hospital for six weeks. During the last of his stay he was strong enough to take an interest in his surroundings. Whenever I came to see him he bombarded me with questions, the endless questions of a child: how and why — how was it possible that the man in the next bed had a needle put in his back and did not feel it? What was the magic? I gave him a brief explanation of local anesthetics. Time and again he would demand details regarding the performance of an operation: symptoms, treatments. These talks revealed a new world for him. Illness, disease, that were not sent by *midzimu* or *abathakathi* — just afflictions that came from nowhere! For he treated my talk of infection as a joke.

At first I was cautious in my explanations, fearing a serious conflict in his mind. But he found a very simple solution for himself, as he had done for the different sects in religion. People, he decided, get illnesses sent by their ancestors, by evildoers, by bad luck. White people were afflicted by diseases from other unknown sources. When natives come from kraals to the town, and are brought into close contact with Europeans, they get ill from both sources. Consequently, he accepted two forms of treatment, African and European.

Once, in my presence, Simon suggested tentatively:

"Won't your father be cross when you take the white man's medicine?"

"No, he won't be cross," John asserted. "When Charlie had an accident he went to the big hospital and they gave him medicine."

"Can one mix the medicines, then?" I asked him.

"Oh, no!" he exclaimed. "The patient will die, or go mad, because the medicines are fighting in the body of the patient."

"Are the white doctors good?" I continued.

"They are good. They can operate. But they don't know about poison, and about protecting people; they can't mix thunder."

As soon as he was sufficiently recovered I took him back to the yard, where life in the meantime had proceeded as usual. Perhaps more people than usual were stabbed, more beer was made, more people arrested, more babies born — certainly more and more children died — but Maggie appeared happier with the new baby, and for John life, on his return from hospital, had become fuller, more satisfying. His practice was flourishing, and if he occasionally felt uneasy at the more frequent use he made of my medicines, my moral support comforted him.

But his happiness was short-lived. News came that the yard was to be closed and the residents expelled. With one voice the natives declared that this disaster was the direct outcome of our visits. The European landlord and shopkeeper, with excellent reason, fanned the flame of dissatisfaction. It was all due to the white friends of John, who were spies of the police. Maggie was refused when she tried to buy at the shop. John was completely ostracized, and he decided to leave the yard.

For some days I did not see him again, and, worried lest

his health was again troubling him, I decided to seek him out. I found him in bed, broken down physically and mentally.

"You remember, Doctor," he told me, "that they have found in the yard bodies of two newborn babies. Nobody knew whose babies they were. The babies were twins, and there was a talk that they have been strangled. This all happened when I was in prison. Then one day two detectives came to see me. I got a fright, because they never come to me, you know. I don't make the beer. I thought they came about my license. When they began to talk to me about the twin babies I felt happier. The stout man with dark glasses suddenly asked me what do I know about this murder. 'Nothing, baas,' I said. 'Twins are bad luck — aren't they?' he asked me. 'So you *ngangas* kill them. Well? You are a witch doctor, aren't you? We know that. Now who was the mother? How old is she?' they asked me quickly.

"I said nothing. But they asked me again and again. They frightened me. I had to stand and my knees trembled. I felt wet. I felt like a trapped animal. They hang you for murders, I remembered. Then I said, 'I am not a poisoner. I don't kill people. I'm only a medicine man.' But they didn't listen to me. On and on they talked of murder and twins; they kicked me. Then I felt my wrists pressed tightly. Tighter and tighter till I cried. And then I dropped. The other man, the tall one, said, 'The man looks ill.' 'These bloody niggers never get ill,' the other said. Then, with great difficulty, still lying on the floor, I said, 'I was sick. I was six weeks in hospital. I nearly died.'

"They called Maggie in and she told them the true story. Then one of the detectives went out, and when he came back he said to the other, 'Quite right. In prison a month. Six weeks in hospital. Discharged fourteen days ago. So

139

that's that.' The stout man closed his book, kicked me again, and said, 'These damn niggers, they go round and round, wasting a man's time.' And then they both left the room without saying a word."

I felt that he meant without a word of apology.

II

SATURDAY night in Swartyard . . .

A pitch-dark night, lighted by the pallid street-lamps outside and guttering candles or paraffin lamps in the rooms; windows and doors orange against the gloom, alive with gesticulating silhouettes of men and women. Outside and inside, tin braziers filled with glowing coals to bring warmth into the cold winter night. In the yard, a shuffling, swaying, noisy multitude. In every room a screeching gramophone blares out its crazy message to the night. Drunken men and women scream and sing and fight. Little groups, with mouth organs, banjos, and drums, make jazz bands that compete with the compelling rhythm in the general din, urging the half-naked bodies of the dancers to a wild frenzy of physical ecstasy. From time to time a couple of these dancers disappear together into the gloom outside the brazier gleam; then back to the orgy of drink and noise. . . .

The anthropologist and I found ourselves in the center of the yard. It was our first visit to the place at night, and tonight the residents were seething with indignation at receiving final notice that all rooms must be vacated by the end of the month. Where could they go? They did not want to go miles out of town to one of the locations. During the past few years they had been pushed from place to place, and now, not to the outskirts of the town, but miles away from the city.

"Like storm and hail destroy a man's work for a year, so do the white people ruin with one stroke of the pen the work of months," a native in the yard once said to me. "Against a storm or hail there is at least protective medicine to get from the witch doctor. Against the white man's bad will there is no help, no hope, and nobody to appeal to." Still — there was beer to drink, so let us drink! Partly to drown sorrow, partly to use beer that would otherwise most certainly be destroyed. It was, besides, the last opportunity of earning money, as the yard was still full of customers.

Saturday night of all nights, and this Saturday of all Saturdays, we must needs come to the yard. In spite of John's constant warnings never to come at night, here we were, moving slowly among the angry, drunken, frenzied crowd, ready to burst out in revolt at the slightest provocation. Soon we became separated. Whilst I was visiting the rooms, the anthropologist walked slowly through the narrow alleyways, concentrating upon her work of observation.

For some time she was unnoticed. Then someone saw the tall, well-dressed European woman, noticed first with astonishment, and then with hostile resentment, the intrusion of a foreigner, and a white woman at that. The news of her presence flew like wildfire through the excited, hysterical mob. Muttered remarks grew to outspoken comments, became shouted threats. At first what was said was merely objectionable to a white woman; but later the utterances became more and more personal, more insolent. The European woman realized the position. An ugly, hostile atmosphere grew with alarming rapidity. She tried to reach the exit, but the narrow passage was thronged with people. She did not know where I was, nor could she reach John's

142

room. She tried to console herself by reminding herself that these people could not harm her: they knew only too well the reaction of the European man to any molestation of his women by the blacks, and also a large number of the actual residents were her friends. But the men were drunk. And she knew very well that she and I were thought to be responsible for the closing of the yard.

A crowd of roughs, inflamed with *skokiaan,* came very close to her, touched her, swore at her in vile language, made sinister suggestions. Some of the women in the yard, now frightened for her safety and the terrible consequences to all of them should anything happen to the white woman, tried to form a protecting ring about her, but they were not strong enough. The roughs pulled them away.

At this critical moment John appeared. A young girl had made her way through the crowd to his room and told him what was happening. In spite of the cold, and Maggie's expostulations on account of his health, he had come immediately, though in his heart there raged a black fury that surprised him. What a fool this clever white woman was! To come to Swartyard at night, on Saturday night, and on this particular night! Nevertheless, with cool authority he appeared beside her and, since actually the people had not intended to molest her, he was able to guide her to the exit — not without sarcastic and obscene remarks from the crowd — to put her into her car, and see her safely away.

It was only then that I learned what had been happening and was able to join her and John and so conduct her myself back to her house. However, I returned and made my way to John's room. I found a heated discussion taking place, and stood listening unnoticed. A next-door neighbor was gravely saying: "Why did she come after dark? Wasn't it enough for her to come and worry us during the day?

Haven't they brought enough trouble, she and the doctor? The women say that they have used our blood against us, the blood they took from us. They say our blood is not good, it shows a bad disease, and so they expel us from the yard." He was referring to the blood I took for an examination for syphilis. This experiment shattered the confidence of the residents in me, for I promised medicines to all, but foolishly supplied them only in the case of a positive Wassermann.

"It serves her right," a shrill voice cried out angrily. "It is a pity she was not treated as we are. We are to be thrown out of the yard."

"The men would have given her a rough time if John hadn't come," the other asserted. "But John always takes the white man's part."

2

JOHN'S health was still poor; he regained strength slowly. The effects of his arrest, imprisonment, and severe illness had combined to make him a physical wreck. Morally, too, he was shaken. His mistrust of the white man had returned in full: even his faith in me had broken down, leaving a painful, open sore in his mind. He refused to come to my consulting room, and so for a time I visited him. He spoke little. The ritual-murder accusation revived memories of the incident of years ago in the Pietersburg hotel, the accusation of assault upon the ugly old spinster. Then he had been young, carefree, strong, ignorant of the cruelties of his fellow men; he had dismissed the affair with a shrug of the shoulders. But now he realized only too well the grimness of so serious a charge as murder. In his weakened state, the shock of such an accusation had been more than he could stand. He felt like a trapped animal, like a man in supreme danger whose eyes are heavily bandaged. Whence would terror next spring upon him? What hiding place from cruelty, injustice, and suspicion was left to him? He could not foresee and forestall calamity now. It struck so swiftly, so unexpectedly.

An idea tortured him. He came out with it one morning after a sleepless night. "It sprang suddenly on me when I tossed in bed. It was painful. The thought came to me that you and the detective were very alike. So alike that you both looked like one man, not two. It was a terrible thought. You must not be cross with me, Doctor. I pushed it away, but back it would crawl, like a beaten dog."

The incident of the anthropologist in Swartyard must have cleared the way to this suppressed fantasy. Whilst I had been kind to him, helping him, and talking to him sympathetically, I had nevertheless continued to question him. What did he know about the killing of twins? Was it a custom of his kraal? I asked him to tell me everything, to say whatever came into his mind in connection with it. I asked him whether it was true that the birth of twins was regarded as a calamity to the whole tribe, leading to drought and famine. Day after day I had questioned him, and John had done his best to satisfy my curiosity, explaining that the Manyika people regarded twins as coming from two fathers, one of whom is not a real man but a snake, a sorcerer, or some other evildoer. That was how baby wizards were begotten. A woman sleeps with her husband and becomes pregnant. The wizard then sleeps with her, without the woman being aware of it, and gives her another child. A clever witch doctor can find out through the bones which is the real child and which the

145

wizard baby. But should there be no diviner available, both babies are killed. Usually the midwife herself strangles them.

He told me that he remembered my smiling at this and saying: "Yes, John; a clever explanation. But I want to know more. Is it true that the mother must go through purification rites, during which she seduces four men, all of whom are killed soon afterwards?" He denied this, adding that some of his people killed twins because they feared that two babies in one womb fought one another and that neither could obtain enough nourishment either before or after birth.

But I was still not satisfied, seeking all the time for more detailed information. "And the stout detective," John said, "did he not do the same? He also asked, 'Why did you kill the babies? I know that you witch doctors do it. Is it not bad luck to leave twins alive?'"

He tried to explain also to the detectives, but in vain. The stout one probed further and further, refusing to be satisfied. It seemed to John as if these white people put their meddlesome hands into his very thoughts, ruthlessly tearing and digging out information. The two men, the detective and myself, thus fused in John's mind into one voice, one set of features, separated and regained their individuality, approached each other till they reminded him of a picture of Siamese twins that he had seen in one of my books. Slowly, one would be superimposed upon the other till the detective and I became one; and then instantly they would spring apart again and become two, widely separated, entirely distinct.

Why had the detectives come to him? There had never been any suspicion connecting him with the beer-selling. Yet they had suspected him of ritual murder. Had I betrayed him? Had I sent the police? When they appeared to drop the matter, had it been a trick? Were my questions, put to him already in the beginning, on behalf of the police? And the woman, too, the anthropologist — where did she fit into the puzzle? Her quiet voice, he realized with a shock, was very like the flat, even tones of the less cheery detective, the tall thin one! The woman's questions recurred to him: —

"Describe, John, how the killing of twins is done. What medicine do they use? And I want to know whether they pray. Do they drink beer? How is the mother dressed? Is the killing done inside the house or outside? Are the babies washed first? How are they prepared? Does the mother really go to the river and allow the twins to drop off her back, and then run away?"

Was the whole thing a trap? Unless they wanted to catch him somehow, why all these ridiculous questions? Were the Swartyard people right? Perhaps his so-called white friends were really the treacherous enemies his neighbors declared them to be. "Never trust a white man. He is like a puff adder in the dust, that strikes backwards." How often had he heard that said! Was he a dupe, a cat's-paw? Had the time come when his confidence in Europeans would make a laughingstock of him? A target for the jeers and gibes of his people? So suspicious had he become, so resentful, that he found it impossible to continue his visits to me. He disappeared the instant the anthropologist entered the yard.

I knew him to be involved in severe inner conflict and understood this hatred and bitterness towards me and all white people, though he himself said nothing. Consequently I did my utmost to encourage him to express his hostility, to talk out his feelings with regard to the white people in

147

general, the detectives and the anthropologist and myself in particular. Occasionally I almost succeeded, for he would be on the verge of allowing his aggression to come out, of saying what he felt; but the affection, the respect, the confidence that he had felt in the past, which had carried him beyond his own fear, had weakened so that all my tricks of persuasion failed. He remained obstinately silent or answered in monosyllables. The old relationship, based on admiration, confidence, and the desire to please, had not been restored.

While the internal conflict in him was unabated, his present situation became, without my help, impossible for him to comprehend. Doubts, uncertainties, conflicting thoughts and desires, were, like the nagging Maggie, continuously with him. I decided that I must interfere and break down his resistance. Ordinary kindness now was not sufficient, and therefore, as in the case of similar psychoanalytical patients, I put what was going on in his mind openly and frankly before him.

I explained to him the essence of the aggressive instinct, of the unavoidability and necessity of hating people whom we believed to be hostile to us. I told him that hatred, like love, cannot be conquered: it must emerge in one form or another. His present refusal to come to see me, to talk to me, was that kind of hatred; it hurt me very much and led us no further; but it hurt him even more than me because he required the advice which he knew very well the anthropologist and I could give him.

So I talked to him, day after day, until I won. And the months that followed were the most successful of the whole period of our relationship. The material flew like a stream that has been artificially dammed, and, his resistance suddenly removed, he brought me endless dreams, to which

148

he associated freely and with ease, came out with most intimate information regarding his life; and he also introduced me fully and unreservedly into the secrets of his art, explaining the use of his herbs and roots, how they were treated and administered to patients, describing in full the ritual of digging, which I had previously witnessed.

3

THE European generally believes a witch doctor to be possessed of some mysterious knowledge concerning potent and magic roots. This certainly did not apply to John. He had no knowledge of any single medicine he used, neither did he understand the indications which were mostly vague and of a general character. The same herb or root was used in various diseases, the ritual of administration being the only part of the treatment that was changed. It struck me that most of his medicines were used for what I would term "lovesickness," and very few for physical ills. John had learned the roots in his childhood from Charlie, but since then he had increased his range in a very peculiar way. He would suddenly feel the urge for a new medicine; then, on the following night, he would dream of his father indicating such and such an herb or root; and in this way his pharmacopoeia grew. I understand that other witch doctors act in a similar way. John himself did not believe overmuch in his herbs, relying more upon his horns and bones — an art which turned out to be very interesting from a psychological point of view.

"A patient comes. The doctor must find out his fortune. It is no good treating a patient who has bad luck, unless you can change it beforehand. There are three ways of fortune-

149

telling. The very first is the use of the horns. Then the throwing of six nutshells. And last the throwing of the bones." In a difficult case, he would use all three methods.

The patient would sit in a chair and look at John, nervous and worried. John, sitting opposite with an air of dignity and importance, would slowly take out the two big horns and rub them in his hands for a minute or two. Then he would make a cross with his hand upon the patient's forehead and touch the patient's head with each horn.

One of these horns is known as the male and the other, slightly smaller, as the female. He would put the horns into a calabash, and they would begin to move. (He appeared to hold the calabash tightly, but I found out that the wrist was loose and gently shaking, so that actually he made the horns move according to his wish. The patient, of course, was not aware of this; to him, the horns were moved by supernatural forces.) It was necessary to rub the horns thoroughly on his hands and on the patient's forehead so as to establish a contact between the patient and his ancestors. Then, after all this ceremony, he would interpret the movement of the horns entirely at random, for each time, no matter how they moved, he would give a totally different reading.

Actually, his interpretation depended solely upon information gleaned from the patient and from the patient's reactions to his suggestions. For example, he would say: "Male horn says this man got a wife; he got poisoned from a woman. They took the earth from his feet and mixed it with medicines. The girl herself did it. His father was very jealous of him. Female horn says he got two children. The people who poisoned him were his own family. I don't say it was his father, but he must not go home, he will get worse. I will give him medicine to fight his father and his family."

150

In a second case during the same hour he gave the following interpretation: "Male horn says poison in the blood" — as he remarked to me afterwards regarding the patient, "He was looking a little bit rich."

"The poison was through the cattle. Then the female horn says he won't be long alive. He will soon die because the horn moves away from me. The spirits are refusing him." And John's judgment was correct: the patient looked exceptionally ill.

These horns, incidentally, are made of clay, in a conical form about three inches long and an inch wide; they are of a grayish color, and were kept in a bright yellow calabash.

Then he threw the nutshells. In this case, the interpretation was easy, for it depended upon how they fell on the floor: with the mouth upwards, which he termed "open," or with the mouth downwards, or "closed." For example, if five were closed and one open, it meant that the patient did not believe the doctor, was very worried, and withheld information from him. If four were closed and two open, it signified pregnancy. Six closed and none open meant that the patient was sure to die. All open was a very good omen, meaning recovery and luck. Two closed and four open — "the wife has the changes." There were other interpretations depending upon the fall of the shells, of as much logical base as the foregoing.

He once threw the shells for me. Three fell closed and three open. Then he put some powder on them, looked at the bones for about three minutes, and then as long at me. Then I had to pay him half a crown; for the shells don't talk without money! Then he said: "You are half lucky and half not. You are very busy, but sometimes your heart is aching. If you would have been a native, the shells would say that you may have a quarrel. Doctor has a daughter." He said it half-questioningly so as to get my confirmation, and I nodded. "I think you will have trouble when your daughter wants to marry. I think Doctor's father is dead." This was not true. And then he went on talking, very confused and trying to correct his mistakes by my reactions to his statements.

The throwing of the bones was much more complicated. His bone lore consisted of forty pieces: twenty-eight bones, six nutshells, and six dominoes. Among these were also a few pennies. All these pieces must be kept in a small sack and the pieces thoroughly shaken together before beginning a séance. After shaking up the pieces in the sack, snuff was added, and he rubbed some ointment on his hands. The pieces were then thrown forcibly on the floor and examined, first the six nutshells.

Four were closed and two open, and this meant that more rain would come and that the wife was in the family way, and that if a person was very sick he would die. Then he looked at these bones that were supposed to be those of an elephant. The bones in general were ordinary pieces of bone belonging to various animals, an inch long to three inches at the most; and though I doubt if one would be able to classify them anatomically, I soon managed to recognize them according to John's classification — elephant-bone, tortoise-bone, bones of a buck, of a mamba, of a zimba(?), cattle-feet, bones of sheep, goat, pig, hyena, castrated male sheep, calf, lion, and baboon. The interpretation depended upon how the pieces of bone fell — with the convex surface upwards, or "closed," or the concave surface upwards, which he called "open" — and also upon the mutual position of male and female bones of the same species and their interrelation to the bones of other animals.

152

It is quite obvious that this provided endless combinations and as many interpretations. John's technique depended very much upon his quick grasp of the patient's trouble, and to a certain degree of the symbolism of the bones. For example, if male and female bones were together, it meant union and good luck; if the lion's bone were far away, it meant weakness; and so on.

After witnessing a number of his sessions, I soon found myself as proficient a witch doctor as he, and to his delight and amazement I proved it to him on several occasions, with the advantage, of course, that my medical knowledge of the case and a deeper psychological insight than John's helped me to "obtain from the bones" a more correct interpretation than his.

4

BUT while our relationship proceeded smoothly, the external circumstances of John's life became increasingly hard. His practice, interrupted by prison and illness, had gone downhill; his reputation dwindled; and the hostile people in the yard wanted to know why, if he were the marvelous *nganga* he claimed to be, he used the European medicines. The Manyika patients appeared suddenly to remember that he was not properly qualified, since he had not gone through the prescribed initiation ceremony. They knew that he had left home young and uninitiated and that he had never revisited the kraal. No wonder, as recent arrivals from Manyikaland remarked, his drugs had lost their healing power. Various stories of unsuccessful treatments were circularized, and John's numerous competitors and enemies eagerly took up the adverse criticism.

Also, life in Swartyard became more unbearable than ever. A series of incidents confirmed the distrust of the residents in white men. Police raids became more frequent; hardly a day passed without some man or woman being arrested; large amounts of beer were constantly destroyed, and the ease and rapidity with which the detectives discovered the hiding places excited suspicions that a spy was in their midst. On top of everything else came continual demands for the payment of the poll tax. Health inspectors increased their visits, poking their noses in everywhere, grumbling at the lack of cleanliness and order. The women were furious. John suffered repercussions of all this. Even the landlord selected him as a culprit, when the closing of the disgraceful slum grew from a speculative threat into a certainty. The woman shopkeeper refused to supply provisions to Maggie; both the shopkeeper and the landlord, themselves Europeans, reiterated to all Swartyard — African, Eurafrican, and Indian — that when they were ejected at the end of the month they could only blame John and his white friends.

John was no fighter as a rule, but under all this pressure became obstinate. Far from acceding to the threats and demands of the Swartyard people, he appeared to have overcome his own suspicions, and he did his best to regain the friendship of the anthropologist and myself, to seek help and advice.

The latter he badly needed in his muddled family life. During all his troubles and conflicts Maggie was always more of a burden than a help. The warm affection he had felt for her in the happy days in Pietersburg completely disappeared. The baby, about a year old now, was still breast-fed, and sexual relations with mother thus being taboo it gave him an easy excuse for neglecting her. For

154

Maggie to become pregnant now, at such a period of poverty and distress, would be a calamity.

Other women were equally taboo. It was a family tradition, he explained to the men who laughed at his self-imposed celibacy, that while in practice a *nganga* must lead a respectable life. He must be married, beget children, and must never be a *nyatsi.* He remained unshaken when Swartyard women tried to tempt him, citing numerous loose-living urban *ngangas* whose kraal-bred fears of sexual taboos had weakened. He was a Manyika, and such were the ideals of his ancestors, the moral code of the great doctors of his family.

Maggie, however, was not entirely deluded. Unsophisticated as she was, she accepted most of the traditional taboos unreservedly, but she guessed that John kept the sex taboos with such rigidity because it suited him to do so. She was quite sure that he did not like her. As for other women, she did not believe in his abstinence, though she dared not mention her suspicions. Inwardly she feared that her own infidelity had caused her husband's downfall.

But she was wrong about her husband. For two years he knew no women. He affirmed this to me repeatedly, and I have no reason to doubt him, for by this time he would not have been ashamed to admit adultery to me. Not that he was devoid of love desires; he knew them in his dreams, which frequently revealed them strongly. But even then he never permitted himself fulfillment. Always some obstacle came between him and the actual consummation.

The idea of going home now began to occupy his mind more and more. In this entangled situation there seemed to be but one solution: to run away to Rhodesia — without Maggie, of course. There he would sleep with a Manyika woman. The image of the Manyika *murowi* again began to

155

have a strong hold on him. For days he dreamed and thought of nothing but Manyikaland. But he stayed on in the yard.

5

WITH the return of physical health John became again optimistic. His good spirits returned, though nothing occurred to justify a rosy outlook. Perhaps the carefree environment of his infancy and early childhood, the absence of any tyrannical insistence on cleanliness, the unstinted love of his mother whose milk literally flowed unceasingly (for a native mother never denies her baby the breast), together with the easy sunny South African climate, had combined to produce John's ever-ready optimism. He felt no forebodings about a possibly rainy day. This groundless optimism was a real hindrance in his present life, for it paralyzed his initiative and impoverished his energy in the fight for better conditions.

This unfounded optimism is more or less natural in the kraals, where the earth may reasonably be expected to supply the infant peasants with their simple needs. But in the town, with its restrictions, competition, economic difficulties, and higher standards of living, such an attitude is disastrous. Certainly, with John it was a tragedy that he took no precaution to prevent his steady march downhill. Long ago I had warned him that sooner or later the yard would be closed. Yet he made no arrangements until the eve of the eviction. Then he hired a room with a friend, paying twenty-five shillings in advance, and suggested that Maggie should go to Pietersburg. Childish idea! He must surely have known that she would refuse to leave him by

156

himself in Johannesburg. For this, as usual, he blamed his bad luck. And as for his practice, he did nothing to improve it, but projected his troubles on others: enemies, witches, and bad luck.

The European conception of fate was unknown to John. His explanation of the causes of suffering was more concrete. These causes emanated from ancestral spirits and sorcerers. So John recognized a concrete cause of his troubles; a cause that existed, not in himself or external life, but in a world which Europeans would call "supernatural." Yet to him this supernatural world was real and natural. He could fight these causes only by means of magic and the performance of rites. Unfortunately, in his present complex circumstances, this method of approach amounted to inactivity, protracted suicide. If only the people around him would change; if only he could get medicines that would change his luck, disarm his enemies, all would be well. So he told himself. But this would mean returning to Rhodesia, for he believed only in the power of Manyika herbs. And this in turn involved defying Maggie, making preparations, saving money.

No. All this was impossible. So he remained in Swartyard.

The last two weeks in Swartyard, before its final closing, I spent in John's room, while he related stories of bad luck, of being bewitched, of poisoning. He talked of nothing else. There was the typical kraal atmosphere of fear, superstition, and taboo, with, however, the difference that in this Johannesburg slum there prevailed an undercurrent of hatred and hostility against the white foreigners, their laws, their language and religion, whereas in the kraal, people feared the chiefs and headmen and elders. In the kraals, however, the fear was combined with respect, everyone was struggling under the same difficulties and hindrances, so that their suffering was lessened, as is that of the poor when there are no rich about them.

As far as I could guess from John's hints, the Swartyard people talked of revenge, of using force to get justice. John laughed at these childish threats. Fight the white man? He knew too well the supremacy and power of Europeans. "No," he would say. "We must not fight the whites. They can kill us in an hour."

He told them a dream, which he repeated to me. "I saw plenty of our people with spears, singing and shouting. The white men came and laughed at us so much. They just stood and laughed. Then other white people came and killed all our people in twenty minutes."

The singing and shouting, they all agreed with John, meant that they wanted to complain to the Native Commissioner, to demand work. "They laughed at us," John continued his interpretation. "That is a bad sign. My father said laughing in a dream is very bad. Laughing means killing. One said the white people could not kill all our people in twenty minutes, but I answered: 'Couldn't they? Haven't you seen the aeroplanes that fly in the air? From those they can shoot all the people. You don't know the cleverness of the whites.' I heard that they go from Salisbury to Johannesburg in three hours. It took me two months to walk. No, we cannot fight the white people. People who talk such silly nonsense just want us to be killed.

"One evening there was in my room an old native who was very strong in his attacks upon the white people. He said that I was wrong. He asked me to come to a meeting with him where I would hear clever people explaining how to fight the white people. At these meetings he heard of a country where all people, white, black, and colored, were equal. I laughed at him. But I said I would go to the meetings. I only wish I could ask Tembu what he thought about it. Tembu knows everything. But he has gone as suddenly as he came."

I was surprised that he did not ask my opinion about fighting the Europeans, and also about the meetings. But a few weeks later he told me that he was attending these gatherings, and I managed to persuade him to take me to one of them.

6

THE meeting we attended was held at one of the locations in a poorly lit hall, not very large, crowded with young men and women. John searched for a familiar face, but this time saw few people he knew. We had come in late and there were no more seats available, so we stood at the back, leaning against the wall. On the platform, an African, neatly dressed in European style, was addressing the gathering in good English. Others followed him, but the speeches had one common note: the protest of the black man against the injustice done to him by the white world.

"The white people say the devil is black, but we have no devils in our religion. To us, the devil appears to have a white skin." The audience applauded, and John looked pleased. One speaker dealt with the iniquity of the poll tax, by which all native men had to pay a pound a year from their meager earnings, apart from other indirect taxes paid in common with all citizens. Unemployed men, who could not pay, were hounded out of their rooms and thrown into prison. A man in the audience told a story that evoked cries of "Shame!" and "Disgraceful!" A funeral procession had been held up by the police and the mourners arrested for not paying their poll tax, the corpse being left in charge of a woman.

The speaker took up the point. "There are bad men among all people, and the policeman by the nature of his job is a ruffian. But he is not the one to blame. The real tragedy is that the people who make the laws hate us. It is such people who make compulsory pass laws and make an unoffending and sober African a ready target for the police. The ordinary man in the street does not hit us as the policeman does, but he wounds us in a way that hurts more. He is responsible for the disgraceful condition of the city slums, where the African is forced to pay exorbitant rents for places the white landlord would not think fit for his beasts. The liberal Englishman is no better than the Dutchman in this, and the Jew is just as bad as either. They all want to squeeze the last penny out of us and give us as little as possible in return."

John told me in an undertone: "Listen! He is speaking of Swartyard."

The speaker went on: "Where are we to live? In 1913 they passed the Land Act, by which they drove us from the land, our natural dwelling-place. Now they have passed the Urban Area Act, and tell us to get out of the towns and go back to the land we do not possess. We stand between the devil and the deep sea. What are we to do? Where are we to go?"

Another man mounted the platform and spoke of the difference in wages paid to white and black men for the same work, the hypocrisy of the liquor laws, and the contemptuous behavior of petty officials. But the speaker's voice was monotonous, his delivery irritating. The crowd began to get restless and inattentive, and at last someone in the audience shouted: "We know all this. Go and tell

160

it to the white man." There was an uproar of shouting and laughter.

All the while there had been sitting on the platform a man who had particularly attracted my attention. He was a black man, tall, imposing of aspect, calm and dignified. He had been sitting in silence, listening carefully to each speaker. Now, when the audience gave voice to its restlessness, he rose. His appearance quieted the people. His voice was deep, resonant, uttering words clearly, distinctly, without haste, so that each might sink into the mind of the listener.

"My friends," he said, "you are right. It is useless to go on repeating our grievances; the white man is deaf to our cry of sorrow. To him we are unskilled laborers, nothing more. How we live, what we eat, how we amuse ourselves — of this he does not want to know. He gives us less care than the horse in his stable, who at least is fed and sheltered after the day's work."

He proceeded to deal with reprisals. It was useless to talk with bitterness, he said. "There must be no desire for revenge. The whole position, the whole system, must be changed, the black man, no less than the white, must be a partner in the destiny of Africa. The white politicians are telling lies, they are hypocrites when they talk of civilization. White civilization, they talk of. Whites, who by means of civilization hope to keep millions of blacks in slavery. We must develop along the same lines as other civilized races, white, brown, or yellow. God did not measure out the heart and brain according to the color of a man's skin. I don't think the white people really believe in the inherent inferiority of our race. That statement is but a salve to the white conscience. For consider: the same white people teach us that all men — blacks as well as whites — are equal

161

before God, when they want us to become Christians. It is only when we want more money, better work, better opportunities that our black skin becomes such a hindrance to us. And yet, in spite of our disabilities, some of our people have achieved European standards. There are among us doctors and lawyers, men who have qualified on equal terms with Europeans overseas. Let us and the white people, too, remember what our brothers, the Negroes of America, have achieved.

"There is another sinister weapon used by the white people to keep us back. They say that the African wishes to marry European women. And that it is bad to mix black blood and white. So they claim that to protect their mothers and sisters, the African must be kept down. But do they honestly believe that we prefer their women to our own? Because cases of rape occur when thousands of young Africans are herded together in towns and mines without their women, does this prove their theory? Ask them what happens in Europe when armies are living among civilians. Whenever you get masses of men segregated together you get these incidents, irrespective of color. Are the white men guiltless when they are alone among the Bantu, away from their white women? How many native women have they not violated in such circumstances? The million people of mixed blood in the Cape — do they not come out of such acts of violation? As for us, we do not wish to mix with white people in the way they think. We want to become a civilized nation, but we have no ambition for our children to have light skins. We wish to take part in building up our country, instead of being a burden and a problem. We claim to use the resources of nature, and the discoveries of science, that will help us to better, cleaner, happier, and complete lives. My friends, take the advice

162

of an older man. Leave fighting to animals. Suffer quietly. But learn. The world is changing. The old society is slowly falling. The old systems are doomed. Before us a new, virgin future lies. We want to prepare ourselves for it. Learn to read and write; learn crafts, trades, professions. Don't listen to those people who urge you to go back to kraal life. Kraal life is all very well, but it does not belong to the world of today and of the future.

"Become civilized, educated, and the white man will regard you differently. You are ignorant, uncultured, primitive in your way of thinking; though, it is true, through no fault of your own. The white man, it is true, kept you down. Those who realize your position have pity on you. That is no good. Pity does not last, nor does it kill fear. I say fear; because that is at the bottom of the white man's attitude towards us. He fears us. He looks upon us as savages, and he is afraid of us. But we don't wish to be considered as savages. We want to progress, we want education, the fruits of civilization. And today we can get it. We must get it. You must demand it. It is your right. You paid for it with your sweat and blood and money.

"We can learn. And for those of us who cannot manage that, I say there are the children to think of. What you cannot get, give your children. Teach them to desire education. Teach them to desire civilization. Then they will help our people."

7

JOHN was strongly moved by these words.

He told me that he could not sleep that night. He lay thinking far into the night along the lines suggested by the speaker. Education . . . civilization — be a proper doctor? He could not see himself in the position of the old man, nor even of Tembu. But he could imagine it for his little son, Daniel. He himself would have to live and die a *nganga*, or perhaps a waiter. But his son would rise above that. His son would be educated. That great African had talked about a virgin future. His son would reap and sow in that future. . . .

For some time he hardly missed a meeting. He came to feel passionately with the speakers, looked for stronger protests. He attended Communist meetings in preference to others because there the speeches took on a more fiery character. He told me that he did not entirely agree with all they said. For instance, they denied class difference and racial difference, but how could there be no distinction between rich and poor, black and white? He smiled at the stories he heard of Communist Russia. How could there be a country where rich and poor, black, white, and colored were all treated alike? Yet the main burden of their speeches impressed him. One conception particularly lodged in his mind: the ideal that all people were born good, that the bad in them came with the changing fortune of their lives. He spoke often of this theory. "All of us were born good; but the white people made us bad with their cruelty and oppression, and also through our sorcerers and poisoners," he would add as an afterthought.

More and more he began to crave the company of Tembu, until eventually, on my advice, he went in quest of him to one of the Bantu clubs, and there he discovered him at last.

It was a Friday night, the club's social evening. The experience was entirely new to John. The hall was crowded; the people seemed happy — in sharp contrast to their everyday demeanor. They were the same Africans, but how dif-

164

ferent in their dress, behavior, and speech from most of the Africans he knew! It was guest night, and most of the men had brought their wives, sweethearts, or friends. Almost everyone was clean, dressed in European fashion, with taste and discretion. For the first time John saw African women with artificially reddened cheeks and lips, gowned in long flowing evening frocks. Until he grew accustomed to this use of make-up, the conservative in him revolted from this artifice. But custom made him admire their appearance.

At first he was worried by the absence of the vernacular; everywhere he heard English. But it was explained to him later that same evening that the great aim of the club was to give a cultural home to all Africans irrespective of tribe and origin; to eliminate tribal feuds and prejudices. Here, all black people were to be united in a common bond of color, culture, and ideals. It was therefore essential that they should speak a common language. English was the obvious choice: a rich and beautiful language spoken by half the world, including their brothers, the American Negroes. This explanation pleased John; being a Rhodesian, he was naturally a champion of English.

He was gratified to find that nobody asked him questions, especially regarding his profession. He would have felt embarrassed had he had to admit to these educated people that he was a *nganga,* for he was afraid that his now cultured countrymen would look down upon witch doctors. He did not know that educated Africans, and Europeans, too, for that matter, are often treated by worse quacks than African witch doctors: he knew nothing of the legion of tea-cup readers, fortunetellers, phrenologists, dieticians, spiritualists, and all the innumerable "healers" to whom Europeans of all classes of society flock like sheep to be shorn. At least John was no charlatan: he believed in his horns and bones and the magical properties of his medicines.

Tembu was genuinely pleased to see him again, but did not show the enthusiasm that John had expected. Hardly had John greeted him and inquired about his health when Tembu had to rush away. He came back, indeed, but was so often interrupted to answer questions and arrange matters for guests and newcomers that John was left continually alone. He felt hurt by this neglect on the part of his friend.

"I felt that Tembu had changed and didn't want to see me. I was very hurt and disappointed and got ready to go away again. Then he came back and said he was sorry, but it was not the same Tembu I knew." He felt himself incapable of recapturing the atmosphere of intimacy that he had experienced in the beginning of their friendship. Yet, like a disappointed lover, he cherished the vain illusion that by some magic the old relationship would be restored.

John felt bitterly Tembu's change of attitude. It was John's tragedy that he failed at this period of his life, when he was ready to slough off the kraal mentality, to find an African, like Tembu, to take up where I as a white man had to leave off.

III

MEANWHILE the time drew ever closer when Swartyard was to be finally closed, and still John made no effort to find himself new quarters. In a mood of bitter stubbornness he seemed to be waiting to be forcibly ejected. He was convinced that he and his people were the victims of a chance caprice of the white officials. In common with his neighbors he felt helpless, impotent as ants robbed of their home by the antics of a small boy with a stick, poking into their heap and destroying in a few minutes the labor of a lifetime. In their own way John and his fellows had been happy in Swartyard; they had at least been able to earn additional and indispensable money. Moreover, their sense of insult was increased by the fact that the authorities had decreed only the blacks must leave Swartyard. Those of mixed blood were to be allowed to remain, although they were just as guilty of illicit liquor selling, gambling, and prostitution as the blacks. "It is for the sake of the African people that this is being done," was the answer given to a question from John.

John raged inwardly. The suggestion that the eviction was being carried out from humane motives he found insupportable. To our intense astonishment, John, always so submissive and meek, suddenly burst forth into a furious tirade; his voice, loud and trembling with passion, betrayed his uncontrolled fury. His rigid attitude, the unusual defiance of his hawklike features, added to his resemblance to a bird of prey tensing its talons for the attack.

"You say the white people want to help us. Who will believe it? Who will believe the white devils? Tembu was right. The devil is not black; the devil is white like all of you. The white people want to suck our blood, and throw us away. You say they want to help us, but I say they want to get rid of us! Well, let them give us back our land, then we will gladly go away, live by ourselves, away from you all. We don't want white devils."

Suddenly, he stammered, tried to recover himself, stopped. He wanted so passionately to explain the reason of segregation as he had learned it from Tembu and others. But words failed him. And, with the first sign of failure, as usual, he collapsed as suddenly as he had flared up.

His tragedy was that of so many Africans. Neither their kraal life nor their early training, nor their later education, serves to strengthen their will power or imbues them with the perseverance necessary for achievement. Renunciation and flight were John's choice in any situation requiring strength of will and endurance of pain. Similarly, John could never say no, even when refusal was imperative. He preferred to make promises which he knew he could never keep. He had not reached that stage or personality or development that belongs to the healthy human being who is not afraid of being obstinate or amiable, assertive or submissive, active or passive, as the occasion demands, steering clear, however, of extremes in any one direction.

John, moreover, had an additional tragedy which shadows the life of almost every African. The circumstances of his life, the clash of his two worlds, constantly caused inner division. Every African leads a double life in the full sense

168

of the psychological concept. For there is no remotest kraal but has its contact with European civilization; missionaries, government officials, traders, and labor recruits have spread European influence. The lure of money-earning possibilities, of European settlements, has brought African men and women to the cities from the remotest corners of the continent.

2

EVERY African, to a greater or lesser degree, lives by two codes of morals and laws, prays to two gods: Mwari and Christ. John's psychic life force was being dissipated in seeking a way out of this dilemma. It is a path made more difficult by the white man's insistence on keeping the African enslaved to the traditions of the fathers. And on this, the pretext that a gulf of two thousand years separates black from white, the European withholds emancipation.

This black man's conflict was particularly severe in John. On the one hand he loved the white man's life, loved civilization. On the other hand, more than most natives, he was bound by his profession to his past, for he was destined to perpetuate his father, the great *nganga*. In spite of his close contact with Europeans, his belief in the supernatural remained as strong as it is in the kraal native. His implicit belief in his *midzimu*, his ancestral spirits, had not been shaken in the least, though he often neglected the sacrificial requirements in connection with them.

Nominally he was a Christian. He had a warm feeling for the Church, linked with pleasant memories of his schooldays. He loved Christ, loved the ritual, loved singing hymns. But his passionate, deep devotion belonged to Mwari, and

169

even more to his father and grandfather. Here again he was torn between two worlds.

John's difficulties were heightened by his lack of a sense of reality. In spite of his long contact with civilization, he still had no idea of cause and effect, did not understand people, could not analyze a situation or foresee the development of events. He remained simply a false optimist. When a situation became unbearable, he submitted to suffering, or whenever possible took refuge in flight. He fled from his home when competition with Nathan became unpleasant, fled from the conflicts between love and professional duties in the bewitched kraal, fled to Pietersburg, constantly ran away from us, his white friends, when we made demands upon him.

3

JOHN'S especial, personal tragedy was what has been called Hamletism. Hamletism is a psychological phenomenon characterized by indecision and hesitancy in situations demanding direct action. Many hypotheses have been put forward to explain Hamlet's incapacity to revenge his father's murder. Some explain Hamlet's difficulties by his temperament, oversensitiveness, too much introspection, inborn lack of decision; others see the causes of his failure in external circumstances, which were stupendous. The modern psychologist, rejecting these explanations, maintains that Hamlet was by nature capable of action, and the task was a possible one. As I have explained more fully in my book on Psychoanalysis, Hamlet's hesitancy cannot be explained in terms of conscious reasons, for his hesitation is due to an internal conflict to fulfill his filial duty and some special cause for repugnance towards it. But Hamlet himself is not conscious of this special cause; his conflict is inaccessible to his own introspection, for it is unconscious, as explained by Freud.

Claudius has murdered Hamlet's father and married Hamlet's mother. Hamlet is in a state of hysterical melancholia akin to madness. Since he had never ceased to love his mother, his father's death, and his mother's second marriage, came as a terrible shock to Hamlet, reactivating the repressed infantile love-desire for his mother, and the desire to take his father's place in her affection. The usurping of that place by a stranger, and the fact that the new lover is an uncle, make the internal conflict in Hamlet more acute. After the death of his father he is thrown unaware into the old Œdipus conflict which is normally solved in adult years.

Claudius has committed in Hamlet's eyes two crimes: the killing of Hamlet's father and the marrying of Hamlet's mother — crimes which the psychoanalyst has proved to exist in the fantasies of childhood. Thus the reality has fulfilled Hamlet's forbidden and successfully repressed desires, and this is the cause of his tragic fate.

John's tragedy, at first glance, may seem to lack the stature of Hamlet's, and one may be inclined to ridicule at the start any comparison between John the witch doctor and Hamlet the Danish prince. But we must not confuse social with psychological states. No two human beings love alike, nevertheless a herdsman may be compared to a king in his love-expression. Even John's external situation is very similar to Hamlet's. True, John is not a prince, but he is a son of a famous witch doctor, with an illustrious ancestry of doctors and chiefs. He was heir to the *nganga*, Chavafambira, just as Hamlet was to his royal father. And John's father also died in very mysterious circumstances. From his mother also he heard hints that his father was poisoned by his uncle Charlie for killing his younger brother; and Charlie, like Claudius, married his brother's wife. We see thus that Hamlet and John are in a similar situation: the father killed, and his place usurped by the uncle.

In their attitude towards the mother there is an equally striking similarity. Hamlet loved his mother deeply, was never able to wean himself from her. His attitude towards Ophelia does not appear to be one of love. When he reveals himself to his mother, at the end of the third act, his language, his whole attitude, are surprisingly mild, at times even loving and full of pity despite the horror he feels of his mother's crime. Contrast with this the bitterness of Hamlet's words to Ophelia. John's love for his mother was more than the ordinary love of a devoted son.

During the most friendly period of our association, the following dream appeared to him: "But I have one dream that cannot be right. I dreamed of my mother. I slept with her in one bed. I had the proper thing with her. In my mind I knew it was my mother. I haven't seen her face. I slept with her. I got up. She got up, too. And we were talking, talking all the time."

He told me this, and continued afterwards to talk about his mother and how wonderful she was, how they loved one another, and how devoted he was to her as a child. He related many dreams connected with her. The following is very typical.

"I was in Rhodesia, where my mother's house was. There was no house. Big grass was growing. I found three chickens, very old, black. One was in the middle, standing ahead of the other two. He talked to me. 'Why have you lost your mother like this? There is no more a house now. You must come back and look out for these chickens.' From there I

172

answered: 'I will come back.' When I went away I met plenty of little boys, and I was the only big man there. They were going to the native school like the Bantus for circumcision. We all went to the mountain and came to a hut. I went into the hut and the boys came one by one and I cut them one by one. I was alone the big man. Very soon an old man came and helped me to put my medicine. But I did the cutting."

This dream showed his longing to become the head of his family. The three chickens, he himself said, were his two brothers and his sister. Without him, his real father being dead, there was no house. Charlie he ignored altogether. In the second part of the dream he visualized himself already not only the head of the family, but of the whole district.

In his relationship with women, John was never successful; he was never fully in love, never fully gratified. Whatever the external reasons, he never had a successful love affair. His explanation that medicine had greater lure for him than women was rationalization. But it was not medicine that was the lure but the desire to replace Charlie, of whom he was jealous all his life. His willingness to enter into a psychoanalytic situation was prompted by this same desire: to overcome Charlie by the knowledge he would gain from me. For the same reason, he was always studying medicine from Ba-Vendas, Zulus, and many other doctors, for the purpose of spiritually murdering Charlie. The custom of the tribe, and John's whole temperament, did not up till now favor a direct attempt at replacing Charlie.

The argument may be raised that in native society it is natural that one brother replace another, and that John could have had no objection to Charlie's replacing Chavafambira. But John did object to it, and showed his hos-

173

tility towards his second father from early childhood. In both Hamlet and John there existed a conflict between duty to custom and tradition and repressed inner desires; this unconscious conflict led in both to a loss or deficiency of will power. In Hamlet's case, the weakness is localized to the one question of killing his uncle; in John's case it was more generalized, for there were many other factors which were responsible for his inertia and lack of decision.

When the closing of Swartyard was imminent I offered John money to take Maggie and the child back to her kraal. The problem was resolved for him without his needing to make a move of his own. He felt such an immense relief from the unbearable tension which had till now suppressed him that he was like a hunted animal, pinned in a corner, who is suddenly shown a way of escape.

IV

FOR several months I heard nothing of John in spite of my frequent letters to him. Finally I decided to visit Maggie's kraal myself.

It was not an easy matter, for I knew only the sub-chief's name, and it transpired that there were a number of small kraals in this district that were known by this chief's name. The actual drive from Johannesburg took little more than four hours, but the discovery of John's hut took more than a day. As it happened, George's hut, where John was living, was hidden away from the main kraal. I had to cross the swift stream which I recognized as the one John had described to me in his recollection of the circumcision rites. My car stuck in midstream. A dozen oxen and as many young natives finally rescued me, and from one of this gang, a bright, clever lad, I finally learned John's whereabouts. "Oh, yes, the foreign *nganga,* you are looking for," he said, "with his lame wife. There is a lot of trouble in that place," he warned me. And, indeed, as I found out from John, there was more trouble than I could possibly have suspected.

Maggie and John were overjoyed to see me. Orders were given for a special hut to be cleaned for me, the car seats became an improvised bed, a primus stove appeared on a wooden box, and smooth skins to cover the earthen floor.

The three of us had tea and supper together and talked far into the night.

John began the account of his recent trouble by saying: "You are mistaken, Doctor, if you don't believe in bad luck. If your dead people are against you, you can do nothing. Besides, I still haven't killed a goat to them."

The present tragedy centered around Mawa, Maggie's mother, whom I was surprised not to have seen. With tears in their eyes, interrupting one another every now and then, they told me a typical African tragedy caused by that very kraal life which the Europeans are so prone to idealize.

When John and Maggie arrived at the kraal they had found Mawa almost unrecognizable, since they had last seen her, so terribly had she aged. She had shown no feeling at all, when her daughter and son-in-law returned, but had remained sitting in a corner of the yard, immobile and lifeless, staring in front of her with empty eyes. "Maggie," John told me, "was so frightened and heartbroken that she fell on her knees in front of her mother. She was crying. And then she took the old hands and kissed them and touched them with her weeping face. But Mawa made not the smallest sign of remembering her own daughter. Her hands remained as Maggie left them. I knew that Mawa was mad." Maggie began to weep as John told me this.

"And then a sad life began for Maggie and me. You know we loved Mawa. She was so nice, quick. Her eyes so lovely. But now she was gray, old, and thin. There was so much sorrow in her eyes."

I saw Mawa next day. She was in a state of deep melancholia, sunk in an unalleviated apathy and despair. Only her emaciated casket remained. The Mawa of John's descriptions, so brave, so attractive, so vital, had disappeared.

"Maggie was very devoted to her sick mother," John

176

went on. "She washed her, fed her, even tried to make jokes with her." John was obviously moved as he recalled the affection displayed by his wife, and I am sure that he had not thought her capable of such emotion. On the other hand, I must confess that John acted more bravely than I myself would have expected. Whether it was the sight of the poor mad Mawa, or the poverty and degradation of the whole family, or the absence of George, who was visiting patients in a distant kraal, or some other factor, it was nevertheless true that he showed himself a man of action, and behaved as the protector and savior of the whole family.

Deserted by George, the family was living in a pitiful state of destitution when John arrived. John's two children, who had lived in the kraal for a long time previous to his return, were scarcely clothed at all. They must have been starving for weeks, for even now they looked still subdued and apathetic, their faces weary and dejected. But John's popularity and fame and the absence of George, now the district's chief *nganga*, enabled him to build up a practice in an unusually short time. People knew that Mawa and her family depended upon John's earnings and so they paid more promptly than usual. John soon had a number of goats and chickens and several bags of Kaffir corn, so there was plenty of food and the children recovered sufficiently to play and run about again. Mawa, however, remained in the same state of melancholic immobility. Still, with Maggie's care she took more nourishment and looked less emaciated.

John knew that insanity came through poisoning, but who had poisoned Mawa? How was it done? How had the poison entered her body: through the heart, stomach, or head? To discover this was a more difficult problem than feeding and clothing the family.

Seated on a stool beside her, crouched as usual in a corner of the yard, John threw the bones for her. When Mawa saw them spread out before her she became agitated, screaming and shouting and even attacking John with her fists. Her frenzy distressed him, because the co-operation of the patient was essential to diagnosis and treatment. He gave up the idea of solving her problem, hoping that his own mother might disclose it to him in a dream. He would go to bed, night after night, with his thoughts fixed on his dead mother's image.

There was open talk that George and his second wife, who was still living with the children in the next yard, had ill-treated Mawa. The second wife was known to be a witch, hated and feared by everybody. Passers-by and neighbors had heard a woman screaming in the middle of the night, and Mawa was once found in the witch's yard, half-unconscious, with a bleeding wound in her head. May, Maggie's youngest sister, remembered that George often put certain medicines into her mother's food, and she had noticed that since then Mawa had grown duller and more spiritless.

On rare occasions, people said, Mawa would suddenly and without apparent reason become enraged. She would hit the children, break whatever she could lay hands on, pouring out all the time a flood of foul obscenity. These periods of excitement usually lasted a couple of days, and throughout them she talked incessantly, incoherently, "mostly nonsense" as the people remarked. Since George had left home and the witch no longer came near her, she had not been attacked by these excitable fits. But signs of restlessness sometimes betrayed a hidden fear, and an actual attack came when John threw the bones.

John and Maggie were convinced that George's second

178

wife was responsible for Mawa's insanity, but they feared her too much to take any action. John, since he found it impossible to get Mawa's co-operation, had to give up all idea of helping her. And in spite of protective medicines and various rituals performed before going to bed, he and Maggie found that they could not sleep at night. Maggie's dreams came to add to John's uneasiness. She continually dreamed of snakes attacking herself and her mother. Then she dreamed of four mice; not real mice but the super-natural mice that never leave their hole. She tried to hit them with a stick, but they ran away.

John knew that seeing mice meant that Maggie would get pimples on her body, and these, he also knew, came from sleeping with other men. But seeing the peculiar mice meant something more: death in the family. His thoughts turned to the accursed *abathakathi* in the next yard. This brought to his mind another recent dream of Maggie's. She had seen creatures coming from the sky. One of them had a long knife and was going to attack her; she cried for help, she was so afraid of the knife. Added to these signs of disaster, John himself dreamed of black fish, and woke up to ask Maggie if there were any fish in the hut. Then he fell asleep again and dreamed of a very big fish in the water. He knew that black fish meant the old witch next door. She was continuing her work of poisoning, and poor Mawa suffered through her. He must kill her. But how? George would certainly protect her, and John's own medicines would then be rendered powerless. Besides, Charlie had not taught him the art of poisoning.

If only he could take Mawa away from this place, he said once to Maggie. She had suggested that he write to me. John had agreed, but the days passed and he did not write.

During the next two days I examined Mawa. I found her

suffering from manic-depressive insanity, which expressed itself in cycles of excitement and melancholia. At present she was in a state of depression. Unfortunately I could give John and Maggie no hope concerning the outcome of the disease, and strongly advised them to send her to a mental hospital. This idea provoked indignant protest from both. "Do you want her," John asked me bitterly, "to be together in the yard with all these hundreds of men and women I have seen with you? But you know that the white people don't understand the mad natives. They keep them there to die." They insisted that I should give Mawa medicine, and so I gave her a mixture, and when I left the kraal I warned John to watch his mother-in-law carefully, especially when she became again excited.

Unfortunately, my warning was amply justified. Mawa, after a month, passed into another phase of maniacal excitement. At first no one took it seriously, regarding it merely as another trick of the witch. But soon they realized Mawa was a raving lunatic and dangerous. She attacked the small children, and even Maggie received several nasty blows. One morning, all the chickens were found scattered about the yard strangled. Everyone knew that Mawa was responsible, or rather, the witch who had chosen her as an instrument for the crime. But the *midzimu,* to whom John and Maggie prayed assiduously, with the prescribed sacrifice of many goats, finally revenged themselves upon the *abathakathi.* One of her children, a little girl of four years, was one morning found dead, strangled.

Someone must have informed the police in Pietersburg, for two of them appeared next day and, after investigating the affair, took with them the body of the murdered child. Mawa was arrested, tried, found guilty of murder committed while insane, and sent away to an asylum. John

180

attentively followed all the proceedings at the trial, at which he had to give evidence, and accompanied Mawa to the asylum.

I went myself to visit Mawa. I found her to be suffering now from paranoia with fears of being killed or poisoned. As before, in the kraal, John insisted that there was real ground for these fears. The witch, he reiterated, had in very truth poisoned Mawa and made her do these terrible things. I advised him to return to the kraal, for if Mawa recovered at all, it would be only after a very long time.

At the time I did not realize the cruelty of my advice, and even now I cannot forgive myself for the casual way in which I suggested his return when now there was nothing in the kraal to attract him. It must have been a terrible blow to him to hear me sending him away. "What will I do there?" he cried. "I am only too pleased that Maggie and the children are there. For me to return to the kraal again would mean to fight with George." And I realized that he was longing again for Johannesburg, which was only thirty miles from the asylum.

As it happened, I was not able to visit the hospital again for several weeks, and John, paralyzed by conflicting desires, returned neither to the kraal nor to Johannesburg, but remained near the asylum. He knew one of the native warders there, a Xosa named N'Komo, and followed up the casual acquaintance, which soon turned into an intimate friendship. He lived in N'Komo's house and accompanied him wherever he went.

2

I KNEW N'Komo very well myself. In education, intelligence, and the understanding of human nature, he was far above John. His handling of the insane was an art in itself; he knew practically every native patient by name, was familiar with his life history, his past illnesses, and the progress of his mental disease; in fact, his powers of observation and deduction were so developed that the doctors themselves often relied as much on N'Komo as on their own examinations. He was also fluent in the various native dialects and languages, and he spoke English well, so that he was much in demand as an interpreter. Thus he was, in a very real sense, the representative of these unfortunates. His tender, sensitive expression when listening to the difficult, incoherent talk of the patients was often indescribably poignant.

Through N'Komo, John became interested in many of the patients. He had had cases of insanity in his practice and was proud that he had been able to cure them; but he could see that these men were different. N'Komo allowed him to visit the patients with him, and later on I offered to take him myself to the male yard.

Whenever he entered the big yard of the male inmates, John was struck anew by the sight. It was indeed unique, and made a tremendous impression on every newcomer, African or European. The yard was a huge quadrangle with a number of doors on each side. John realized with astonishment that none of them had handles. In this quadrangle were about five hundred male patients, of all tribes and ages, talking, shouting, jumping, the brilliant sunshine making grotesque shifting shadows of their antics. Some of the men lay on the ground, baking themselves in the hot sun. Near them several human statues sat or stood frozen in fantastic attitudes. A tall Indian, almost naked, stood in the middle of the big square, monotonously intoning prayers, bending double so that his head almost touched the ground. In a corner sat an old, wrinkled native, a witch doctor. "Also a *nganga*," N'Komo ironically remarked to John. It was a sad story. The man had been sent to jail with a life sentence for practising witchcraft with dire results; the authorities had transferred him to the asylum. Now he crouched on his withered haunches, stretching out his claw-like hands to throw imaginary bones for imaginary patients, to whom he gave imaginary medicines. A young boy, deaf and dumb, ran about the yard, biting anyone he could. Almost next to John a boy had an epileptic fit and was hastily taken to the ward.

"The poisoners," John declared vehemently when we were outside the enclosure, "who have made men mad are far worse than those who cause death." He genuinely suffered for and desired to help all these unfortunates, to find out the cause and perpetrator of the poisoning. But they seemed utterly self-absorbed and showed no interest in him, he complained to me. It appeased him to hear from me that such patients behaved in the same manner to everyone; there was no external stimulus to which they reacted; it was as if they had lost all contact with the world; they lived, indeed, in a different land.

In a corner next to the enclosure for violent, dangerous patients, a group of men were talking of the riches of which they had been robbed. "I am a chief; I have many, many

183

wives and cattle. But my brother has taken my women and keeps me here with these dirty Kaffirs," a middle-aged man said in a sly, irritated voice.

"You liar," an elderly Bushman retorted promptly, speaking Afrikaans. "I am King George, and I know all the chiefs. You are not a chief! You are mad! If you don't keep quiet, I will give an order to have you hanged. You see all these people?" he went on, addressing the group. "They are my soldiers, my policemen. They will do whatever I tell them." He ended his threatening tirade' with a shrill cackle of laughter.

John found himself at a loss. Was the old Bushman, his face hatched and cross-hatched with wrinkles, really mad, or just playing the fool?

A shadow fell across John. He looked up and saw that a tall native of exceptional physique had joined the group and in a deep voice threatened to destroy everybody. He was, he said, the chief magistrate, the tax collector, chief of all the whites, sent to punish the people. His voice rumbled on and on as he explained that he was in the lunatic asylum because the white people had put him there, fearing he would punish them for taking the land from the natives. Suddenly he stopped his oration and, squatting down in front of John, addressing him quietly, said: "All my people, my servants, and soldiers are outside in motor cars, waiting for me to come out. You'll go with me, won't you?"

John wanted to laugh, but was unwilling to provoke the ire of this chief-magistrate cum-tax-collector, so he moved away and joined a solitary figure whom he recognized as Barlow, a Xosa boy, who began immediately to intone his lamentation. He suffered from religious delusions. "Christ came to me last night," he proclaimed in his monotonous

184

singsong voice. "He told me that I was chosen to punish all the white people."

He glanced furtively at John, then looked away, plucking nervously at his clothing. Still without looking at John, except with an occasional sly glance, he went on to say that he was a saint. Everyone else had committed great crimes. With a sudden entirely irrelevant and disconcerting smile, he assured John that he was Satan, too. Satan was his dead mother. This place was Sodom and Gomorrha; a place of judgment. He was God and Satan. He was their son.

John remarked to me: "The Christian religion muddles some native brains. I hear so much silly talk when these people think they are God, Jesus Christ, or Satan. But I have not heard a single one imagine himself to be Mwari or a *midzimu*. Yes, the old religion of our fathers is better for us. The Christian religion makes trouble in the native brain. It is the talk of sin that makes all the trouble. Our Mwari and *midzimu* don't talk to us as Christ and the preachers do."

Once, when he was alone in the yard, a feeling akin to panic descended upon him. Here he was, in the midst of hundreds of poisoned madmen. Perhaps he would become infected with their poison, become like them! And with horror he reflected that he had no protective medicines against madness. Could he prove his sanity? Perhaps they would keep him here! But for all that, he continued to visit the mad people. In the evenings he would discuss the patients with N'Komo, and during the day with me. He would tell me their bad-luck stories. "Many of them came to the asylum from prison. How cruel the white people are! If these men had committed murder, why didn't they hang them? Why torture them, make them mad!" John was sympathetic and good-natured, and his heart would swell with

185

sorrow for all these tortured black people, hurt by the whites and by their own people, too. If only he could instil by magic some superhuman powers into his people! He would lead them to rise and fight, destroy this terrible hospital and all the big buildings, smash the whole white super-structure that places such bitter and intolerable burdens upon the black man.

He would often be carried away by his fantasies of helping the suffering black humanity; and at these moments a different man stood before me. Beneath the armor of servility, meekness, and cowardice I saw a will to help and a readiness to sacrifice. I saw at these moments the emergence of a new John. However, when it came to the question of practical help for the inmates of the asylum, he could offer only to throw the bones for them.

Not wishing to discourage him I agreed to this. Still, I must confess that by this method of approach he extracted from the insane a wealth of information far exceeding any that I did. Most of the patients not only willingly submitted themselves to his interrogation, but regarded his efforts with confidence and trust. John, with his bones, horns, magical formulae, and rituals, meant to them the real medical man. And I wonder if it wouldn't be advisable, from a psychological point of view, to employ *ngangas* in the treatment of insane natives. In any case, there is nothing to lose, for our methods fail lamentably.

Several patients talked about their sexual troubles to him. One said: "I am an African. I am afraid of the white people. I am afraid of my own people. My father wants to poison me. I have been fifteen years in this hospital and every night God and judges standing in the sky force me to sleep with my mother."

These statements worried John. Fears of fathers and

brothers! Sleeping with one's own mother! How like his own dreams, and the dreams of his friends and patients! Who was mad — the men in the asylum with these delusions, or the men who walked in freedom outside with dreams so similar to these delusions of the insane? If incestuous dreams were a sign of insanity, was anyone sane?

John had argued with N'Komo about the abnormal ways of love-making practised by many of his patients in the asylum. N'Komo had used them as proofs of madness, but John laughed, declaring that if this were true, hundreds of natives in the compounds and in the crowded city yards would need to be put into asylums, for in such places love-making between men was quite usual, as it was between women also.

"I tell you, Doctor. You think only mad people do these things. Listen! I was walking along the street in Johannesburg, not far from Doornfontein Station. It was about eleven at night. I saw the pick-up van standing by the pavement. Then a native girl ran out of a yard with a white policeman after her. My heart was sore for the poor girl. She looked so frightened as she ran past. Presently the policeman came back. He had the girl. Some other men joined me. The policeman said to us: 'Have you ever seen a man dressed like a woman?' And it was true. He showed us the hair under the *doek*, straw in the dress for breasts, blue paint under the eyes, red paint on the cheeks and mouth. Yes, the man made such a good girl that only the sharp eyes of the policeman had seen this."

So John pondered the old, old problem of insanity, but his observations and studies ended sadly. One of the patients attacked him with a knife, intending to kill him. "Yes," screamed the unfortunate madman as he was dragged into a cell. "Yes, he is a white man! I know him! He helped

187

the white doctor prick me and take away my blood. He is a white man! I must kill all the white men!"

When John related this tragic incident to me in the presence of N'Komo, he sat still, his head bent. Then he began to cry bitterly, with a storm of tears like a child. He wept from pain, from fear, from the soul-searing turmoil of internal suffering. He also wept for the poor unfortunates in the yard, for his own unhappy people, and for all who had to live out their lives in this unhappy world. At last the paroxysm passed, leaving him desperately tired. The whole incident, he said, was an expression of the *midzimu's* anger, a warning to refrain from betraying his own nation. And, still conscious of the pain from the wound in his arm, he remembered how he had betrayed his own profession to me, association with whom seemed doomed to bring him to disaster. He was on the verge of a nervous breakdown, and I gave him a soothing drug. A few days later I took him back to Johannesburg.

3

BACK in the city he found his old friends easily enough, and one of them offered to let him share his room in Sophiatown. I supplied him with money, Simon lent him blankets and, what was still more valuable, brought him patients who very much appreciated John's return. Gradually he began again to practise. He kept away from me, and I guessed that, after his recent experience in the asylum, he had resolved not to be too much involved with white people.

Simon and other old friends hinted that, as he had seen the result of hobnobbing with Europeans, perhaps he would

188

now have enough sense to keep clear of them. Furthermore, they strongly advised him to stay away from meetings. There had been considerable trouble lately in connection with these; police had come, and many people had been arrested and thrown into prison. John should leave that kind of thing alone and devote himself to his horns and bones. A *nganga* must stick to his profession.

John agreed. With the black people, illiterate, raw, and heathen, natives of the kraal, was his proper place. He blamed me freely on the rare occasions when he came to see me. He said that I had taken him from his old life, where he had been happy, and had given him nothing in return. Like the missionaries who had given a new religion, but had helped to take away the land.

So he went to Simon and his friends, but found no happiness there either. He fitted no longer into their life of orgy and drink. One evening he went with Simon to a dance. The small room was packed. There was a shilling entrance-fee. For two days and nights they danced, drank, and slept with women. But John gained nothing. The whole affair appeared ugly to him. His head ached. He was cut and bruised at the end of it, and presumed that at one time he must have been fighting. He felt tired, dispirited, degraded. So where, he asked himself, did he belong? To these wild dances, and these uncontrolled stupid people, Simon's friends? No. Nor to the Bantu club and the educated African circles; nor to the white people. He was a man alone: a *nganga*. He must devote himself to helping people, engross himself in his practice. But he must remain friendless, aloof from other men and women, like his grandfather Gwerere, who was even buried apart from the others.

He left Simon's place unnoticed. He was drunk, and inevitably caught by the police. He paid ten shillings fine and left the cell with a bruised body and a swollen and distorted face. He did not speak to Simon for a week.

But as the weeks passed, he drifted slowly back into the rut in which he had lived before my advent. He became a *nganga* again, and even began to practise witchcraft. Although he was not conversant with the art of poisoning, he began to use his medicines to that end.

Outwardly, he seemed content. His practice was not so good as before, but his wants now were very simple. He became dirty and careless in his appearance, more and more the type of witch doctor he had formerly despised. His very personality seemed to have changed since he had settled in Sophiatown. I did not lose contact with him altogether, but my influence on him dwindled, although we remained friends.

PART FOUR

Under Suspicion

I

I CANNOT with impunity tell what happened
to John from now on, naming the actual scenes of events
and the actual people who figured in them. Reluctantly I
must resort to disguising both the scene and the characters
just enough to ensure anonymity without in any way affecting veracity.

After I had known John intimately, I extended my interest beyond him to the whole African community. I got to
know many witch doctors, kraal and urbanized Africans,
raw and educated men and women. Many of them became
my friends. As John once remarked: "I can see that you,
Doctor, are a true friend of ours. I say so to my patients
and people. They will like you when they meet you."

Among the people we met in Sophiatown who practised
witchcraft and medicine there was much talk of a certain
ngoma named Emily. She lived in the Blesfield location,
not far from the Sophiatown slums. We heard much about
this woman and her remarkable cures. At first John was
frankly skeptical and scornful. Various actions ascribed to
Emily by her patients did not fit in with the practices of
ngomas among his own people in Manyikaland. He even
suspected this woman of being a rank impostor. But as
we heard more and more about her, our curiosity increased,
and one day we went to see her, pretending that John was
a patient.

We were met on the *stoep* of Emily's house by her husband and sister. They acted as her assistants and interpreters at séances, and they "prepared" the patients by impressive narration of miraculous stories. My presence did not surprise them because, they said, many white people came to ask her advice.

We found other patients waiting on one small verandah to see the *ngoma*. To all of us Emily's husband told the story of her life. She was born at the time of the great *rinderpest*. Many would remember the devastation wrought by that disease. But on the day of her birth that dreadful scourge disappeared, cattle became well again as suddenly as they had been afflicted; so from her first day in the world her miraculous powers became apparent. Nor was she like other girls. She refused to do any work; she brooded often for hours; she scarcely associated with her companions; sometimes she would disappear for days; once she disappeared for a week.

She had been ill, feverish, complaining of a sore throat, actually losing her voice. One night she felt a choking feeling as though fire were burning inside her. She left the hut and went to the river. For seven days she stayed under the water with the little people. These people were spirits, and Emily talked to them for seven days. A one-eyed woman led her among them, and at the end of that time gave her two bundles of roots, one white and one red. With the old woman behind her, Emily climbed up a black pole and out of the water. She came back to her home. For a long time after her return she was very ill. On her head and arms was white paint, which the one-eyed woman had put there. Through this sign the people knew that Emily was chosen by the spirits.

Then a great *nganga* came to the kraal. He took Emily

194

under his care and taught her witchcraft and the use of medicines. After that, Joseph Mazulu, the greatest doctor in Pondoland, pierced her ears, putting medicine in the incisions. Since then she had been able to hear the spirits talking. For a long time the people thought her mad. Once a white policeman wanted to arrest her and send her to the mental hospital, but the great doctor protected her. John remarked to me that it was true that white people often sent *ngomas* to the asylum, because they think them mad. "And now," the husband concluded solemnly, "the spirits come down to her every day. They stay with her and talk to her. But when people make her angry, they disappear, and that is bad. She gets angry when people quarrel with her and refuse to pay the money. Then she falls down like dead, and the spirits go away. They don't like quarrels. When this happens Emily loses her voice and feels like one dead."

One at a time we paid our fee to the husband and went into the house. John's turn came and I accompanied him into a hot, semidark room. Straining my eyes in the gloom I made out the immensely fat form of the *ngoma* seated on a wooden chair in a dark corner. I was awed and astounded by her aspect. She was enormous. Her face was so puffed that her eyes seemed tiny beads tucked away above the smooth swellings that were her cheeks; the nose lay flat and bloated on the swollen lips; the cushion of flesh forming her chin rested on her chest. The swelling breasts were covered by a sleeveless blouse that exposed her arms, smooth and soft like those of a huge black baby. The soft, flexible leather skirt of the woman outlined the great abdomen. The skirt was lavishly embroidered with blue and red beads. Slung over the *ngoma's* shoulder, crossing her breast and back, were the round bead strings from which

195

dangled her calabashes at waist level under her arms. Each calabash was covered by an elaborately worked bead cover. Round her neck she wore long strings of pearls. Her head was uncovered. Her woolly hair had been teased, augmented with black darning wool, and was braided from the center of her forehead in a loop over her left eye. Round her, on the earthen floor, sat visitors and relatives. Silent and absorbed, they watched Emily, following in awed suspense every word and gesture. The *ngoma* talked incessantly. She had a deep, resonant contralto and she used it to great effect. The voice changed its tempo, rhythm, timbre at her will. It was always effective; it always influenced the listeners. She handled her audience with the confidence of the supreme artist who believes implicitly in herself.

John was powerfully affected by the gloom, the tense, hot atmosphere, and the subtle artistry of the *ngoma*. He shifted steadily forward, peering intently at her face. At last, in answer to his supplication, Emily consulted the spirits on his behalf. First her voice, soft-pitched at the time, deepened and hardened. It struck a final, firm note. Then, eerie in its contrast, came a full minute of complete silence. In the hot, dark, crowded room everything was still. Only the breathing of the people could be heard. The effect was awesome and terrifying. Then she began talking to the spirits for John.

She used, not her normal voice, but a thin, high-pitched whisper, like a winter wind blowing through a tiny crack. John listened intently. The *ngoma's* eyes closed. Suddenly they opened again, deep-set glimmering bulbs pushed into her great puffed face. She told John he was lucky, the spirits were talking from the top of the room for him. Closing her eyes again she continued her whistling whisper.

It seemed to John, he told me afterwards, that another sound mingled with her whisper — a sound which seemed to him like the dropping of water from a distant rivulet, faint but clear, distant, yet refreshing.

We waited intently for the message of the spirits. The stuffiness, the stench of human sweat, was overpowering. Emily said that John must wait awhile: she had sent the spirits to his qwn country; they must have time to return. Later, John commented to me that I must not trust Emily because spirits do not and will not fetch anything from far away. Besides, they will not talk with anybody where others can overhear them. "The spirit was cross. This was right. She, too, must be cross to be able to see these spirits. My mother was the same. When she was fighting and was cross with Patrick or Charlie, she felt sick, got cross and then she would talk to the spirits."

Still, when, after a time of depressing silence, Emily began interpreting the spirits' message, he listened intently. She told him he was suffering from the shaky sickness. And, indeed, John was actually shivering from head to foot in a state of nervous tension. He must use *rutsanga*, the water reeds, Emily continued; if possible, he must get them from the middle of the river and from under the water, as the roots that are constantly shaken by the water are the best. They shake more than the patient, and the sickness goes from the patient to the roots.

"Your eyes are yellow. It means you have also the yellow sickness. You will have to catch a yellow bird. But before catching the bird, make cuts in the hands, forehead, and the back of the neck, and put the powdered *rutsanga* roots into them. The cure cannot be finished at one time. The spirits will tell more. You must come again."

We came again, and several times after that. I disclosed

197

my identity to Emily, and she became very much attached to me; she was indeed an unhappy woman, suffered from a serious endocrine dysfunction which was responsible for her enormous stoutness, was most depressed about her sterility; she was also an extreme hysteric. She was easily influenced, and I was able to hypnotize her in a few minutes. Later on, my ordinary command for her to fall asleep was sufficient for her to close her eyes and relapse into a trance. She was prepared to do anything for me, talking to the spirits, asking them to help me and bring me luck in all my work.

John also became a friend of hers, and later on something of an intimacy sprang up between them, the emaciated but still handsome *nganga*, and the huge, fat, ugly *ngoma*. Not the close intimacy of two people sharing common things, but the distant intimacy of consultant and client, interested, but careful, guarded.

Then at last during one such visit John disclosed his identity. She said she was not surprised to find he was a *nganga*, and pretended to have known it all along. They became friends; they were often together. Malicious scandalmongers in the location said that they were lovers. John fiercely denied the accusations; yet he spent weeks in Emily's house, acting as her assistant in place of her husband, who was frequently in jail for illicit liquor selling.

John's old comrade, Simon, did not approve of the new friendship. Partly it was jealousy, since he had hoped that, with Maggie in the kraal, he would have John more to himself. John resented this.

"A funny man, Simon," he would often complain to me. "He does not like me to be friendly with anyone. The white people were bad, and now he wants me to drop Emily, this *ngoma* who helps me with money and patients, and teaches me the art of fighting poisons and talking to the spirits. Simon is jealous."

Simon, in his turn, argued with me that John was married, and had to support his family and not go about with other women. He ridiculed the story of Emily teaching John medicine. What could he learn from a woman? he asked. Maggie often wrote to Simon to intercede for her with John, urging that he should persuade John to send home part of his earnings to her. This was common practice, Simon argued, among all town natives. But John would indignantly answer that he had no intention of doing so.

"The money of the others goes to feed their own cattle and work their own land," he said. "I have no land and cattle at Maggie's kraal. Why should I send money for George's cattle? I am not going to waste my money on a stranger's land." Nevertheless, he sent Maggie a few shillings now and then; and once he sent five shillings to Mawa, who was still in the asylum. It was easier to do this than have Simon always nagging; and, more important, these occasional advances would help to keep Maggie safely in the kraal.

Simon, however, was a persistent man. Raw, illiterate, ugly, he was obstinate and tenacious, and was not to be appeased with small concessions. He regarded John as his possession; John was his teacher, his friend, his sole companion, and he would give him up to no one. Simon was as nagging as a wife. "No good will come of an association with people like Emily and her husband," he used to repeat again and again. "You wait. They will bring you to ruin yet."

But the end of John's friendship with her came in a different way. After a long association with her he came to see her human ugliness. He still believed in her powers

199

of witchcraft; but as a woman, as a person, she eventually became distasteful to him, and he gradually dropped her. And Simon naturally exulted.

2

ONE afternoon a Nyasaland native, Mdlawini by name, came to consult John. He came from the Blesfield location. Something terrible had happened to Emily. He had gone to seek her help. For a long time bad luck had pursued him: he had lost his job; news came from the kraal that the cattle had died; and finally all his money and belongings had been stolen. He came to Emily to find out which enemies had bewitched him, and to get protective medicines against them.

Emily told him that his dead uncle was very cross with him and that, apart from this, he had many enemies. She said she would find out from his *midzimu* who these enemies were. And then for a long time she neither moved nor spoke. She seemed to be asleep.

For a long time silence reigned, till a shadow crept into the room. It was Emily's husband. He seemed agitated. Without a word he quickly went to the shelf by the door, grasped a bottle, fumbled with the latch of the tiny window, opened it, and hurriedly threw out the bottle. The sound of breaking glass had just reached the ears of the people when the door was pushed open and two native policemen appeared. Everyone was scared, not so much at the policemen as at the possible effect upon Emily, for they knew that sudden awakening was fraught with danger.

One of the policemen made his way noisily and roughly to Emily, seized her by the shoulder, and demanded in a

200

loud voice that she should divulge where the liquor was hidden. Then Emily awoke. First a shudder passed over her; then she slowly opened her eyes, gazing stupidly around her. Then, without warning, she was seized with uncontrollable fury; she began hitting out like a maddened animal. She seized a chair and threw it at the policemen, grasped anything she could lay hands on and flung it about the room, and, all unheeding, swept a pot of boiling water to the ground, scalding both her legs.

The effect was terrifying. Emily was attacked by one of her fits, her whole body trembled and shivered, and she fell to the ground, suffocating. A terrible sound issued from her tortured throat: a sound he would never forget, like the sound of a saw cutting slowly through soft, moist wood.

Mdlawini stopped. He seemed overwhelmed by the events he had to relate. John came to his help with leading questions and finally got the rest of the story from him.

Emily's sister ran to find the white and red roots given to Emily by the old woman of the river. Their magic power would help. But she could not find them. The huddled, frightened people watched Emily's face turn purple, almost blue. Her eyes, wide open and staring, were bloodshot. The tongue protruding from the mouth as though it wished to leave the dying body. The hands moved helplessly. She was gasping for breath, but there was no more air left in her body. She got up for the last time and then she fell flat on the floor. Only a few minutes had elapsed since the beginning of the attack. But . . . Emily was dead.

The story shocked John immensely. "She died through the white people," he repeated to me continuously the same afternoon. His memory of her was so vivid that he could not believe that she was dead. Then I seemed to feel in John the stirrings of a desire to fight, to assert himself, to

201

step into Emily's place, as a soldier on the field of battle takes the place of a fallen comrade. There was in this new urge a mixture of guilt at having dropped her so suddenly, a desire for revenge, and an inner conviction that he had been chosen to become a great diviner. He suddenly felt a special sympathy for the Nyasaland man who had brought him the story. He decided to carry on where Emily had left off. For the first time in his life he even applied the methods used by Emily.

He ordered the room to be darkened, and gathered the initiates of the séance in a circle around him, with Mdlawini in the center. Then, imitating Emily, and talking in a strange theatrical voice, he called on the spirits. Half an hour of protracted ceremony followed, during which time he touched the horns, threw the bones, uttered strange formulae, till, with a peremptory order, he commanded all to leave the room. He and Mdlawini remained. Simon and the others were bewildered. For the first time John had made use of a ritual that was the prerogative of a *ngoma* or an *isanussi*.

Alone with his patient, John became absorbed in strange thoughts. The sudden remembrance came to him that Maggie's lover, so he had been told, was a Nyasaland man. What if Mdlawini were the lover who was responsible for his present downfall? For he was now sure that his misfortunes had begun from the time when Maggie had contaminated his medicines while he was achieving fame in Kroonstad. The events of his life since Maggie's betrayal sketched themselves in an endless ordered line before him. Maggie's betrayal had caused his downfall — but was it entirely Maggie's fault? In the end she was only a woman. The man who had seduced her — wasn't he the real culprit: wasn't it upon him that vengeance should fall? Charlie

202

had told him long ago that no help would come for a *nganga* who did not revenge himself on a man who destroyed the potency of his medicines. Was it Mdlawini, or was this another trap for him? If not Mdlawini himself, it might have been his brother, his friend, certainly one of the same clan or tribe. And by the law of his people, every member of a tribe has to be included in vengeance for the crime of a single man.

The room was still, John sat silent, apparently ignorant of his patient's agony. Unaware of it himself, John began to take his revenge.

He spoke gravely and deliberately. "You are in danger. Your people are bad people. Your people in Nyasaland are against you. Have you been fighting with your father, your brother, or your uncle?" His voice rose half interrogatively. He watched Mdlawini's expression. At the latter's involuntary nod, he continued: "Yes, this uncle, he is going to kill you; soon. Very soon."

"But he is in Nyasaland," Mdlawini objected.

John smiled. "A poisoner can kill from any place. In Nyasaland the poisoners have been taught by the Indians. They can take any shape or form. They can kill from afar. But I will protect you with my medicines. However, it will take some days for your safety to be sure, as my medicines have to travel far, right to Nyasaland. So you must be very, very careful for the next few days and nights. Perhaps the poisoners will get to know that I am arranging your protection, so they may attack you at once. There are no secrets from them. Just as a *nganga*, so does a poisoner know what you do and where you are."

Suddenly John sprang upon Mdlawini. "Have you slept with women, here in Johannesburg?" And, not giving him a chance to answer: "Perhaps with the wife of a *nganga?*"

203

But Mdlawini looked so stupid that John decided he was far too much of a fool to be a lover. Again silence descended upon them — silence that was agony to the patient.

Mdlawini shivered. How could he detect his enemy if he were able to assume any form? As though in answer to his thought John said: "Your enemy may come as a little child, a dwarf, or a ghost. Most probably a ghost." He leaned forward, emphasizing his warning by striking one palm with another, dropping his voice to a graver note.

"In the middle of the night, if you see someone moving about don't talk to the unknown figure. Do not look at it. If you speak, or if you look, you will be changed instantly into a small animal, and killed."

He paused, still staring intently from his heavy-lidded eyes. "Have you an assagai or an ax? No? You must keep a weapon next to you. After three or four days you will not need to worry. You will be immune from your enemies. But until then, be on your guard."

He sent Mdlawini away, hinting, however, that medicines have no effect until treatment is paid for. Long afterwards he was unable to explain to me the real intentions behind such a stern warning as he had given the man, for his bones gave him no instructions for it. But, whatever his intentions, a terrible tragedy resulted from his advice.

3

DEPRESSED, angry, and helpless, Mdlawini set off for home. As he walked from Sophiatown to his location there was plenty of time for thought. The picture of Emily's dreadful death kept appearing before his eyes. If that powerful *ngoma* could do nothing to protect herself, what hope was there for him, constantly pursued by bad luck? In the town he walked slowly, desperately trying to distract his thoughts by looking at shop windows. Not far from the post office he passed a curio shop which attracted his attention. Outside it, on the pavement, stood a decorated barrel containing different types of assagais, some long, some short, stabbing assagais; some plain, some with elaborately fashioned handles; but all sharp, cutting, like John's warnings.

His overwhelming need for a defensive weapon galvanized him to an act foreign to his nature. Making sure that no one was looking, he seized an assagai, slipped it under his coat, and hurried away. So great was his dread that he would be discovered and the weapon taken away from him, that he ran most of the way to the location. There he still further shortened the wooden shaft and concealed the blade quite easily upon his person. He felt, with the weapon near, a little less helpless.

That night he wrapped himself in his blanket, fully dressed, setting the assagai beside him and reassuring himself as the heavy hours dragged on by repeatedly touching it. His sleeping quarters were in a room for many others, and for some time he alone remained awake. But he was utterly tired after having walked nearly twenty miles that day, and soon fatigue overcame his fears. After a period of fitful dozing he finally fell asleep and slept heavily.

Suddenly he awoke with a jerk. He had felt a touch. His hand instinctively closed over the assagai. The blood hung in his ears. His straining eyes made out a blur in the doorway — a vague, white, moving shape. Slowly it crouched, then lay down.

Mdlawini felt cold sweat upon his body. The room was full of sleepers, but he dared not call to them, for he knew that it would bring disaster. The hand grasping the assagai began to tremble.

The white blurred figure moved again, and he was sure that he could hear a peculiar groaning sound. He must be quick or it would be too late. Without speaking, without looking, he must strike.

He threw aside the blanket, rose to his feet, and leapt at the figure by the door. His blade flashed down, between the shoulders, through the ghost's heart. The thing died without a sound, so perfect was the stroke.

No one stirred. No one had heard. Satisfied, Mdlawini went out. He must not look at the thing he had killed: that was the law. If he looked it would be suicide. So he slept on the veld, and all next day he wandered, not daring to return until nightfall, when, he concluded, the ghost would have been removed. He was taking no chances in the matter of looking at it.

He was convinced that he had killed a malignant enemy: a ghost in the form of a man. And the conviction was in no way shaken when he learned that he had killed a young countryman of his, a good friend, whose white blanket he would normally have easily recognized.

He slept in peace that night. Only towards dawn was he awakened by the police who had tracked him down. He made no statement when they arrested him. At the police station he merely said: "I killed him with the assagai."

II

MDLAWINI was a raw, illiterate native. His contact with the white man had been brief and superficial. Like a newly transplanted shrub, he had not yet thrust roots into his new soil. Now, after his arrest, he mistrusted the world more than ever. Both blacks and whites were his enemies. The Europeans seemed to be hunting him; they wanted to kill him; he had been told that he would hang for murder.

The endless questioning and manhandling of the police were agonizing. When, after the preliminary examination in the Magistrate's Court, the advocate sent by the Government came to his solitary cell, he too was met by the sullen hostility the prisoner had shown to the Europeans. This man happened to be a personal friend of mine and from him I obtained full details of the murder, which agreed with John's version that was known only to me. He implored Mdlawini for his own sake to open his heart to him; but to Mdlawini he was white, and therefore against him.

After some days Mdlawini made a statement, in an indistinct, mumbling voice, which the interpreter said was a confession of the crime. But to the advocate he appeared to say far more. It was the eternal tragedy of the illiterate native who cannot make himself understood to the Europeans, even to his protectors and friends. The white man accuses him of childish stubbornness and stupidity. What a lack of sympathy and understanding!

Mdlawini was standing alone, friendless, facing a hostile world, far from his own people and lacking the protection of his chiefs and ancestors. What was the use of explaining to the advocate and the magistrate? He must have felt that nothing he could say would alter the white man's attitude, for, as far as possible, he kept silent. The whole procedure of the court was entirely foreign to him.

At one time he looked pleasantly surprised to see a number of his friends in court. But his disappointment was pathetic when they began testifying against him. As they described how he had run away, he looked slowly round the crowd of European and African people that filled the small courtroom, as though searching among them for a protector. Suddenly he noticed John sitting on one of the back benches, and a ray of hope lit up his face. Indeed, John seemed to nod encouragingly at him, moving his fingers as if in a ritual performance; and Mdlawini smiled at John to show his faith in the *nganga's* powers and express his gratitude for his presence.

Finally, the magistrate announced his decision: the accused was committed for trial for the murder of David Mahali. Mdlawini was taken back to his cell. He went, apparently reassured by his faith in the witch doctor.

John, on the other hand, felt anything but assured. The gestures that Mdlawini had interpreted as ritual had in reality been merely a nervous movement, for he was desperately afraid of — he knew not what. The news of the murder had come as a shock. He had known the murdered David. He recollected giving him some medicine for luck only a week before. He did not connect his fortunetelling with the crime. He heard people say that Mdlawini had

killed the youth in revenge and that he suspected David of
stealing money. There was gossip, too, concerning a quarrel
over a girl, and John readily accepted these as motives for
the crime. Nevertheless, he noticed with relief that none
of Mdlawini's friends appeared to know of his visit to
him. He felt uneasy, however, when he noted the man's
demeanor in the magistrate's court, so calm and subdued,
and began to doubt the motives suggested. "No," he said
to me, "such people don't kill out of revenge."

He was convinced that Mdlawini was the victim of evil
forces which had made him kill an innocent man. He
thought of Emily's interpretation of Mdlawini's trouble,
and his own advice. What could have happened? Perhaps
the *umthakathi* had taken the form of the younger man and
then, at the crucial moment, left it. A feeling of guilt overcame him. He felt that he had failed as a protector against
witchcraft.

Now he reproached himself. Why had he not told
Mdlawini the truth he had told so many others, that he was
a medicine man and not a witch doctor? Mdlawini might
have gone to a real witch doctor who would have given
him proper poisons with which to kill his enemies. Yet
John did not care to admit that he was at fault. If anything,
it was the fault of Charlie in not teaching him the art of
poisoning, as he was in duty bound to do. Also, Mdlawini's
enemies had been too powerful for an ordinary witch doctor,
John consoled himself further. Hadn't they killed the powerful Emily when she was on the verge of disclosing the
evildoer? He recalled Mdlawini's expression in court, and
now the man's face seemed to him to have had the look of
one under a spell, as dull and lifeless as the faces of the
victims of poisons that he had seen in the asylum.

Perhaps Mdlawini had gone mad. There had been a

smile on his face which John now interpreted as a sign of insanity. Many insane natives smiled like that. But this brought him no consolation; rather, he reproached himself further, for it seemed that his fraudulent imposture had resulted in a double tragedy — David dead and now Mdlawini mad.

In this frame of mind, conjecturing thus, a new fear came to him. Mdlawini might tell about his throwing the bones; and then he might be arrested for practising witchcraft and be implicated in the murder. A very reasonable fear indeed, in view of the laws of the country. He did not know what to do. He had an impulse to run away, back to Manyikaland; but his pass was not in order, his tax had not been paid, he had not a penny to his name. Besides, he was no longer the weakling who ran away from every situation. I noticed more and more, at that time, fantasies of fighting society rather than fleeing from it.

Four months passed between the preliminary examination and the trial. For John it was a period of fear and uncertainty. He could not attend his patients and could not remain in his room. He went away for days at a time. Eventually he was arrested on a charge of failing to pay his taxes and was sentenced to a month's imprisonment. It was not the first time that he had been in prison, but now he actually felt happier and safer there than outside; and he hoped inwardly that he would still be in prison when Mdlawini's trial began. But he was released before then, and when the trial reopened he was again in court, following the procedure with the closest attention.

I was sitting next to him, and hardly recognized Mdlawini when he entered the dock. He seemed lost in the big box. John looked sympathetically at him, a small, ragged figure facing the imposing red-robed judge, then from him to the jury — nine of them — a lucky number; and he remarked to me, with pleasant surprise, that they seemed just ordinary people, such as one met daily in the streets. He might even have waited on them. The idea astonished him; it seemed to form a contact between them and himself; he felt he had the right to plead with them for a favorable verdict.

First the prosecutor read a paper concerning Mdlawini and the killing. A doctor described the dead body. Then some natives were called. They were friends of Mdlawini, but they spoke against him, to John's anger and indignation. That his own people should speak against a friend, a native, in front of white people! It was nauseating to hear how willingly and freely they answered the prosecutor's questions, and how they hesitated or kept silent when Mdlawini's advocate questioned them. Early in the trial it became clear to John that the prosecutor was trying to prove that Mdlawini had deliberately prepared the crime, and this horrified him even more.

After the morning interval, Mdlawini was taken to the witness box, and with the help of the advocate, the judge, and the prosecutor, he told the story of the murder. The tone of his voice, his manner of speech, the simple way in which he told of his misfortunes, impressed everybody. He related how he had gone to Emily, told of her terrifying death, of his visit to another witch doctor and the latter's advice. When he came to the description of the actual stabbing, he began to cry, but soon recovered and finished his story with great self-control. He replied as well as he could to questions put to him by the judge and members of the jury, but during the cross-examination his answers became confused, especially when pressed for the identity and address of the witch doctor. He still relied upon John to save him with his medicines and would not betray him.

211

As the case against Mdlawini became blacker, John grew more nervous and agitated until, with sudden decision, he left the court. I followed him out, anxious about his actions and the whole affair. I tried to persuade him to keep away from the court, but he wouldn't listen. He insisted on re-turning, and as we re-entered we found the prosecutor in the middle of his speech. He was relating an analogy to the case.

"A traveling circus came to a small town, bringing a number of wild animals; among them a lion. The lion escaped, and the townspeople were greatly alarmed. There was in the town a man of a very nervous disposition, suffer-ing from a fear of wild animals. The man went about with a revolver in his pocket from the moment that he heard of the escaped lion. Late one afternoon he went to the house of a friend. A servant was busy sweeping a lion skin hung on the wall. The nervous man, imagining the lion every-where, mistook the servant and the lion skin for the escaped beast, and killed the man.

"Now let us imagine another situation. Friends of the same gentleman decide to play a practical joke upon him. One of them disguises himself very cleverly in a lion skin, so cleverly, in fact, that at first sight it is quite easy to think he is a lion. The man hides behind a tree and suddenly rushes out to frighten his nervous friend, who immediately draws a revolver, fires at the supposed lion, and kills the man."

In the second case, the prosecutor said, the murdered man was the victim of his own joke, and the murderer would be blameless. But in the first instance he could not plead a reasonable mistake, for no sane man would make such an error. Anyone who did so must certainly be con-sidered guilty of murder.

212

A similar case, he said, existed in Mdlawini's situation. Mdlawini did not take reasonable steps before killing; especially as he knew that the man he suspected of stealing his goods slept in the same room, as was revealed in the evidence. Moreover, the accused knew that the deceased David had been wearing a white blanket for some days, and why should he have forgotten these facts? He might have been confused for the first few minutes after waking, but his mind must have been clear when he took the assagai to stab his victim. He remembered neither to look at nor speak to the spirit, and he managed to stab swiftly and precisely through the heart. The wound, as the district surgeon had shown, required skill, accuracy, and presence of mind.

The defense might plead that Mdlawini had killed David in the belief that his life was endangered by evil spirits, a fear that the witch doctors had magnified. But where were these witch doctors? One of them was dead; the other could not be traced.

John was again seized with an impulse to leave the court, but this time I restrained him; though I am sure he heard little of the rest of the prosecutor's speech.

The next morning the counsel for the defense addressed the jury. John was disappointed; he could not follow his speech.

The advocate asked the court to imagine Mdlawini's state of mind in the days preceding the crime, when he returned from his visits to Emily and the unknown witch doctor. Mdlawini a cunning, ferocious murderer! He ridiculed the suggestion. "Look at this man. Can you imagine that he planned a murder in cold blood, stayed away until the removal of the corpse, and then returned to be arrested? Why did Mdlawini go away? Because he had been warned not to look at the ghost, dead or alive. Why did he return? Because the danger was over.

"To the primitive African, the belief in witchcraft is real and logical. There is no such thing as imaginary feeling. There is no such phenomenon as imaginary pain or imaginary vision. It might appear so to others, but not to the sufferer. The African fears malicious spirits which he actually sees and hears. He lives in constant fear and turns to the witch doctors, in whom he places unconditional belief and trust. Mdlawini had a reasonable belief in evildoers. His fight against them was reasonable. That evil spirits were acting against him, as he first intuitively guessed, was definitely confirmed by the woman Emily, and by another witch doctor. Certainty brought terror and fear, and prompted him to take desperate measures. Thus he was driven to the tragedy of that fateful night.

"Civilized people find it extraordinarily difficult to get away from our way of thinking, and therefore find it very hard to grasp what is going on in the mind of a man whose ways of thinking and acting are foreign and almost unintelligible to us.

"The State has provided but one law for all, whether black or white, primitive or civilized; but in the administration of that law it has not prohibited a human interpretation. But we deny that there was intent to kill any human being, much less the deceased David, and we plead, my lord and gentlemen, for the verdict of culpable homicide."

Little as he understood the foregoing, the concluding words of the speech made a deep impression upon John and hope lighted his face. The judge began summing up after the interval; and now Mdlawini must have sensed the importance of the moment; for the first time he showed signs of uneasiness. He gazed pleadingly at the great white man in the red robe who held his fate in his hands. He

214

obviously wished so much that he could gain the sympathy of this man, wishing that he might talk to him as to his own father — tell him his life story, his home tragedy, his longing for his kraal, for his wife and child, tell him, above all, how sorry he was for the killing.

The judge spoke slowly and dispassionately. The defense claimed that the accused had no intent to kill the deceased. The defense maintained that the accused intended only to kill a ghost, and that he formed this impression on reasonable grounds. The Crown, on the other hand, suggested that the primary motive for the crime was enmity and revenge. It was for the jury to decide whether the case was one of willful murder, or whether the plea of the defense was justified. The judge dealt at length with native beliefs and fears, and the role of witchcraft in their society. He urged the jury to accept the suggestion that the accused really did believe that he was killing an evil spirit. The question for them to decide, however, was whether that belief was reasonable.

John grasped the gravity of this injunction. Now his only wish, he whispered to me, was that the judge would state his opinion clearly. For the more he listened, the less could he determine what was in the great man's mind. Who was for Mdlawini and who was against? That was the question. The judge's speech seemed to him like the zigzag track of a train in the Manyika mountains.

The jury retired to consider their verdict, and the court was filled with an atmosphere of uncertainty. A man near John said emphatically: "The poor devil will hang." Presently the jury returned.

There followed minutes of awful suspense, and then the foreman announced: "Guilty of murder, with a recommendation to mercy." The decision was unanimous.

2

MDLAWINI did not understand. Only when he was told, in his own language, and was asked if he had anything to say before sentence of death was passed upon him, did he realize the true state of affairs. And then he could say nothing. His heartbroken stupefaction was laconically translated by the interpreter as: "The accused has nothing to say."

But Mdlawini's ordeal was not over. He was made to stand up and face the judge while the latter, addressing him in English, pronounced the sentence of death, adding, however, that since the jury had recommended him to mercy he would do all in his power to give effect to their wish.

Mdlawini was taken back to his cell. The advocate told me afterwards that at first the man was too dumbfounded to show any reaction. But soon he began to weep, the soft, silent tears of a hopeless, abandoned human being.

I experienced great difficulty in quieting John. My assurance that, so far, all such cases had been commuted, and that apart from this, there would be an appeal against the verdict, was of no avail. John was utterly disillusioned by this sample of the white man's justice.

I tried to dispel his fears of arrest, but he feared far more the vengeance of both his and Mdlawini's *midzimu* than any punishment by the white people. He was agitated, nervous, and soon fear gave way to bitterness and rage. Outside he gave vent to his feelings, shouting and gesticulating wildly, repulsing Simon who came up to him and tried to calm him. "That is the white man's place of justice," he exclaimed to a gathering crowd of natives. "Today

216

Mdlawini, tomorrow you . . . and you and you!" He pointed to one after another of them. "Which of us is safe?" His voice became hysterical, like that of preachers threatening the heathen with hellfire. A uniformed native quietly advised them to disperse and to take the speaker away, telling them: "The white man does not like to hear his laws criticized. There will be a lot of trouble for black people from such talk."

Again Simon tried to drag John away, but the usually quiet and passive man was difficult to handle now. He had always despised Simon's cowardice, and now the man's interference infuriated him. He shouted even louder. His speech became raucous, a mixture of English and vernacular.

It was a shame, he said, that they should let Mdlawini hang. If they would stick together like the white people, innocent men would not suffer. Yes, Mdlawini was innocent. He had not killed a man but a ghost, which had disguised itself in the form of David. He, John Chavafambira, the Manyika *nganga*, knew it through the bones. And he had had a message from his ancestor, Gwerere, whom all knew to be the famous *nganga*. "David Mahali is not dead. He wasn't murdered at all. He is alive in his kraal in Nyasaland."

Simon, now seriously alarmed, came to fetch me and, at the sight of a white man, the crowd dispersed. "Keep quiet, you fool," Simon now urged John, speaking more authoritatively than before. "If they arrest you and find out through your talk that you were the witch doctor Mdlawini visited, you will hang together with him."

John made no reply. The sight of a policeman approaching, and my presence, sobered him. He allowed himself to be quietly led away.

217

III

LATE the same evening Tembu and another African came to me with the news that John had been arrested. They had not witnessed the actual arrest, but at the Main Road where it happened they had found a small pocketbook with John's name and my address inside it. This was why they had come to me. He had guessed from various rumors, said Tembu, something of John's role in the Mdlawini case. It was obvious that he thought it my duty to save John.

Tembu's last remark irritated me. There was no need to instruct me in my duties to my fellow men. I had been fulfilling them as well as I knew how for a long time. I had even been victimized because of it. I had been compelled to leave a consulting room in a fashionable block of flats, outwardly on some trivial pretext, but actually I suspected because John and other natives came often to visit me there.

And then, a moment or two after Tembu's arrival, Simon arrived with the full story. He had guarded his friend like a child after the incident outside the court, and had taken him back to the location. They had walked slowly, and by the time they reached the location dusk was upon them. Soon they came upon a huge ox-wagon, heavily laden, laboriously climbing the steep hill. A native child of ten

218

or twelve years was leading the oxen. Behind the wagon some motorists, impatient at the obstruction, were hooting angrily. The native boy tried to force the oxen to the side of the road, but the weary animals, thin, old, and underfed, frightened by the noise and the excitement, stopped in the middle of the road. The child grew desperate and began lashing the animals fiercely with his whip, encouraged by the adults sitting on the load and by the motorists behind. But the more he hit the oxen the more obstinate they became. Apparently a vicious circle had been created which no one made any attempt to break.

At last someone got hold of the youngster, snatched the whip from him, and loudly demanded his arrest. A policeman was called from the location, but the youngster resisted arrest, screaming and shouting while the policeman cuffed him severely. John, incensed, confronted the policeman. "You have no right to hit the boy like that," he said. "He is only a child. You ——" He got no further.

When Simon came up he found John lying on the ground, handcuffed to the arrested child, his face bruised and bleeding. Simon realized that nothing could be done now. For a black man to interfere with the police was a serious crime in the eyes of the white men. He watched John and the child being taken away, utterly despondent that, in spite of all his care, the fate he had so carefully guarded against had finally overtaken John. Realizing the seriousness of the position he had hurried back to me.

Although greatly relieved, for I had feared that John's arrest had been in connection with the murder, I found the visit of these three men distinctly embarrassing. I read in their faces, in their tone of voice, in the manner of their speech, thinly disguised under their servility before a white man, the accusation that they dared not put into words.

219

Simon said: "You must save John. If they find out there will be trouble for us all." Tembu made no such demand, but his silence was eloquent. I made no reply to Simon. I tried to console myself by reminding myself that I was not responsible for John's downfall; I had done everything possible for him. He had reverted to witchcraft because his one ambition in life was to become like his dead father, a witch doctor; and no effort of mine could prevent him. Neither could I change the attitude of the white people towards the black. Fear . . . it was a question of terrible fear: the fear of the blacks for the whites; fear that dominated the whole of South Africa. How could I, one small individual, root up the curse of humanity?

I wanted to utter these thoughts openly; but would they understand me? Now, when danger threatened one of their men, I was held responsible. Judges never understand the men they try, I told myself, and then caught at the word. Try? . . . Yes — I was on trial now. The colored man, silent, lifeless, with a masked face, appeared to be the judge; Tembu, vindictive and inwardly aggressive, the prosecutor; and Simon, the simpleton, the jury. Was I to place myself in the hands of these hostile men, and protest to them my innocence? Didn't I myself, a Jew, belong to a people ceaselessly driven from pillar to post? It was useless telling them so. They would not understand me, as that morning the court had not understood Mdlawini, and would not understand John tomorrow.

Yet John must be saved, but how? With these men watching me, silently judging me, I could think of no solution. Finally, I excused myself and asked them to come next morning.

When they had gone I felt relieved. But still I could not rest. The thought of John gave me no peace. John was not in actual danger so long as he did not let escape some remark that would lead to a confession. But would he have the sense to realize that? Would not the fear of prison and the fate of Mdlawini blot out all consideration of caution from his mind? Would he perhaps commit suicide out of fear of death? For fear can be unbearable; so unbearable that even the worst reality may be preferred to the torments of anxiety. It took a strong man to combat fear, and John, though no longer a coward, was still a weakling.

A desire came to me to review my knowledge of John, to delve deeper into his personality. Perhaps I had been wrong in the psychological diagnosis I had made of the Manyika. I took out the voluminous notes I had made about him and tried to forget the sophisticated interpretations I had previously made, the comments I had written at the time. In order if possible to obtain a more impartial attitude, I tried for the first time to see John the human being and not the subject of psychoanalytical studies. It seemed to me that in spite of my sympathy and external freedom in relationship with him, he nevertheless had remained chiefly a psycho-anthropological specimen: the main aim had been to collect his dreams, his fantasies, and find out the workings of the primitive unconscious mind.

On consideration the conclusion was inevitable that John's behavior ever since Mawa's insanity was that of self-destruction. He unconsciously ran into dangerous situations, and like many others who inevitably finish in total destruction, he depended upon extraordinary luck to save him. Then it struck me that his self-destructive actions might be the direct result of his sudden and abrupt severance from me. I knew very well from experience that no patient could be dropped, in the state of a so-called positive transference, without serious risk of his mental health. Why

had I not taken the same precaution with John? Because —
I had to confess again — John had been to me only a subject of experiment, and the whole analysis nothing more
than a case of psychic vivisection.

Now in the stillness of the night my main concern was
for John's safety and well-being. A new man separated
himself from the pages I was reading. The human: the real
John.

2

I WENT over in my mind John's treatment at the
hands of white men. I remembered an old African's description of Europeans to me: "They are all enemies of the
blacks. Some, like the English, suck us dry while they remain
polite and gentle. They even make us smile while they rob
us. We call them the rats, because the veld rats eat away
the dirt from the feet of the sleeper without waking him.
Others, like the Dutch, are cruel, rough, very cheeky to
us. They are like thunder and fire, cruel in their rage. But
call them Lord, Saviour, Father, and they will have mercy
on us. They always tell us that our fathers were very bad
people because they fought their fathers. Then there are
the Jews. They have no say in the government. They are
like jackals, glad to squeeze out of us whatever they can on
the quiet."

Early in the morning I went to Tembu. I felt that I must
hear just what this educated black man thought of me. I
found it always difficult to be long with some Africans
of his class; they never spoke to the point, they always
hinted, made indirect references, were always too polite
and obliging. Even last night, little was said openly. So I

decided to force the issue. Did they accuse me of being responsible for John's present tragedy? Did they accuse me of indifference, of actual treason? One who perhaps informed the police? Maybe they regarded me as a secret agent, a spy of the government, as Simon, Maggie, and others had suspected me in Swartyard. And how could I prove that I was not the informer?

Tembu met me with friendliness, anxiously waiting for news. I was circumspect. Perhaps they were right, I said, to suspect the white people of insincerity and even treachery. A natural reaction. All painted with the same brush. The atmosphere of suspicion and mistrust was destroying social intercourse. Finally, I put a direct question: —

Did they believe me to be a real friend of the Africans, and honest in my relations with John? Would they trust me absolutely if I declared myself to be prepared for anything to save John?

Silence. Finally, Tembu spoke: —

"A few nights ago I and a friend visited a European. We discussed the new native bills that, by abolishing the Cape franchise, are depriving us of the last vestige of human rights. Our host was indignant in his protest. While we talked I had need to leave the room. You know. Our host took me to the servants' quarters outside, to a dirty, foul-smelling latrine. On our way there we had to pass a similar place in the house. It was clean, well kept, not like the other. I ask you, Doctor: What are we to think?"

IV

JOHN'S case was heard in the magistrate's court. I briefed a lawyer to defend him, but scarcely any defense was necessary. At that time the police were very much in the limelight. Corruption and abuse of power have become a public scandal, especially in regard to the victimization and exploitation of Africans. Summary evidence was called, and the magistrate, who must have deemed it wise to be as lenient as possible, explained to John that it was a serious thing in the eyes of the law to interfere with a police officer in the execution of his duty, but that in the circumstances he would take a lenient view. Sentence was imposed of a fine of three pounds or a month's imprisonment. The fine was paid.

I was disturbed. It was not safe for John to remain in Johannesburg; another such event might have dire consequences. I must get him out.

I told John finally that he must go back, at least for a while, to Manyikaland.

He was too dazed by the turn of events fully to appreciate what I was saying. He thought of it as some trick to console him. I told him to get ready with all haste, to see nobody; under no circumstances must he allow any patients to consult him. I further urged him for safety's sake to stay with a friend, and he promised to go to Simon.

Two days later I went to fetch him. Only with great difficulty did I find Simon's house. It was a tiny place of one room and a veranda. Seven people lived in it: Simon and his wife, and their four children, and Simon's wife's lover. On the small veranda I found seven more people encamped: Maggie, her three children, Maggie's sister, and two of the latter's friends, a girl and a boy of about seventeen years of age.

John was dirty, his clothes spattered with mud. His face and eyes looked dull and ashen gray, like the autumn clouds above him. Quietly he told me what had happened since he left me.

Arriving at his room to fetch his blankets he found a message from Simon that an old patient whose case was urgent was waiting for him at Simon's house. He hurried all the long way from Sophiatown to the location in cheerful anticipation of earning some money. On his arrival he found no patient, but Maggie and the rest of the family. At first he had been pleased to see them, though embarrassed by the suddenness of their arrival. He welcomed them warmly and wholeheartedly. He had always wanted to take his son Daniel to Manyikaland. But Maggie's suspicious attitude crumpled his good humor. She brushed away his explanation of the present situation as nonsense, invention, lies. She knew that he wished to get rid of her, and she knew that he would tell her any lie that suited his purpose when he could not face a situation. She was therefore firmly convinced that the danger of which he spoke was another excuse to run away from her.

Far from showing John the sympathy and understanding he needed so badly, she nagged at him the whole night, dragging up the past. She tortured him deliberately, pouring over him a torrent of hatred and abuse fomented over

225

long bitter years of injured pride and broken heartaches.

John hated quarreling. He left the veranda, spending the little that remained of the sleepless night on the wet ground outside.

He implored me to assure Maggie that his story was true. But Maggie mistrusted me as much as she did John. She remained on the floor with the youngest child at her breast, and the other two clinging tightly to her, refusing to listen to me as I tried to reason with her.

Finally I said I would take John by car to his kraal in Rhodesia. Both John and Maggie were surprised. John had not expected me to take him myself. As for Maggie, she took this as further proof of our conspiracy against her. She rejected the offer in unmistakable and none too polite terms. She was not going to be left alone after taking all this trouble to come to Johannesburg.

"What can I do with such a woman?" John asked me in despair.

Maggie could not be altogether blamed. For nearly a year her husband had left her destitute at the kraal. Mawa was still in the asylum. George, entirely under the influence of his witch woman, starved Maggie and her children and thrashed them when he was drunk. It had not been easy to come to Johannesburg. And now here was John contemplating a new flight that meant she must go back again to the kraal. From Manyikaland he would never return to her. His desire to take Daniel with him was proof of it. But now she sensed somehow that danger threatened her husband. He looked ill, worn out physically and mentally: he had again that look of a hunted animal. Torn between the fear for herself and anxiety over John, Maggie suggested a compromise. She would let John go on the condition that her younger sister, Ann, should go with us.

Again the simple Maggie was trying to secure John by the identical method of many years ago, when first her marriage had shown signs of crashing. Then it was Nellie who was the bait; now the younger Ann was cast for the role. By binding John to the young and sensually attractive sister, Maggie hoped to retain John as her husband. If she could get him to take Ann as his second wife, the bond of her own marriage would be made more secure.

But I refused to take a young native girl on my travels, and Maggie was adamant that either Ann must go or John must stay. We had reached an impasse.

Pressed for a decision, I told John that he must make up his own mind. He promised to be at my house the next morning, with or without Maggie's consent. I left assured, for John had dared so much that I expected him to find enough strength of mind to oppose Maggie.

But he did not come. Worried, I went to the location to discover the reason. I found him standing at the gate with his little son beside him. "I was going to walk to you," he said. "I had no money."

This was untrue, for I had given him money the day before. But he looked so overwrought and ill, and had so much the appearance of a man in terrible danger, that I decided to waive the discussion and argument, and go. I also agreed to taking Daniel with us.

That same morning the three of us set out on the Great Northern Road to Rhodesia.

2

GRIM and withdrawn, John sat in the back of the car that sped towards Manyikaland, to his home. I did not disturb him. I knew how he suffered, especially on Mdlawini's account. At best, Mdlawini would have to spend years in prison: a life of torture, hard labor, years of shame.

I tried at last to rouse him, shouting: "John! Aren't you excited at going home after so many years?" But he did not answer; he did not appear to hear. He sat stupefied by his thoughts: horror of the past; fear of the future.

The car reached the Rhodesian Border. More morose than ever, John settled down in the seat. He gazed malevolently at the officials. How he hated these white people! To him the officials put not one question; he might have been a dog, some part of the baggage of the white man.

"Why is it," he asked me, "that a white man has it so easy and can make it easy for us? But when we are on our own, the same people put endless questions about the pass, the tax, the illnesses?" In his own way John was expressing the protest and indignation often heard from educated natives against the white man's potential power to liberate the black citizens from various restrictions by a scrap of paper or by a single word. Psychologically, they maintain, their status is that of serfdom and slavery.

As the car moved rapidly along the road I became mildly interested in his reasonings. It began to dawn on him that he was uncomfortably hot, and at last he removed his overcoat. I expected to hear something from him about his native country, but he remained as silent and morose as ever. I found out later that the idea of love of a country was foreign to John: his emotional attachment is confined to his kraal, district, and chief. Rhodesia to him was a conglomeration of nations, as Europe is to the European.

That night, to my amazement, he appeared in my bedroom at the hotel where we were spending the night.

"Please, Doctor," he said, in his soft, husky voice; "please, Doctor, I am sorry I must wake the Doctor up."

I was tired. I opened my eyes and looked stupidly at him. "What is it? Couldn't you wait till morning?" I asked irritably.

John's voice dropped, so that it was almost inaudible. Then he managed to say: —

"I have killed Maggie."

There was silence broken by the sharp striking of a match. In the yellow radiance of the candle John stood, hands clasped, eyes cast down.

I imagined John was referring to his medicine-man trick of poisoning people at a distance and did not take his announcement seriously. He must have seen this in my face, for he reiterated with grim emphasis: —

"I killed Maggie. I put poison that I got from your room, Doctor, in her tea the night we went away. Now she is dead." And then the monotonous tone changed, vibrating with suffering as he said: "What shall I do now?"

It took me a few moments to realize the meaning of his words; and when I fully understood what he said I must confess I was gravely alarmed. My first thought was for myself: So I have smuggled through a murderer! However, I tried not to show my uneasiness, and asked him to tell me in detail what had happened.

When after I had left Simon's house Maggie refused point-blank to let him go with me, he had burst into a fit of rage, torn off his clothes, ripped his shirt to pieces, got hold of pots and pans and hurled them to the ground. He remembered shouting, bellowing aloud, that Maggie was driving him mad. He could still see the silly, frightened faces of neighbors peering into the room. Maggie stood bewildered. She thought he actually had gone mad. Never before had she seen him like this.

"'You want me to live in a prison,' I said to her. 'All my life you spoil everything for me! In front of everybody you make me look like a child. But now I'm not listening to you. I will go back to my own people. They love me. You have made me almost forget that I am John Chavafambira, son of the great doctors. I will show you that I am a man, you lame bastard!'"

Maggie made no reply, and John, exhausted, had flung himself upon the floor. Immediately, Maggie and her sister and Simon's wife were upon him, stripping him of the rest of his clothes. They left him under the blanket, bitterly humiliated.

It was dark. Maggie sat in a corner. He could see her eyes mocking him. He heard her say to her sister: "John will stay here." Her smug tone revived his fury. He must get his freedom. Stealthily he slipped out of the blankets, crept across the floor to the corner where he kept his medicines, secured one little bottle of poison that he had taken one day from my consulting-room, and crept back to the blankets. For a while he lay there, fingering the bottle. It had a black label with POISON in red letters.

Maggie was drinking tea, cup after cup.

How greedy she was in her eating and drinking! He could see her unwieldy form in the dim light from the door. She shuffled across to the stove. Her sister went out to fill the kettle. There was no one else in the room. He went swiftly to the table, poured some of the poison into Maggie's

230

half-finished cup, and quickly returned to his place on the floor.

Ann came back with the full kettle, and Maggie lazily returned to her tea. John watched her, amazed at his unconcern as she finished it. After some time, Maggie fell fast asleep.

Maggie had settled herself in a corner. Ann attended to the children. Used to Maggie's ways, she had thought nothing of the fact that Maggie had gone to sleep.

John did not sleep. Uneasiness began to assail him. Very early in the morning he got up. Maggie lay terrifyingly still. He put on his clothes. Daniel woke up. A good omen. He always felt that his son should be with him. He dressed the boy silently and together they left the house without disturbing the other sleepers.

And then guilt and fear paralyzed him. He realized that he hadn't the courage to go to me. That was why he had remained at the gate waiting.

John handed me the poison-labeled bottle. I looked at it and then burst into a fit of uncontrollable laughter. Cruel though my behavior was, I could not help it. And John stood, bewildered and indignant, staring at me with that bleak, hawklike stare. The poison was merely an innocent sleeping draught, labeled poison in accordance with the strict letter of the law. No harm would have come to Maggie if she had swallowed the whole bottle. I hurriedly explained to John the nature of the poison he had given to his wife, and told him that the worst that could happen to her was a twenty-four-hour sleep from which she would awaken with a heavy head.

But when John left me I still could not sleep. The idea that John could be a murderer stunned me. My personal pride was injured. Though I had known him for nearly two years, I had never once suspected that he was capable of such a crime. On the other hand, I must admit that I was pleased to discover that the old John, lacking courage and endurance, was disappearing, and that there were steadily growing within him self-assertion and the instinct to fight his way through life.

John was ready for revolt.

PART FIVE

Kraal-land

I

DURING the last stages of the journey home John became a different man. His sudden relief from guilt broke the constricting shell that had been hampering him. He began to take a lively interest in what was going on, shedding his habitual dignity, gesticulating and cavorting like an excited child.

When we visited Zimbabwe Ruins he walked with pride. He guided me through one of the temple's narrow entrances. Naturally, he had heard a lot about these "churches," as he called the ruins of the temple and the acropolis. He made a significant remark: "Charlie used to talk about this place. He even said he saw these churches. But I don't think it is true. Now I can tell them at home all about these places, and ask my father Charlie questions, because I think he told lies about seeing it."

At Marandellas we stopped for some time. We were walking down the street when a woman hailed John. He stopped, looked, and then, realizing who she was, greeted her with enthusiasm and emotion. She was from his kraal, a relation: it was a complicated relationship. "Charlie's present wife's brother-in-law's second wife's daughter," he told me. To John it was quite simple, although Charlie was his uncle and stepfather. This uncle-stepfather's present wife, no relation to John at all, had a sister married to a man who had a second wife, and the woman at Marandellas was his second wife's daughter. I gave up trying to understand. With this meeting the last of John's glumness dropped from him.

About lunchtime we arrived at Rusapi, the trading and transport center for the kraals in the Inyanga district. In his early travels from the kraal to various Rhodesian towns John had to come first to Rusapi.

As he talked to me, he was constantly interrupted by acquaintances, friends, and relatives. Even the acquaintances greeted John as if he were a near relative or very intimate friend. Like all oppressed people, the Africans develop a strong feeling of sympathy with their fellow sufferers. The dangers to which they are all exposed and the persecution to which they are all liable unite them in a feeling of "oneness." They all greeted John as if he were a near relative or very intimate friend.

But the enthusiasm displayed here was nothing compared with the emotion I witnessed at the chance meeting of Edna and John.

We were walking in the main street of the village when a large, stout woman, with a baby on her back and an older child running after her, rushed up to John. So stormy was her approach that I was afraid that this huge mass of black humanity would overwhelm him. She was crying like a baby. "John, John," was all that I could hear for a long time. And John, too, had unmistakable tears in his eyes. Edna was his sister, a daughter of his first father, who had two wives: Nesta, John's mother, and Nelima, Edna's mother.

Out of politeness I moved away from this meeting of brother and sister after so many years. I gathered that news was exchanged like lightning. In a few minutes they had told each other their life stories, marriages, number of children, material position, and so on. Finally John introduced me to Edna, who wholeheartedly expressed her gratitude and esteem for me. Edna really intended to remain in Rusapi, where her husband was working, but now she immediately decided to go to the kraal to take part in the family rejoicings.

I expressed my regret at not being able to offer her a lift, as the car was full. John professed to agree, but then occurred proof that he was a far better diplomat than I had ever imagined. We parted from Edna and a man named Richard, also a relative from the same kraal, expressing our hopes of seeing them again in the kraal next day. An hour later we left. Hardly had we passed the outskirts of the town when John, feigning surprise, exclaimed: "There are Edna and Richard and the children! Poor people, they will have to walk all the way." There indeed were John's relatives trudging along the road. I obviously could not allow a woman and two children to walk, and in the end we literally squeezed four more people into the car already packed with luggage. I am quite sure this chance encounter was staged.

When any African tells you that you are near your destination you may rest assured that there are a good many miles before you. John's estimated fifteen miles to the kraal proved to be over fifty, and the last ten miles, after we had left the main road, were shockingly bad, so that it was dark when we arrived.

As we neared the kraal the road climbed steadily into the hills and mountains. In a picturesque valley between two mountains, where a small waterfall rushed down the ravine, we found a gathering of some twenty to thirty natives — men, women, and children — sitting round a fire drinking native beer. John and Richard joined them, finding many friends among the party. For the first time I saw a South African native beer-drinking party in its natural surroundings. They were all free, genuinely enjoying themselves without any fear of being trapped or persecuted by police. To me, after so many years in Johannesburg, their carefree behavior seemed strange. And John, who so often says the right word at the right moment, remarked: "You see? Here we are free to drink whatever we like. No pick-up vans."

It was impossible to reach the kraal by car. The last two miles we had to go "by walk" as John put it. Edna went off to her own kraal. It was late in the evening. We walked towards high mountains. The full moon rode in a cloudless sky. The air was very clear and transparent. The night, still and calm, filled me with awe, so utterly silent was it.

John chose a roundabout way to the kraal so that our arrival would be a surprise. We talked little, and in whispers. We crossed a river and John said softly: "This is the river of my dreams. From here my mother Nesta used to watch me going to the mission school." And he pointed to a hill on the opposite bank.

We climbed a steep hill, at its top an enormous stone. A deep crack ran right through the whole length of the granite mass. Trees grew around it. "It is the grave of my grandfather, Gwerere," John told me. "And the crack is the place where the stone opened to swallow his dead body and then closed up again. My father planted the trees. Since his death Charlie looks after them." Saying this he accelerated his pace and hurried past the grave. "Nobody comes near the place, especially at night. We come here only for praying and beer-drinking in times when no rain comes," Richard ventured to add. I remained for a while to absorb the atmosphere that distinguished this simple grave. There was dignity and reverence expressed by this huge stone, encircled by trees on the top of a hill commanding a view of the whole district; and the comparison with Rhodes's grave in the Matopo Mountains was unavoidable. Gwerere had expressed his burial wish in much the same way as had the European. He had said: "When I die, put me next to that stone, and I will disappear there, and the stone will be my grave."

My native friends had outdistanced me: John, dignified in his dark blue overcoat, compared favorably with Richard, barefoot and in rags. But Richard had the quiet composure and inner assurance of a son of the soil, while John's whole demeanor was that of a proletarian who has no solid ground to stand on.

There was not a soul to be seen, not a sound in the still-ness of the night. Then, suddenly, an ear-splitting shriek shattered the silence. It came from the mountain to the east, where legend says King Solomon mined for gold. "Someone has been to the man eater without a fowl," John whispered. "I mean the mountain I told you of, Doctor, that swallows people. Look to your left and you will see it."

"No, it is not from that mountain," Richard ventured to contradict. "The sound came from the one in front of us, where Johannes lives, the new preacher of the gospel against the white man's God."

Presently John whispered to us to keep absolute silence. There were the dark shapes of huts, visible against the sky-line. John was jumping about like an excited child, whispering to me: "You will see how they will meet me. I will not say a word. Let them recognize me."

As we drew near a dog barked. Others joined in. Richard indicated Charlie's dwellings. We came to a small open door. A bright fire blazed within. Five people, mostly women, were seated around it. John pushed me toward them, hiding behind me. Two women stood up and came out. They turned out to be Sarah, Patrick's wife, and Junia, John's sister. Looking bewildered at the sight of a strange white man late at night, they rushed back and shouted for help. Then John stepped forward. Sarah, reappearing, recognized him. "John!" she screamed. We began to regret the whole idea of surprising them. Junia rushed up to John, looked at him, and then became hysterical to an extent which I have seldom seen. Neither of the women welcomed John; on the contrary, they turned away and began to cry. They must have cried for an hour or more. It was the crying of helpless, bewildered human beings overcome by something too big and too sudden for comprehension.

John remained silent. In the stillness of the night he might have been listening to the shadowy footsteps of his mother and father and the host of his ancestors pressing close about him. The brilliance of the moon made black the shadow in which he stood, except where the glow of the fire made a wedge of warm gold. Below us the hills rose and fell, wreathed sometimes in woolly mist, for all the world like vast herds of animals in lush valley grass. As far as the eye could see lay the hills. So often one finds things described disappointing when seen in reality, but the view from the kraal was indeed magnificent, the never-ending rise and fall of the landscape held a serenity, a sense of infinity dwarfing and obliterating man's petty concerns.

John quietly returned to Richard and me, and the three of us walked slowly up and down the smooth beaten patch near the hut. For he told us that the women must be given time to recover before he could greet the others in the hut.

Finally the shrill wailing ceased. Only then did John go up to Junia, gently kiss her, and say: "It is me — John; you must not cry." He then shook hands with Sarah and explained my identity and presence. Junia was still shaken by sobs. John said she would cry right through the night.

Sarah led the way into the hut. Charlie was still absent, and John felt irritated at this. He was anxious to impress his father, and it was annoying to find him away. Presently, Amos, John's elder brother, arrived. He had a gentle, spiritual face and was maudlin with drink. He recognized John instantly and embarked on a drunken lamentation in a soft, feminine voice. He spoke like a careful child who cannot yet pronounce sounds correctly. John regarded him with smiling tolerance.

"This young brother of mine," began Amos, shaking his head slowly, sadly, "he did not write to me for fifteen years." He swayed a little on his feet. "I beg your pardon," he bowed with alcoholic solemnity towards me, concentrating on his articulation, "he did write to me once when I was in Gatooma. Only one letter in fifteen years. This cheeky little brother of mine. Yes, Doctor, I am telling the truth I swear. All people know that I am honest. They say I am lazy, but no one will say that I am telling lies." He looked round the hut, his eyes wide and foolish, a fatuous smile on his slack lips. Then, drawing himself up tipsily, his face taking on an expression of sententiousness, he continued: "I love my brother John, and my heart is very sore when he does not write. This bastard. I am very sorry, Doctor."

He sagged at the knees and fell on his haunches. It seemed likely that he would fall asleep, but, recovering himself, and addressing himself to a point midway between Richard and John, he said, his voice trembling a little:

241

"Thank you, Doctor, for bringing back John." Then, in a louder voice, possibly because Sarah had clicked her tongue against the roof of her mouth, unable to control her irritation at Amos, he said: "Yes, I had beer. What else can I do here? I can't work, I have nothing. They call me now the stupid Amos, but I was clever, Doctor. You can ask the teachers at the mission school." And with that he abruptly finished his lamentation.

Amos made a deep impression on me. He reminded me of the Christ-man, Count Myschkin, the hero of Dostoevsky's *Idiot*. Closer acquaintance revealed many striking similarities. Both were other-worldly, imbecile to us, disinterested in mundane affairs, good-natured, prepared to sacrifice their life to others, yet at the same time incapable of constructive action. Amos was deeply religious, and the most Christian of all the natives I have met. To him Christ and the Gospel were realities that replaced his Mwari and *midzimu*; in him, the inevitable conflict between two Gods was the least apparent. In this respect he was luckier than John.

John turned to me. "It is true," he affirmed, "Amos was very clever. Cleverer even than Nathan. But someone poisoned him, and since then he is not quite right in the head. Whatever he has he gives away, money, clothes, and he works for anyone who asks him, without receiving money."

It was late already, but I was eager to witness the meeting between father and son, when Charlie arrived, and so I stayed on. In the meantime, John talked to his stepmother. The antipathy that I knew had always existed between them had not lessened with the years. She made one or two acid remarks about Daniel which showed that she was by no means pleased with John's return. She rightly sus-

242

pected that he had come to take over the family practice and oust Charlie. I — the European — must have increased her fear.

At last Charlie came. John eyed him with contempt, the old antagonism returning. Charlie must have changed enormously. Before me was a flabby, wrinkled, dirty and dissolute old man, more dead than alive. He greeted John in the traditional manner, hailing him as a *"nganga,* befriended even by a famous white doctor, who was not ashamed to accompany his great son to his father's house." But he insolently ignored the boy Daniel and I could see that this hurt John deeply.

Nor, he found later, was this the only way in which he was to be hurt. He was continually being reprimanded, by Charlie most often, for he had forgotten so many of the countless little taboos and restrictions of the kraal. The same night he received a sharp rebuke for inadvertently standing with his back to the fire. "Does my son," demanded Charlie sternly, "wish to be turned into a baboon that he stands with his back to the fire?"

Such things happened over and over again. Once while we were crossing the river a band of children even began shrieking and mocking John because he had omitted some ritual act which he had so completely forgotten as not to be able to recall it. I once innocently added to his confusion by offering him some ham from my provisions at breakfast. John had unconcernedly consumed ham with me on many occasions, but now the horrified stare of those present reminded him of the pig-meat taboo of the family. Charlie openly lamented the heretical behavior of his son.

"They go to the city, our young men, and they become slack, mannerless, forgetting their upbringing and the respect due to their religion and their elders. Our nation is

243

not what it was. What will your own child know about our ancestors?"

"I am like a child," John said angrily. "It is worse here at home than it is in the town."

But I advised him for the sake of domestic peace to observe as far as possible all the meticulous restrictions. Even so, he still tripped on occasions. A few days later, Katie, his mother's bosom friend, who had nursed him as a baby, came over from her kraal to visit him, and he was tremendously pleased to see her again. "Soko!" she greeted him, her yellowish old eyes glowing with affection. John returned the greeting with the same cordiality, impulsively seizing her hands, and would have kissed her had not a look of venomous anger from Charlie's wife brought him to his senses. He had acted with the greatest indecency, he explained later to me, in greeting a woman of the same *mutupo* as himself in so emotional a manner, without having first bought her permission by handing her a coin or some other valuable.

"He was so long away from us," Charlie said again, shaking his head. "This is what life in Johannesburg has done to him."

"And the way my little brother spoke last night of our religion, of the Church, of Christ and of the Virgin Mary, was blasphemous, horrible," Amos added. His manner was apologetic, hopeful of improvement, but John did not relish the criticism.

Sarah was more open in her hostility. "Yes, that is what our young men do when they go away," she exclaimed bitterly. "What do they want to come back for?"

244

2

THIS feeling of strangeness in his own kraal, and among his own people, began seriously to disturb John. The inner conflict — town versus kraal — had been accentuated by his return, and for hours he would discuss the situation with me. At night he dreamed incessantly. One dream particularly impressed him. He was in Rhodesia. Three women were washing in a big river. The river was in angry flood. The women were naked. They came nearer and nearer to him. He did not look at them. They called him. One came forward, seductive and voluptuous. He felt ashamed. Then he noticed that each woman held a long white stick. He had seen an old man holding such a stick in his hands. The women wanted to hit him with the stick because he did not look at them. He went away but they followed him till he reached a big house. Inside he saw an old, old woman. He told her about the three naked women. She went out to them, screaming. He left the hut by the other door.

The dream frightened him. Who were the seductive women? We both agreed that his return must have awakened his natural desires for a Manyika woman. The old man, he knew, was Johannes, the preacher, who was a constant topic of conversation in the kraal. Johannes intrigued me, too, for from what I had heard of him he appeared to be not only a religious fanatic, but also a "political" rebel. John was not pleased at the man's presence near the kraal, for he suspected an alliance between him and Charlie. We both decided to make his acquaintance.

Very early one morning, before anyone was stirring, we

245

hurried off to the mountains and climbed to the cave of Johannes. There we found an old man who greeted us with entire unconcern. He spoke as if he were delivering a sermon; in a thin, old, sexless voice, he told us of the present, of the past, and of the future, which he said were but different sides of the same mountain. We were both disappointed in him. He was not the vital force that we had expected, but merely an old man in his second childhood, suffering from a religious obsession. Although later events were to prove him a dangerous enemy to John, we returned to the kraal somewhat reassured.

For the next few days I saw very little of John. The news of my arrival had spread, and from far and near came patients seeking treatment. Around me gathered men, women, and children, paralyzed, blind, imbecile, demented, crippled, sterile women, impotent men. A feeling of helpless fury soon began to invade me. A whole district with no medical men, with *ngangas* as stupid and ignorant as Charlie! Betrayed by the intensity of my emotion I looked for a scapegoat, and turning to Charlie, who was watching with jealous and vindictive eyes, I openly demanded why his treatments had no effect. But Charlie remained sullenly silent, and I soon felt it was stupid of me to attack him, for actually it was not so much his fault as that of the white men.

Meanwhile rumors had soon spread that John had come home to replace Charlie. The people were openly dissatisfied with Charlie, telling us spiteful tales of his loss of memory and bungling because of his old age. He was accused of being envious of youth and generally malicious. People maintained that he used his profession to harm, not to cure. Many deaths, we were told, had lately occurred in his practice, and these were attributed to his underhand

246

poisoning methods. And they cited Amos and Patrick as proofs of his malignity. We were continually being warned by friends of coming trouble.

Charlie, for his part, began openly declaring that John and I were conspiring evil against him, and brought himself to a state of nervous tension and irritation that reacted throughout the kraal. Meanwhile, we kept our own counsel. But there was a new complication which had been forecast by John's dreams. He became completely infatuated with a young girl, a stranger to the kraal. She was of exceptional beauty, judged even by European standards — what the anthropologists would describe as a Hamitic type, well proportioned, in contrast to the average kraal woman with her huge buttocks and pendulous breasts; smooth-skinned, with an oval-shaped face marred by none of the skin affections so common among native women; the nose wide and yet at the same time clearly modeled, almost Grecian; but the most vital part of her features was her eyes. They could have been those either of a saint or of a great sinner. I myself was conscious of her rare beauty, and openly expressed to John my admiration of his choice.

I was sincere in my approval, for it pleased me to discover John's new criterion of beauty to be no longer that of a primitive kraal-man, but that of an educated black man. And I wondered whether the Manyika witch, who had obsessed his thoughts ever since leaving the kraal so many years ago, could have approached this girl for beauty. One thing was certain, however — the image of this witch, that he had carried for so long, had at last been superseded, and I never heard him mention her again. I am sure that only another Manyika girl could have achieved this.

John made up his mind to marry the girl, and she for her part was also attracted to him. When she was with him,

247

she taunted, teased, and yielded to him in turns. When he was away from her she filled his every thought. She was unlike anyone he had ever known. He knew that his love was reciprocated, but how could he marry her? Her parents would demand many cattle. He investigated his position and found himself the owner of a paltry three or four head of cattle, although Nesta and his first father had left him quite a number of cattle and goats. But Charlie declared that some had died and that Patrick had sold the rest. John did not believe this, but could do nothing.

For a time his love affair overshadowed all other interests, but in the meantime the kraal had divided itself into two camps. There were more enemies working against him than he had thought. Young men, jealous of him, were telling Charlie all kinds of stories about him, fanning the old man's enmity against him. The women, on the other hand, were solid for John.

At last the storm burst.

One evening he came home late from seeing the girl. Questioned by Charlie he gave some vague excuse. Then, to everybody's surprise, he turned on his stepfather with angry, biting words.

"My second father, answer this question. Where are the cattle of my first father and my mother Nesta? You do not answer! I will tell you. You have robbed me of cattle and land. Is that right? You did not teach me or Nathan the proper medicine. Is that right? No, my father. It is time that you carried out for me the initiation ceremony, for I should begin to practise now, in the proper way of my fathers, so that I may occupy the place you must soon leave for me."

A buzz of conversation broke out. The remark about the vacant place was, to say the least, daring. But to my sur-

248

prise, Charlie agreed with complete mildness to do what he asked. He would perform the ceremony in seven days, as he had first to instruct John in the use of poisons, and also he must inform the people of the district of the great event. To John's other accusations he made no reply.

John appeared disappointed. I knew that he was prepared for trouble and wanted a fight. Charlie, as we know, had been his enemy ever since, as a small child, he had ousted John from his mother's hut. He had been convinced that it was Charlie, and not Samuel, who had poisoned his father. Charlie had poisoned both his brothers to marry their wives and enrich himself with their children, their land, and their cattle; and now, he was sure, the old man was even conspiring to rob him of the young girl. She had hinted to him that her parents had already agreed that Charlie himself should marry her and pay them a *lobola*. "And where will the *lobola* come from?" John demanded. "From my cattle!"

He remained now in a state of constant irritation. He was desperately in love; he hated his father; he was nervous of the approaching initiation. The whole life of the kraal was now tiresome and entirely foreign to him. He became aggressive, and the thought of coming to grips with Charlie worked him into a state of impatient anticipation. At last he would assert himself, demand his rights, be worthy of his manhood and his ancestry. Whereas, in Johannesburg, it had been I who had wished to see John more self-assertive and pugnacious, now I found myself continually having to advise patience and caution.

II

I SOON became aware that restlessness and tension were by no means confined to John; his personal and individual grievances were but part of a wider, more general unrest. I perceived a leaven of irritation, stirrings of revolt, throughout the kraal. We heard rumors, threats. Sometimes there was bitter talk about Charlie's delinquencies; more often we heard sinister allegations against Johannes. I felt that sluggish rivulets of discontent were filling up, even as the narrow cracks of fissures all about the kraal, empty now, would fill quickly when the rains came, overflowing and flooding.

To make matters worse, the tax collector chose this particular time to visit the district. He demanded all arrears of government tax, together with all outstanding rents, which must be paid to the landlords, most of whom were resident in London. The inhabitants of the kraal were thunderstruck at having notices served upon them to the effect that they and their families might be moved at any time to a reserve in the mountains.

The thing was incredible. Because of a depression that they could neither avert nor understand, it was possible that they might be removed from the land on which they had lived for centuries! Taken to a reserve even now incapable of supporting its inhabitants, who were having food sent to them by the government! Ugly rumors started of a general revolt throughout Manyikaland. The stories of bloodshed in Northern Rhodesian Copper Mines served to give point to them.

The widening of the zone of threatening disruption gave John a feeling of elation. His own personal fight for his beloved acted as the driving force to his desire for self-assertion, but circumstances had given him the whole of Manyikaland as a stage. Was he not the obvious leader of the people, he, John Chavafambira, hereditary *nganga* of the district? Self-confidence swelled within him. His chance was coming. He determined to win the girl he loved, oust Charlie, defy the powers that oppressed his people. In his daydreams he saw himself not only the savior of the girl, but the liberator of his family and his tribe. My presence inspired him with still greater confidence that the final victory would be his.

He no longer showed Charlie open antagonism and defiance. On the contrary he treated the old man with some show of deference, for without the due initiation as *nganga* John had not the requisite status for a leader among his people.

Meanwhile the mounting flood of passion and resentment seemed to be sweeping the whole kraal into a whirlpool of terror. Everywhere the people clutched at any slender hope, or fastened on Charlie, Johannes, or the government, as the forces dragging them down to death and destruction.

At home, in the fields, in church, at meals, or in bed, conversation surged and eddied round recent events: the sudden return of John accompanied by a white man, the notices served by the government, the activities of Johannes in the mountain. Even the weather was phenomenal; not in the memory of the oldest among them had there been so severe a winter. The tragic and rapid sequence of events gave the people a sense of suffocation, as one has at a ritual ceremony, or in the hut of the *nganga* with patients pressed uncomfortably together.

There was expectancy in the air. Everyone knew that something overwhelming was upon them; that their peaceful, ordered life, lived as their forefathers had prescribed, was to be shattered much as a hillside is dynamited by a railway gang. They had seen such an explosion. But afterwards, after the upheaval, what then? What was their future? Darkness, like a blanket, was choking them in its heavy folds. Who would read them the riddle and lighten their darkness? Where could they go for a sign? Every occurrence, every phenomenon in nature or in human beings, became pregnant with meaning to be interpreted for good or evil by the elders.

Rumors and stories multiplied — wild tales of thousands of natives killed and imprisoned because they refused to pay the tax. Young blood preached revolt, recalling feverish sagas of old wars against the white, the foreigners, aliens who seized the land of their forefathers.

But the excited voices were drowned by the increasing evidence cited by the more responsible members of the community who knew only too well the futility of using violence. They capped saga with saga. Had not the first Mutassa chief and his famous blacksmith, who forged magical weapons to destroy the Portuguese invaders from the sea, been betrayed to the whites? Chief, blacksmith, everyone had been slaughtered.

The Christian ministers, black and white, could not fail to note the unrest and turmoil rife in their flock. All the people were Christians now and attended their churches more frequently in this time of stress. The pastors warned

252

them continually against violent measures, which would react so surely on themselves. But Biblical quotations and examples taken from ancient history had little or no appeal to these tormented beings. At last one missionary promised that he would plead their cause with the government, and this pacified them a little.

The kraal stood shoulder to shoulder in its firm refusal to pay the tax. Whenever the tax collector arrived the defaulters, warned in ample time, invariably managed to hide. Life in the kraal became paralyzed. The lands were left untended. Why till fields that at any moment they might be ordered to leave? It was fantastic. To leave the soil from which they had sprung, where the stones, the trees and the flowers, the very blades of grass, spoke to each one of his life, his childhood games, his loves, his work! To tear them away would be to leave a bleeding wound on them and in their land; to rend a man from the land on which his ancestors had lived and in which his parents were buried was to commit a crime screaming to heaven for vengeance. For, in a world that was slipping from under their feet, protection and succor could be sought only from these ancestors. In them they resisted; to them they prayed.

Surely, they asked me, surely this last outrage could be averted. "You can help us. You must help us with your advice. You are a white man yourself." But they reported to John: "All in vain." The white doctor, they said, hides himself like a coward behind the shield that he is not a Rhodesian, that he has no power with the authorities. "We do not believe these words, John. Your friend will not move a finger to help us."

"You must believe the doctor," John assured them. "They will not listen if he speaks for us. They will say, 'This man is mad, or else he is a traitor. Why does he speak for these blacks? Why is he against his own people?' The doctor is very clever. He is good and kind. But he has not the power. The ewe cherishes the lamb. Can she save it from the rock that crashes down the mountain?"

So they continued to come to me with their grievances and their difficulties, showing amazing confidence in me. It was as if, laying their tragedy bare to me, they hoped I would reveal it to the conscience of the world. They could not realize how little they counted to the rest of humanity. How could they appreciate that, in the event of a clash of interests, their white overlords would not even give them a thought? Patiently, laboriously, I endeavored to explain that the root cause of oppression was not color, but fear. In Manyikaland the Europeans feared the natives, feared their progress, feared that they would lose the chance of exploiting them.

My efforts met with scant success. How was it possible to explain to these people, so narrow in experience and contact with others, the ills of the world? The people preferred their own solution.

"It is because our chief never visits us, because he does not arrange the proper feasts and sacrifices," some maintained. Others asserted that Charlie was to blame. "He grows slack and selfish." A third group blamed Johannes, who had angered God and their ancestors. Others again said, "Our young people go to the town and live there. They do not propitiate the spirits of their forefathers. They forget their ancestors and fail to bring sacrifices to pacify them."

It was decided to go to Charlie and demand the killing of goats and cattle and the arrangement of a ritual feast at the grave of Gwerere.

And then a dreadful thing happened. The *midzimu* showed their anger.

254

The horror originated in the hut inhabited by John's cousin Francis and his wife and three children. The baby, a fine strapping boy of six months, had been restless and peevish of late. Charlie's medicines were useless. Day and night the worried mother gave him the breast, but he was not pacified. Secretly the mother took the child to the *nganga* of a neighboring district, and he, to her terror, found that her baby was doomed, for he was cutting his two upper teeth before cutting the lower ones. This abnormality was a disastrous omen. The child must be killed because of it. If it lived it would bring disaster not only to the parents, but also to the family and clan. The *nganga* further suggested to the unfortunate mother that some old men were trying to poison all the children of the kraal.

"Charlie and Johannes!" thought the distracted woman as she walked home, trembling at the probable fate of her little son. To Francis alone did she reveal the misfortune that had befallen them, but the news leaked out and soon the whole kraal knew.

Charlie openly demanded the sacrifice of the baby. He must have realized his own unpopularity and rejoiced that a scapegoat had been found. Stupid as he was, he understood that the killing of the child, the ritual ceremonies, the dances and beer-drinking connected with it, would distract attention from himself and Johannes. Perhaps, too, he might evade John's initiation ceremony, preparations for which were now in full swing.

Charlie's wife had made the old man's life a misery since the advent of John and his son Daniel, and particularly since the decision about John's initiation. The difficulty arose from the fact that she herself had a son by Charlie, a bright, clever lad of about thirteen years of age, and for years she had made Charlie teach the boy the art of medicine, though this was against the last wish of his elder brother, John's father, who had told him to instruct John and Nathan alone. It was not easy for the old *nganga* to break his solemn oath to his dying brother, but he had been pestered by a nagging and ambitious woman. And from the moment that she knew of her husband's promise to initiate John, she had made his life a veritable hell. Day and night she talked incessantly of her son, threatening to stop John's initiation at all costs, even if it meant appealing for help to Johannes.

Francis stoutly declared that he would not sacrifice his child, that he was prepared to kill as many cattle and goats as Charlie or the chief decreed necessary, but should any harm come to his baby he would appeal to the white man's law, which hanged murderers.

The frenzied parents' harangue was received in depressing and ominous silence. The elders made no reply. Francis and his wife returned to their hut more afraid than ever for their son. They had been ostracized by the kraal. No one would come near them, and when confronted in any spot where this was impossible to avoid, the fanatical hostility in their eyes was painful in the extreme.

Their closest friends dropped them with one exception: John. Francis could scarcely believe his eyes when, late one night, John and I walked into his hut. John was the last person he expected to see, for how could the future *nganga* risk association with the bewitched? Yet John visited him. And John was friendly. "We are cousins, Francis. We have always been friends. I come to help you. I can't do this. But the white man, he will help you."

I began explaining to the unfortunate parents the absurdity of the superstition regarding the cutting of teeth. My words fell on willing ears: human beings are ever ready

256

to believe what they desire. As it was inadvisable to mix John up in this affair, I had decided to speak to Charlie himself. With the heartfelt blessing of Francis and his wife, we left their hut that night after a full discussion of the whole situation. We walked back to the huts on the hill. John was restless, and presently told me in a low voice that a woman was shadowing us, probably Charlie's wife.

Early next morning a meeting was called, at which on my advice John was not present. The people were evidently surprised at my intervention and my determined attitude and plain speaking. I told them in unmistakable terms that, should the child be the victim of murder, I myself would report the matter to the government, so that death and imprisonment would be meted out to those directly and indirectly responsible.

Charlie, for all his denseness, grasped the situation. After I had spoken there was a surprised silence. Then Charlie made an announcement.

"Our ancestors," the throaty old voice proclaimed, "came to me and spoke to me in the night. Our *midzimu* agree to accept the killing of a white he-goat in place of the child. They took me through the night and showed me herbs which shall be rubbed on the child's gums to prevent these teeth coming through before the lower ones. And they told me," he went on craftily, "to proceed with the initiation ceremony according to the manner of our forefathers. They told me to initiate at this ceremony my son John and also my son Lucas."

Charlie must have fervently hoped that this concession to his wife would ward off further trouble. But he was mistaken, for events now began to happen with dramatic rapidity.

III

IT SEEMED hardly credible that the life of a peaceful, isolated kraal could change in so short a time. Locusts, droughts, tax collectors, in themselves destructive enough to the well-being of the people, were nevertheless accepted phenomena that bore no supernatural significance. But the cutting of upper teeth, as in the case of Francis's baby, the birth of twins, and similar events, trivial in themselves, were interpreted as omens of catastrophe and produced in the people a restlessness akin to panic.

And now another event came to aggravate their anxiety. A fire broke out in the school while the children were absorbed in their studies. Luckily no one was hurt, but everyone was puzzled at the cause of the outbreak. Nothing of this kind had ever happened before. The matter was serious. It affected every member of the community. No longer was it a question of the fate of one abnormal child, or of paying taxes; the lives of their children were at stake. Open revolt broke out against Charlie. Savage shouts rang out. "Down with Charlie and his wife!" He had not only failed to protect them, he had also shown himself powerless to discover the culprit. Charlie must go. They demanded a new *nganga*, and the eyes of the people turned to John. He was, in fact, declared their leader, for he had behind him my prestige, the friendship of Francis, the backing of the teacher, of his

258

own old schoolmaster, and of Amos, together with the unqualified devotion and loyalty of the women. He was, besides, a man of the world, who could advise them in matters affecting taxation and the like. Not only as *nganga*, but as leader and guide, they needed him.

The same evening he addressed the people: "I will be your *nganga*. It is good for me to do that. As my father, Chavafambira, protected your fathers, I will protect you. But only a fool burns his own porridge. Therefore Charlie must not be hurt. Only he can perform the initiation ceremony so that our ancestors will listen to my voice when I speak for you, and accept the sacrifices when I kill cattle and goats to them in your name. Your leader must be properly initiated, otherwise how is he to speak to your *midzimu*? Besides, Charlie has not yet fulfilled his oath to my father. He has not taught me the art of poisoning. Without this, how can I punish your enemies? You are angry with Johannes. I must be able to poison before I can deal with him for you. Also, I can throw the bones, but only as the Ba-Venda do, not in the Manyika fashion. This, too, my first father placed in Charlie's hands for me. So I say, go to Charlie. Tell him that my initiation must take place at once. When I am *nganga*, then I will be your leader, in the sunshine of daytime, and also among the shadows, before our ancestors and our God."

So the ultimatum was given to Charlie that John's initiation must take place the following Saturday, and that in the intervening three days Charlie must teach John all that his oath to Chavafambira entailed.

"Charlie's wife," John had warned the people, "will plead for the initiation of her own son, Lucas, at the same time as I am made *nganga*. This you must refuse. It will lie with me to do this for Lucas at the proper time, in accordance with the custom of our profession, by which the elder teaches the younger."

Charlie accepted the ultimatum and John's instruction began forthwith. John was not vindictive, and now that he had Charlie at his mercy he treated him with courtesy and deference, though he found that he had little to learn from the debilitated old man. It seemed sad to him that the all-powerful Charlie of his childhood had shrunk so in dignity and knowledge. Charlie showed John everything, even allowing me to come and watch on many occasions.

Meanwhile, the brewing of the beer kept all the women occupied, and the atmosphere was definitely more cheerful, until fresh trouble broke out among the people. John, according to custom, was secluded in his hut pending his initiation, and therefore knew nothing of developments in the kraal till he caught an angry murmur, like bees swarming. Soon rumors reached him that the people had decided to expel Johannes. Charlie and his wife had been seen visiting the mountain, and the people suspected a conspiracy. John hastily explained to those of us who managed to visit him that at all costs the people must be kept from harming Johannes, since any murder would lead to interference from the authorities. Once the initiation was over the fate of the old people concerned him little, but now it was imperative that they should not be molested. Francis and the others grasped the situation instantly and ran to advise the people accordingly.

But the people refused to be pacified, and finally John was forced to break his seclusion and appeal to them himself. "My bones," he told them harshly — instinctively using the uncompromising tone that effectively dispels hysteria and the words that would command attention — "my bones told me this night that you people are going to the mountain to kill Johannes. My bones told me more. They told me that our *midzimu* is not on your side this morning. For Charlie is no longer your *nganga*, while I have not yet gone through my initiation."

As he spoke, one after another squatted down, till all were on their haunches, the traditional attitude for respectful listeners. Even Charlie's wife followed their example, and John's victory was assured. His voice softened as he told them: "Last night my father came to me. He showed me roots to dig and medicines to use. Suddenly I found myself next to a mountain, covered with flowers, roots, and medicines. On the top of the mountain stood a big box. Next to it stood a man holding an ax, one of those old ones made by our ancestors before we were born. He held the ax in his hands and chopped with it. My father disappeared. This frightened me and I woke up."

All eyes were fixed on him. A stone was dislodged on the hillside, rolled down. The sound could be heard distinctly, so deep was the silence.

"You see, my people, my father does not want me to go to the mountain. I must first become the real *nganga* to fight the witchcraft of the evildoers. Wait, my people. Do not leave me. It makes my heart ache to think of what will happen to you at the mountain."

He spoke so sincerely that all were convinced of his fears for them, and were comforted.

"But who will protect us from the evildoers?" an old man asked timidly.

"My father's father, Gwerere. This is what my dream means. He will protect us. They came to me, they told me to tell you this."

Dramatically he turned and went back to the religious seclusion of his hut.

2

I WOKE early next morning in a state of anxiety, for during the past few days I had begun to worry about the growing dissatisfaction in the kraal. The situation promised to develop into a real revolutionary outbreak, for which the authorities would most certainly hold me responsible. I decided to let John fight out his own battle, and went over to his hut.

I found him depressed and irritated. His seclusion, he complained, was becoming irksome to him. The hours dragged endlessly. The virtual imprisonment, imposed by custom, galled him. His enemies, he was sure, were making use of this time while he was rendered inactive. Charlie's wife, he felt certain, would wreak vengeance on him for not allowing Lucas's initiation. The elders of his kraal, too, he thought, did not really approve of him. They disliked his town clothes and his intimacy with me. He had, of course, staunch friends. Francis, the two teachers, Amos, and above all Sarah and Junia, would watch his interests. But it irritated him to sit in this futile way when he should be up and doing. News had to be brought to him secretly. We, his friends, were forced to slip in one by one, unobserved.

The actual ritual of initiation he fully realized to be essential: he must have Charlie's sanction and the ancestors' co-operation, but this isolation seemed ridiculous. He considered his qualifications and medical knowledge and experience. He had treated patients for years, he had some knowledge of European medicines. He could throw the bones in the complicated Ba-Venda manner involving thirty-two pieces in addition to the Manyika four dice. He understood life, he considered, better than anyone in the kraal. He was better educated, better qualified in his profession. And now to be treated like a youngster, imprisoned in a hut while his girl was hidden from him among a pack of cackling women . . . he wanted to dash out of this stupid thatched prison, snatch her up, and bring her here. . . .

The strength of his passion clamoring for gratification amazed me. Yes, he said, he had never loved before. Maggie — well, he had married her, begotten children, but pity and duty had been his ruling emotion; never a hint of this scorching desire, this unruly demand. Edith? Her thin body, breastless and flat-buttocked, had filled him with repulsion always. She had a good brain, was unusually well-informed; but she might as well have been a man. Marie, Lizzie, Edna, playmates of his youth, fascinating at a distance, but now seen at close quarters, married, with their brood of children, old, worn out with wifely duties, a mass of symptoms and complaints — how unattractive they were!

Only this girl now had the power to stir his imagination and desire. Who was she? I asked him, but he didn't know. He didn't care. He would make her his wife, come what may.

Then he decided to throw the four dice, as Charlie had taught him. He fingered them, recalling their names and explaining to me what they symbolized.

"*Cokwadzima,* the crocodile: it stands for man. *Chirume* means the essence of manhood. These other two, *Nokwara* and *Kwami,* stand for woman and the essence of woman."

He threw them carefully. The male dice alone appeared open, the other three covered.

"It means I shall be in danger, work hard, be disappointed. Hard work without getting anything, because rest, safety, good luck, and luck in love are shown by the female dice. Charlie said the luckiest throw is the male with the essence of the female. The man gets what he wants in life, and his heart's desire." The interpretation showed a deep insight into human nature; I had expected that John would say a combination of man and woman would be the luckiest. John insisted that it was the *essence* of the woman that was important to the man, and the *essence* of the man to the woman.

He gathered up the four dice and threw again. This time both the male dice came up.

"Trouble and fighting. Haven't I had enough of them?"

He stood up, stretching himself. "I must tell you something, Doctor. Francis said there were rumors about you in the kraal. Some said that you are a spy for the white lords and the tax collectors. What else, they said, kept a white man of your position in a native kraal? This is the same talk I used to hear in Swartyard," he added uncomfortably. But now his confidence in me was unshakable, and he was seriously concerned about my fate. Not that he feared anything from his people; they were peaceful folk who would never raise a hand against a white man. But what sinister game were Johannes and his enemies playing? If they had not hesitated to fire the school full of little children (he was sure it had not been accidental, as I maintained), what would stop them murdering me? Of course, white people were immune against African magic — was not this the whole tragedy of the fight against the whites? — but what if they used straightforward methods of attack? He advised me to stay away from the kraal as much as possible, especially at night, and I agreed to sleep at a neighboring trader's house and to return home as soon as possible.

This latter decision saddened him. He sat down again

264

and I made use of his hesitation to talk about myself. He agreed that it would be best for me to return to Johannesburg, but asked me to wait at least for his initiation ceremony.

3

VERY early the next morning the people of the kraal assembled at the appointed spot near Gwerere's grave. Reed mats were spread upon the ground. On one side sat the men, on the other the women. Between them, on his own mat, Charlie took up his position. On the mat next to him, they arranged the calabashes and horns, together with the medicine-stick carved in the likeness of a woman, and drugs, bones, dice, roots, and an ax, specially decorated for the occasion.

At a little distance from Charlie sat the *nganga* elect. This was really contrary to the prescribed ritual, for he should have been in an isolated corner. But nobody protested, for in the eyes of the people John was already their *nganga*.

In a feeble, almost inaudible voice, Charlie addressed first the men and then the women, bidding them drink the beer provided by the hosts, the spirits of their ancestors. The ceremonial clapping of hands testified to their acceptance and willingness to obey. Then followed prolonged beer-drinking to the endless host of names of the departed whom it was desired to evoke and propitiate.

A traditional dance of the spirits followed and then more drinking, after which John, according to custom, was expected to perform a solo dance. This he quietly refused to do, nor did Charlie insist.

So long did the singing, drumming, and dancing continue that John, wearying of the performance, demanded that Charlie should finish the ceremony; and, having obtained silence, Charlie thereupon addressed the people.

"Let us go. All is completed. Spirits, leave the man." Turning to John, his voice gaining suddenly in power, he said: "Go. And make the people well."

The initiation thus in order, John left the gathering, while the people continued drinking till the big pots were emptied. Slowly he walked to where I had been secretly watching, and accompanied me down to the trader's house. Next day I was definitely returning to Johannesburg.

As so often happens when people finally achieve a lifelong ambition, a reaction set in, and John appeared depressed. "The dreams of my childhood are fulfilled," he said as we walked through the open fields. "I am in the place prepared for me by my father. My lifelong enemy Charlie has been laid low. I have sacrificed much to get these things. For this I was born and reared and brought to manhood. Now my way is clear before me, to become the famous *nganga* in Manyikaland, even the whole of Rhodesia. Then why is my heart heavy within me? Is it because my friend, the doctor, is leaving me? Perhaps I should not have come back to the kraal. I have learned new ways in the big town. Life in the kraal is rough. Will I be happy here?"

I felt saddened as he convulsively clutched my arm, as if he would prevent my departure if he could. We came to the trader's house and continued talking for some time, and his heaviness was eased a little. Then Amos and Francis and the two teachers arrived to see me off. Amos, who was slightly drunk, cried bitterly. But it was not good-by for John.

We were destined to meet again, and very soon.

4

THREE hundred miles from the kraal I met with an accident in the car which necessitated my staying in a small village while spare parts could be brought from Johannesburg. I had been there nearly a week when, on the main road outside the village, I suddenly came face to face with John and Daniel.

Our meeting took place, symbolically enough, not far from the spot where John had met the dying man who had led him to the bewitched kraal. And now, indeed, John was once again preparing to follow the same trek as had first led him eventually to Johannesburg. He looked exhausted after his week's journey, and Daniel could scarcely stand. He told me what had happened.

My departure must have depressed him more than I had thought, and on his return to the kraal he had begun to drink. By nightfall he was drunk. Going to Junia he demanded that the girl should be brought to him. She came to his hut, and then followed a night of wild passion, as was possible only for a love-starved man.

With the girl in his arms he forgot the whole world, he told me. For the first time in his life he was as happy after his mating as before. He had no desire to run away from the woman as always before. On the contrary, he felt a delirious joy just looking at her face in the light of the fire that he kept burning all night.

"So Hakata lied," he thought drowsily as he slipped over the edge of sleep.

He awoke again later and awoke in turn the girl pressed warmly to his side. Again he felt the need to talk. He explained that this marriage by the laws of nature would be ratified in the morning by the laws of their people. She was perfectly content. He lay relaxed in his blankets, the girl in his arms, the hut warm and peaceful. Her voice, so young and fresh, was very sweet in his ears. His life was fulfilled. Nothing could hurt him now. Lazily he asked her what was her *mutupo*. "Soko," she answered quietly.

Slowly he released her as he realized what he had done. He had slept with a woman of his own *mutupo!* It was the incestuous crime of which he had been warned so often in dreams.

This was the final abomination wrought by his enemies; this was the revenge brewed in their blistering scorn. To a strange woman his first question had always been, "What is your *mutupo?*" For if her and his ritual animal were the same she would be as a sister or mother. He had never asked this girl her *mutupo,* he realized, hardly crediting his own senses. And I remembered, as he related this to me, that he had also omitted to ask the *murowi* in the bewitched kraal the same question. Who had shut his teeth upon it?

What explanation could there be? Witchcraft. Nothing else.

He sent the girl away. Then, fully dressed, he sat down and considered his position. He was profoundly shocked. He loved this girl. He thought of throwing aside convention and running off with her. But he knew that he could not do that. He could not run away from his own condemnation. Besides, where could he go? Only to the Union, and there Maggie would ferret him out. And Maggie, he knew, would tolerate no second wife but her sister.

Should he stay and fight it out? Times had changed; in the old days he and the girl would have been stoned to death; but now, he knew, he could arrange matters by the

sacrifice of oxen and goats. But he would remain a laughingstock: the *nganga* who went to towns and became so
civilized that he had been intimate with a girl without
asking her *mutupo!* He was humbled, too, in his pride. He,
the perpetuator of the famous Gwerere, to fall a victim of
incest! What confidence would the people have in the bond
between the ancestors and the new *nganga?*

"I have failed," he told me bitterly. There was nothing to
do but run away. For him, no security — always flight. From
his childhood, from the bewitched kraal, from his jobs,
from Maggie, from Johannesburg: flight, always flight. And
he must run away again.

He sent Junia for his son, Daniel, and then for Amos and
Sarah. In simple words he told them what had happened
and announced his decision. They shook their heads, dazed
by the sudden change of events. He picked up the sleeping
boy, and they all walked to the main road. Junia kept
stumbling. John was heartbroken. The small consolation of
escape gave him no relief. He felt that his *midzimu* had
been affronted and were against him. He was a wanderer
in an unfriendly world. Without the help and protection of
his ancestors he could not face life; he dared not even die.

"There was a lump in my throat and a mist before my
eyes. Here was the road again, hard and dusty. When I
walked the first time to Johannesburg, I was young. Now
I was hurt and sorry. Then a monkey cried out and Daniel
woke up. 'Monkeys,' he said. They were quite near the
road; a monkey clan, crossing the road. I stood still and
put Daniel on the ground. Hope came back to me. Here
was a sign from the *midzimu* that I had asked for. The
monkey — our *mutupo*, our family protector. Amos and
Sarah also were pleased.

"The monkeys had crossed the road when a car came

269

round the corner. There were three young white people in it. Then a dreadful thing happened. A mother monkey, with a new baby, was still on the same side of the road as we were, and couldn't cross because of the car. One of the young men got out of the car. To my horror he picked up a stone and raised his hand to throw it at the monkey. Amos and Sarah shrieked. The little monkey and her babe might easily be killed.

"Then I ran to the white man and stopped him throwing the stone. He dropped it, but threw me to the ground. When I fell I hurt my head, you can see, and much blood came from it. But I was happy. To suffer through and for your *mutupo* is the highest thing a man can do. I rose to my feet and found Amos beside me. 'Soko looked so pleased and thankful,' he said. 'Our protectors will never forget you, my brother.' And the white man looked puzzled. 'Fancy a Kaffir protecting a monkey!' one said.

"I felt happy. I came back to Sarah and Daniel. The car drove away. Sarah looked at my wound, but it was not serious. She bandaged it with a piece of cloth from her clothes. Then I took Daniel and left them."

The two of them had made the journey to the Union in easy stages. John had constantly to rest for the sake of Daniel. It took him a week to reach the scene of the first link in the chain with the *murowi*, the scene of the encounter with the dying old man.

"Here I met the old man from the bewitched kraal," he reminded me. "I have thought of my bad luck, of the old man who was a wizard and the girl in the kraal who was an *umthakathi*. She followed me all the years. But now I feel free of her. I saved the monkey and so I am at peace with my *midzimu*. Yes, I have failed. But now I can still be worthy of my great father. Now I will go back to Maggie,

270

because my work in life, according to the sign given to me by the dead people, is to protect the Soko. Is not my little son Soko like me? So I must return to Maggie, because a child needs his mother. I will get work as a waiter again," he went on seriously. "The boy must be educated, for life as it is now, and not as it was when I was a boy. Daniel must be able to look an educated African in the face. Our ancestors will help him. They have sent me a sign."

What had always been a great conflict with John was now being resolved. Now he was learning, at last, that there was no contradiction between the past and the future, between life in the kraal and life in the town. And he saw at last that the only solution for his son Daniel, as for every African child, lay in education.

But decent schooling was almost unattainable for the Africans. Education was not among the few benefits the whites saw fit to bestow on the blacks.

PART SIX

Revolt

I

THE journey to Manyikaland had brought John much closer to me. In the fortnight of sharing the intimacies of daily living — sleeping in the same hut, eating the inevitable mealie meal, visiting friends and attending patients together — we had become companions. The barriers between psychoanalyst and patient, white man and black, had broken down. Like winter-hidden veld roots shooting up at the sun's first spring warmth, unseen resources of self-assertion and leadership flowered in John in the original atmosphere of home and friendliness.

It was a short-lived bloom, unable to withstand the severities of Johannesburg's conventions regulating black-and-white relationship. Here it was impossible for us to be companions. Neither could we resume our old roles of psychoanalyst and subject.

John had long ago ceased to be merely an object of study. I had never regarded him as a patient; within the limits of his grim reality John was a relatively well-adjusted individual. His deficiencies were not characterological; they were the product of his whole life situation, a situation produced by the society in which he lived. John's greatest need was not to know more of his repressed unconscious, but to know the society he lived in, to recognize its ills and to learn how to fight them. If I could no longer be his companion, if I could do little for him as his physician, I could at least teach him what he had to know and to do. It was not going to be easy.

Trouble began the very evening we arrived in Johannesburg. John said he expected bad luck; it followed him every time he returned to this town, as if the curse of the *murowi* he met in the bewitched kraal still had the spell on him.

The first problem was where John should sleep that night. He could not stay in my home; the law prohibited any African to remain on the premises of a white man unless registered as a domestic servant. And while I was bent on teaching John to fight such laws, I would not expose him to the risk of arrest for breaking them. John finally went to Nandi township, a slum for blacks. John hated these "lower depths"; he went there against his better judgment.

For the next few days I forgot about him. I did not think of him again until a week later, when I realized there had been no word from him. I became worried. On inquiry I found out he had left for Blacktown the evening following our arrival. When a few more days passed and there was still no news from John, I went to Blacktown to investigate.

There was no trace of John. The hospital, the police, the mortuary — I tried them all. The solution of the mystery did not come until two days later, when an African brought me a scrap of paper with the words "I'm in prison help John" scrawled on it. It took me three days to get John out.

Before John left for Nandi township I had given him a chain for his bicycle. When the police stopped him to examine his curfew pass they saw the chain bulging from his pocket. I had not known that Africans were forbidden to carry this gadget, which in the eyes of the police was a lethal weapon. He was summarily arrested and a sentence of ten pounds or six months in jail imposed on him. He had, of course, to go to jail. His attempts to reach me failed, for I was not his official employer, and he was sent to a chain gang to crush heavy stones. I paid the fine. After a number of formalities consuming two days of my time, John was free. Thus sadly did the new life we were planning begin for him.

A few days after he came out of jail, I fell seriously ill. For months I could not see John, who in the meantime had found a little one-room shack in Blacktown where he was living with Maggie and the children. When I recovered, I had to leave immediately for Europe.

I went to say good-by to John and Maggie. Life was not going at all well with them. John's torn shirt of dirty gray, his patched khaki trousers, his unshaven face, showed it. It came out that he was drinking and gambling heavily and his practice was very poor. John and Maggie were shocked at the news that I was leaving Africa.

"What for are you going away?" said John hostilely. "You have everything here — you have cars, you have plenty of money."

"No, Doctor mustn't go," Maggie implored. "Doctor must stay here. John is too bad now."

I wanted to explain why I had to go, but I felt that it would be useless. They needed me badly, more so than at any other time; what use explaining?

John asked slyly, "Is your family going with you?" They were not. "You always told me, Doctor," he said chastisingly, "that I should not leave my family alone for a long time. Aren't you afraid that you may die, or that they may die here?"

277

The accent on "die" betrayed a wish as well as anxiety. For nearly ten minutes he berated my callousness.

It was almost a year before I went to see them again. Maggie was alone in the house. She did not know where John could be found. Full of tears, she told me that John had been "so bad, so bad," since I had last seen him.

"Something terrible is going to happen, Doctor. He is loafing, drinking, murdering people."

"Murdering?" I asked anxiously, remembering his attempt to poison Maggie.

"Yes, he murders people." And she began to tell me a story about a woman, a lover, an old husband. She spoke disjointedly. I could not make head or tail of it. I promised to come back the following Sunday and talk to John.

2

JOHN did not accord me a warm welcome. He said nothing for a long time, refusing even to answer my questions. I recognized his old hostile mood. But now I had no way of breaking it. Finally, I came to the point. I told him what I knew of his latest use of medicine, not for healing but for killing.

"Didn't you always say that Charlie and the foreign medicine men were bad because they were helping to kill people?" I asked him.

But it was no good. I had started off badly by pointing out his guilt — never a good way to get a man's confidence. But I could not give up. Too much was at stake. I came back again and again until I got the whole story out of him.

"Well, we have a neighbor, Annie," he finally began. "She lives in that tiny house on the corner where you nearly

278

broke your car the other day in the big hole in the road. One day she came to see me. She had a young man with her — Raphadu, a mine worker. A handsome young man, fancy clothes. He must be very lucky with the girls. Raphadu comes from the same kraal as Annie. Her husband Tom, Annie's husband I mean, was a relation of Raphadu. Raphadu never liked Tom. But Annie he loved. You see, Annie was his first girl — he'd loved no one else really. She always used to choose to be his sweetheart when they played children's games. Well, Raphadu had gone away to work in the gold mines to get money for *lobola*. And Annie's parents made her marry old Tom for ten oxen *lobola*. They came to Blacktown to live. They were very poor and they had no children.

"When Raphadu learned that Annie was in Blacktown, he came to see them. Annie was so happy when she saw him; Tom right away could smell something wrong. When Raphadu left, he started picking on Annie and quarreling with her. His heart was sore. He was a Christian and Annie was his only wife. Tom said to Annie, 'Jesus, you're becoming a wicked and sinful woman. I could see the way you looked at Raphadu.'

"Annie hated all this 'Jesus' stuff. 'You've got sin on the brain,' she told him. 'You think it a sin to go to bed with me. Fat lot of good you are to me. Jesus, Jesus is all I hear nowadays, and you sit on your backside while I do all the work. I tell you this God of yours only loves white people.'

"This made Tom very angry. He told her to shut up and he began to hit her. But Annie was clever. She said, 'Jesus will punish you if you hit me.' So what could Tom do? His hand dropped like a dog's tail before the master. They quarreled all the time. Annie loved Raphadu. I was sure

279

they were sleeping together. But to make sure I took out my horns — the big horns — from the bright yellow calabash. And the male horn, the bigger one, was shaky, so I knew that they wanted to poison Tom. And the little horn, the woman, told me nothing. So I guessed that Annie doesn't tell the truth."

And John explained to me that when you want to find out little things you should always ask the female horn "because a woman talks more and you can make her tell all the little things."

"So I told them," John continued, "that I knew they were sleeping together and asked them if the old jealous Tom suspected it. Yes, Tom knew, Annie confessed. Ebenezer, their miserable meddling neighbor, and his wife Sophy had seen to that. They told Tom one day that Raphadu had come to see his wife while he was away and stayed all day. Tom got very wild, starting the Jesus business again, and called Annie all kinds of a sinner. But Annie was in love now and didn't care. She told Tom she didn't care, that she loved Raphadu and would leave Tom to marry him. Thank God, Annie said, she is not a Christian and must not listen to the church. Tom beat Annie — you know, Doctor, how jealous our men can be. And it was worse with Tom; he was old and in bad luck. He told Annie he would never divorce her, and if she leaves him he will demand his ten oxen back which he paid in *lobola*. Annie wished he were dead. Now I knew what they had come to me for. But I pretended I must find out from the bones what was wrong with them. But first I told Raphadu it would cost more money."

I was shocked to hear John say this. Such a callous, cynical extortion was not like the John I had known. Still I did not offer any criticism and John went on.

280

"I threw the bones for them. I used all my forty pieces, the nutshells and the dominoes and the pennies." This meant the case was a difficult one and entitled him to a higher fee.

"I shook well the pieces in the blue sack and went on rubbing the ointment on my hands and on their foreheads for a long time. I wanted to have a good look at them. They were so frightened and shaky like the horns in my hand. I felt sorry for Annie. She looked sick. But this Raphadu. He was too well dressed for me. Well, the bones were bad. Four of the six shells were closed. It meant the woman was already with a baby. And someone was very sick. The bone of the he-lion was running away. A man is dying, all the strength is going out of him. So I told them that Tom is very very sick. And I could see from their faces that they were glad to hear this.

"In the middle the astragalus bone of a grown male goat lay open — the animal on its back — of course, a helpless man. The bone of a black hare was beside it. The spirit running out of the man. So I told Annie, 'Your husband will die.' 'How soon?' Raphadu asked excitedly. 'Can you give us medicines?' I knew what he wanted but I pretended and asked, 'To save him?' 'No,' said Annie without shame.

"I told her the medicines would have to be put in Tom's food. I gave her the powdered miranda root. Annie watched her husband for weeks. She would come to worry me — my medicines were no good. And then Tom got very sick. His heart and the stomach and the bladder — all was no good. Water ran into the legs. Three months later he died."

Though I knew that Tom had died from a syphilitic infection of the heart, I censured John severely for killing a man. But he laughed, saying: "He didn't die from my medicine. The miranda roots are for the stomach. It was from the bones I knew he will die." Nevertheless for a medicine man to do this was against the accepted ethics of John's profession.

However, this was not the only shady practice John was involved in, I learned. He had become the head of a gang of youthful pickpockets, young boys from Blacktown, slum children who, having no schools to go to, nowhere to play, their parents away all day working, had drifted into delinquency. John knew them well — they all lived near by — and became, out of sympathy, a sort of godfather, giving them luck medicines and throwing the bones for them for luck. He would kill a goat — whenever they managed to "acquire" one — to the dead to protect them against police.

Gradually, the little gang became an organized nucleus of petty thieves. I never found out whether John actually received stolen goods in his own house, but I knew that the young thieves would gather in John's little yard (Maggie would never let them come into the house) before and after every expedition. One day I surprised them there myself. I felt that the matter had become serious. I argued with John for days about the danger he was in, but he was not impressed. It was not until I pointed out the danger threatening his own son Daniel that John saw the light. By this time most of the boys had been arrested and the gang had dissolved.

I asked him how it was that his protective medicines had not kept his clients out of trouble. John shrugged, saying, "They were foolish boys and no medicine can help a fool." John's explanation of his failure — that "the patient did not co-operate" — was the same excuse our own doctors sometimes give for their failures.

Even after this battle was won, I was still faced with the necessity of establishing a relationship between us that

282

would enable me to assume my newly chosen role of teacher. Frequent visits to John failed to break down the resistance I felt in him. The solution came in a way I had not foreseen. A newly published psychological study I had made of John arrived one morning from my English publishers. I took two of the copies, giving one to John and the other to Maggie. I volunteered to read it for him, and Maggie, since it was obviously too difficult for them. I asked him to make comments as we read along. The book made a tremendous impression on John. I had often told him I intended to write a book about him, but he had never believed me. Now here was the printed book with his picture on the first page.

As we read John would make comments, sometimes recapturing a memory or mood that he had forgotten at the first telling. He would declare himself puzzled by some of the psychological interpretations I had made in the book, and there would ensue long discussions about the influence of childhood on the adult behavior.

Gradually the whole panorama of his life unfolded itself vividly before him.

His birth and christening . . . His mother Nesta had never stopped talking of the great affair. In the church, or at Gwerere's grave, and at the beer-drinking in the kraal, he was the baby son, Mother's darling, Father's choice as his perpetuator. It was a carefree life with no trouble, no illness.

The first drama in his life . . '. His mother's remarriage with the hateful Charlie, his uncle, when, bitterly jealous and protesting, he had to go to sleep with other boys in the boys' hut.

And here he was at five or six, beginning to shepherd the cattle and goats together with the other boys and girls.

He had a good ear and a pleasant voice, and soon became the leader of the children's choir. But he was no good at fighting, the others mocked him for his girlish ways. His mother took Charlie's advent matter-of-factly; it was the natural order of things that the brother should inherit the deceased widow and become the father of the children. But John never liked Charlie. "It is time Charlie began to teach me," he would say with annoyance. Nesta was worried.

John's first sweethearts . . . Three of them he remembered clearly. He was hardly six when he learned the sexual practices common to all children, and at ten he was seduced to mutual masturbation by the elder boys in the hut where they slept. During the day he used to play man and wife with the girls, including the "sleeping," as he would say. Once his mother discovered him with his cousin Marie. She was cross. "But Mother, all the boys and girls do it," he protested. "It is silly. It is bad for children," she had replied. "We also used to do it as children, and our parents beat us for it." The comment hardly strengthened the prohibition. Then Charlie came in. He was not at all cross; he only wanted John not to spoil the girls and gave him some practical advice. After that, except for occasional thrashings by the elders and unfortunate fights with the boys, his life was very happy, or so it seemed to him in retrospect.

Growing pains . . . The missionary school where he went together with his lifelong rival Nathan. The first day in school, dressed for the first time in khaki shirt and shorts, overawed by the strange building. The church frightened him, and the reedy and sonorous notes of the organ sent shivers down his spine. The confusing hustle and bustle of the classroom discipline was strange to him. One of the

284

teachers was cruel, cuffing him the very first day for being out of line. In the afternoons he was trained, together with Nathan, for their traditional profession. Charlie was as cruel as the teacher in the mission. John had been good in school. He learned to read and write English and Manyika. Geography was his pet subject. He could not believe that the world was so big. Other countries, other people, intrigued him.

1917. Charlie forced him to leave school, but John refused to remain in the kraal. He ran away to his eldest brother, Patrick, and worked as a kitchen boy in Umtali.

1918. The terrible epidemic, and the death of his mother. His own illness that had lasted nine long months with nobody to care for him save his little sister, Junia, and occasionally Patrick's wife, Sarah.

Then after that he had gone to Umtali, Salisbury, Bulwayo, wandering from one place to another. Always restless, always discontented, always lonely, an African Odysseus.

And now it was 1938. John was nearing his thirty-fifth year. What was his position in life? I looked around the bare little house that he hired from the Municipality for one pound five shillings a month. One bed for father, mother, and four children. One kitchen table. Three broken chairs. In the corner a broken portable gramophone and a few records I had given to him. The room in semidarkness. Their clothes were rags. The children half-naked, barefoot. John did retain a certain neatness and still wore a tie. But the shirt was torn in many places, the trousers patched, and the jacket spoke of very long service. The room was full of smoke coming from the open coal fire in the corner. On the stove there was a huge bowl of mealie meal boiled in water, and a smaller bowl of potatoes. Milk was a luxury. Meat they enjoyed only on the rare occasions when John had to kill a ritual goat for a patient. Corn, potatoes, and bread, with tea, formed their monotonous diet.

John had not a penny to his name. They lived for the day, no further. Should John die, Maggie and the four children would be destitute. Daniel, at my insistence, was being sent to school. But they taught him practically nothing — how could they, with one teacher for two hundred children of various ages crowded together in one classroom?

I often wondered if John's poverty and insecurity were not due to the fact that as a *nganga* he had no definite steady source of income. But then, were the Africans who worked as servants or in factories or mines better off? No African has savings, property, any form of insurance against illness or unemployment.

Many people criticized me for letting John follow his profession of medicine man, which they ridiculed. But such criticism is made only by those who are ignorant of the role and functions of the *nganga* in African society. As long as the African is kept uneducated, starved, and diseased, he will need the medicine man's magic. The sensational stories about African witch doctors current in tabloids and believed implicitly by their readers are largely a product of the imagination. What occasional misuse there is by *ngangas* of their power is no more heinous than that of which white doctors are sometimes guilty.

John in any case was not a witch doctor. He had no knowledge of witchcraft, of magic roots and secret brews. As a matter of fact, he had no knowledge of a single medicine he used; he employed the same root in every disease he was called in to treat. The ritual of its preparation and administration was the only part of the treatment that varied from case to case, the method of application being of a purely psychological nature. John gave his fellow sufferers a belief in better luck, and it was this belief that acted as a consolation and an inspiration for overcoming life's hardships. Far from discouraging him from practising his profession, I encouraged him to continue. All I did attempt was to increase his efficiency, by giving him some of my own knowledge. Gradually John and I established a sort of collaboration in treating John's patients. I supplied John with aspirin, cough mixtures, tonics, vitamins, medications that all of his patients could benefit by in their poor state of health. John agreed to charge nothing or very little for them. I also made him promise to let me see the patients that had serious physical illness. We worked smoothly together. The increasing success John was enjoying in healing his patients enhanced his reputation and increased his practice. But I, on the other hand, narrowly escaped getting into difficulties with the Johannesburg Native Welfare Department. Had I, they demanded, opened a consulting room in Blacktown? No white doctor, they warned me, has the right to practise in Blacktown without their special permission. Not having a consulting room in Blacktown, nor practising there for gain, I ignored the Department and continued collaborating with John.

More serious interference came from quite an unexpected quarter — Maggie. Although my helping John had considerably eased their financial difficulties, she again became just as hostile to me as when I first began the analysis of John. Again she began to say to John: "No good will come of mixing black and white medicines. You're a *nganga,* and you must stick to it." Her hostility increased as time went on; fuel was added to the fire by an incident which occurred about that time.

287

One afternoon Maggie appeared in my consulting room. At first I did not recognize her. Instead of the usual half-torn, faded blouse and short skirt, Maggie was wearing a long dress, a flimsy black shawl gracefully draped about her shoulders. In her frizzy hair she had braided a ribbon of as violet a hue as the rouge she had rubbed into her cheeks. And on her usually bare feet were shoes and even stockings. But it was only after she had gone that I recalled all this. I was very busy when she first came in, and saw her for the briefest moment, only long enough to greet her hurriedly and ask what I could do for her.

She put into my hand two carefully folded five-pound notes. "I want you to keep this money for me, Doctor," she said. "I don't trust anyone. And don't tell John about it."

Seeing the doubt in my face she added, "Don't be afraid, Doctor. It's good money."

I could give her no more time, and in a moment she had gone out to make her long tiresome way back to Blacktown by train and mostly by foot.

It was only after she left that I realized the time, the effort, the expense in outfitting herself that must have gone into this extraordinary excursion. What hours of planning and preparation — and all I had done was hand her a receipt for the money, all I had said was a few hasty words that meant nothing.

3

WHEN John appealed to me at last to do something about Maggie's nagging and to explain things to her, I was glad to accede to his request. I had long wanted to explore the inner workings of this simple woman's mind, which I knew mainly through John's picture. Now, after the incident of the money, I was particularly anxious to talk to Maggie.

I soon found out that Maggie's obstruction was, as I suspected, due to her jealousy of the close relationship which I had again established with John. Maggie was willing to talk to me, but to make her associate freely was not so easy.

"Just think aloud," I said to her. "Let the words slip off your tongue. If you won't look at me when you talk, it will be easier."

"Why do you want *me* to talk to *me?*" she asked, baffled. She refused to tell me her dreams, saying, "What I see in my sleep I tell no one. My dead people will be cross." She went on to say, "I'm asleep, I'm like dead . . . and the *midzimu* come to talk to you then. And if they are too busy to come, they send a message by a snake, a horse, or some other animal. Sometimes they let you know they are with you by other signs. . . . Bad and silly people forget their dreams. And so they don't know what's going to happen to them; then they come to John and he, through his bones and horns, speaks for them with their *midzimu*. John can talk with dead people any time."

Her *midzimu*, said Maggie, came to her every night. In the kraal it was different. The dead were in the hut with the living, there was a special place for them. "But," said Maggie, "of course they couldn't live in Blacktown."

Maggie preferred to retail Blacktown gossip and give vent to some of Blacktown womanhood's grievances against their men.

"Men are loafers, no good. They want to sleep with you! Never tired of it. Make you work for them all your life! Are the white men like that too?"

"White women," I conceded, "do have an easier time of it."

"Easier," she retorted, bursting into amused laughter at my understatement. "What do they do all day with us doing the work for them? Your girls smoke and drink. And how do they find a husband? Is it true that white girls give *lobola?* Isn't it funny? Do white girls also have babies without the church?"

Maggie couldn't understand how rich white girls remained unmarried. "What's the good of their money if they can't get a man?" she asked.

"There are some women who don't wish to marry," I ventured. Maggie was startled. Then, after considerable effort, she came out with the announcement that she herself found no joy in sleeping with a man.

"What's the good of it?" she said. "A woman must never love." And she began relating a long series of Blacktown tragedies of passion.

Maggie, I found out, did indeed hate men. Sex meant nothing to her. I doubt if she had ever experienced true sexual pleasure and gratification. Few women she knew, she said, had such pleasure — a fact that I later verified in the course of an investigation carried out among John's patients.

The dreams Maggie finally described to me gave confirmatory evidence of her attitude towards sex.

Two dreams were particularly outstanding.

"Plenty of horses running straight at me. We were frightened. But we looked straight at them. Then a white lady appeared. The horses ran away."

The same night she had another dream.

"A man was digging a hole in front of my house. I had flowers prepared in a pot. I have covered the hole, made it strong so that the flower should stand firm and grow straight. The man came back, made a hole again. A black snake came out. I chopped off the head, then another head appeared. Then my father called the snake. He followed him. Father and snake went into a pool of dirty water. I saw there cups, plates. I was busy taking them out of the dirty water to wash them clean."

The associations that these dreams provoked were equally significant.

"Horses . . . many men . . . the minister of the Bantu Methodist Church . . . There are no good horses in town. The best are in the kraal. . . . The chief has wonderful white horses and seventy wives . . . it is good to dream of an old white lady. It means all the women help each other. It is good luck if the white people are good to us. The men in the kraal are too much naked. Even the chief. They should be ashamed of themselves." In connection with the second dream she said, "Trouble will come from a man. Someone wants to break into my house. I want to keep clean."

Encouraged by her associations, I guardedly gave her a tentative interpretation of the symbols, explaining to her that the house represented the female body; breaking into the house meant she was afraid a man wanted to violate her body. She protected herself by covering the hole. The straight firm flower in front of the house represented her desire to be a man herself. The snake with many heads, I told her, was a sign that many men were tempting her. This symbolism, I pointed out, was exactly the same as that in the story of Adam and Eve. Maggie did not protest against my interpretation that she did not want men to make love to her, and that was why she had made her father go away with the snake to the lake. "But why was I washing

291

the cups and plates?" Maggie asked. "Because," I explained, "you felt unclean and therefore were busy washing." On the whole she accepted my psychoanalytical interpretation of symbols quite readily.

Maggie, it became soon clear, had a secret of her own. But the compulsion to confess was not strong enough to overcome the feeling of shame. She began to stumble in her speech, the right words came with more difficulty, the periods of silence became longer. Then Maggie began to moralize. Unlike John, she had a strong sense of justice, of right and wrong.

"I think we shouldn't do it," she finally said, quite suddenly, following a train of thought. "It spoils our nation. What'll happen to our girls? Every girl is some man's sweetheart. John too has one. He used to sleep with me once a week; now not even once a month. But I don't really mind. John's too impatient when he wants it. I can wait . . . Funny, the girls who sleep for money are like men . . . impatient, quick . . . but they're fooling. The man thinks she wants him quick, but all she wants quick is the money."

I remembered Maggie's own affair with the mineworker in the early years of her marriage. I listened expectantly for a confession. But Maggie veered away, began to relate a dream.

"Me and another girl were walking in long grass, as high as the bed. The grass was moving without wind. John was coming to me. I ran away. The girl asked me why. I didn't know why. I found a hole, very clean, and meat was hanging. A young man opened the hole. The girl and I stood next to it. We asked for some meat. He gave it to us. We asked for some more. He gave it to us. Then I woke up."

I gave Maggie my interpretation of the dream. The girl and she were obviously both herself. The giving of the

292

meat symbolized her sexual relations outside of marriage. It was then that she told me about her intimacy with the mineworker when John was away in Kroonstad and, further, an earlier incident before her marriage.

"Did John know about this before you were married?"

"No." She smiled slyly. "The man never knows. He's stupid and in a hurry. But my mother found out and I was so ashamed."

"How did she find out? Did you confess?"

"Our mothers or grandmothers examine us every month to find out if we've got spoiled."

Maggie told me in detail how this was done. I reflected that the crude method served more effectively as a lie detector than as a reliable physical test of virginity.

Maggie was worried about her daughter, Isabel, now almost ten. Could I, she asked, advise her how to protect her from the filth of Blacktown? She watched the child, she said, talked to her, threatened her. I had the notion Maggie was putting the fear of God into her daughter. I cautioned her against overdoing it. Isabel might run away. I promised to talk the matter over with John. She was grateful. From now on I knew I would have no opposition from Maggie in carrying out my plans for educating John.

II

IT IS seldom possible to say with any exactitude what part of psychoanalytic treatment produces the desired change in a patient's personality and behavior pattern, what forces liberate inhibitions and infantile repressions. The how and why of cure remain intangible. It just happens. It is the analytic situation as a whole that contributes to it. Dramatic revelations are rare. Recovery is slow and imperceptible; it is not the concrete, tangible change that takes place before our eyes in recovery from bodily illness. Friends and relatives are the first to remark the change in the patient undergoing psychoanalysis; the doctor and patient are not seldom the last to perceive it. Only in retrospect can the doctor trace the steppingstones to recovery.

I often asked myself, was there any change in John? When had it occurred? How? I could never, during the course of our relationship, give an honest answer to these questions. I felt a change had taken place. John's friends felt it. Maggie was definite about it. John had stopped drinking and having women, she pointed out, and he brought money home now. He built a chicken yard in the tiny space between the latrine and the back door, started a vegetable patch in front of the house, with neat rows of pumpkins, tomatoes, cabbages, and carrots. Maggie herself was almost inspired to put up colored clay figures of a

294

lion, buffalo, and other animals at the front gate. It was a sentimental longing for the remembered brightness of beads and scarlet Kaffir bloom flowers of childhood. But such plants meant expense, and the little space before the gate remained bare and cheerless.

Everything looked especially dreary on the Sunday morning in September 1940 when, summoned by John, I came to Blacktown. I had just come through the noisome stretch of sewerage farms that adjoined the location. The stench was still in my nostrils when I was stopped at the high gates to Blacktown, and my entry permit was demanded by the uniformed black guards who stood there. No one — black or white — who did not live inside those spiked iron fences could enter Blacktown. I had refused, on principle, to procure the required permit, preferring to use my stethoscope as my passport; they could not, after all, keep out a doctor on his way to a patient.

In the dust and wind of that Sunday morning the dirty rows of brick houses, scattered in colorless uniformity along streets that bore no names, looked forlorn. The small square windows looked like the expressionless eyes children draw. Nothing to break the monotony; not a shop window, a building, a blade of grass. No pavements, no gardens. Broken taps leaked and made great ruts in the sandy streets. No one cared to repair them.

John was not at home. It was the third time in succession he had let me down. I was both annoyed and disturbed; was this a new relapse? The stuffy little room was full of people. N'Komo was there, Tshakada, Dhlamini, all John's new friends — educated, cultured Africans I had introduced to him. N'Komo was a sick man — he had been living for some weeks now with John. He reminded me of John's brother Amos, ingenuous, unworldly, sympathetic. He was

295

speaking gratefully about the work of the Eduletini Mission in feeding the Blacktown children of school age, left out of the government program of providing tuppence-a-day lunches in the schools. He began to read from the report of the Reverend Harthorne.

The head of the Mission had written: "It is a tremendous joy to see the children having some food. . . . It is hard to come to school on an icy morning with no food inside one, and no prospect of having anything to eat till Mother gets back from work late in the evening. . . ."

But Tshakada, a well-educated clerk in a law office, was less impressed. "I hope," he said bitterly, "the white people can visualize what Father Harthorne was describing, and I hope that this daily crucifixion of innocents will make them squirm."

N'Komo had a suggestion. The report should be reprinted in large numbers and sent to every white man. "Let them see what they are doing. When people see what's going on they respond generously." He had heard, he said, that when the white people got to know that triplets born in Slumtown were lying naked on the bare earth floor, they had taken care of them. It was ignorance, he added placatingly, that caused all this suffering.

"Ignorance, my foot!" came John's voice suddenly from the doorway. "The white man knows what goes on with us, but he runs away. His excuse is that the black child cannot suffer like the white one; that if you starve it, it will not die; that if you freeze it, it will not sicken; that if you beat it, it will not feel. Is it not true, Doctor?"

I nodded. He was only repeating, in his own words, what he had heard me say on the subject of white men's rationalizations.

"The white man," John continued, "knows what goes on

296

here and how bad it is with us, but he closes his eyes. How many of them come here to see how we live? I don't mean you, Doctor, or your friends. But the others; if they'd only say one word for us, to the government, everything could be different. I'm telling you, all the whites are against us.

"Do you want to know why I'm so late? I'll tell you. I came to the station in Benoni ahead of time to get my train home. But would the man give me a ticket when I asked for it? 'Shut up,' he yelled, 'there's no train for an hour yet.' Sure, I knew that, I told him, but I wanted to buy my ticket ahead of time and rest awhile on the bench till the train came. 'You Kaffirs get enough rest, lazy bastards,' he said, and slammed the window in my face. At 7:45 Europeans began to come up to the window for their tickets. Of course they got theirs first. Then just as the train came in, an old native woman and I finally got our tickets. But it was too late. The train pulled out before we could get on. I had to wait two hours for the next one."

John was tired, his eyes red-rimmed. But he was sober, serious. This fatigue differed from the exhaustion that used to follow the wild nights of drink and women. As he stood in the half-open door, the sunlight striking obliquely across the hawklike face, the hand clenched at his side, the erect figure surging forward, he looked like a seeker after something.

He had just come from a mission, he said, as he dropped down on the floor next to me.

"I've been busy these last few weeks," he said wearily, "trying to stop a fight. It is time to stop this fighting among our own brothers. Ah, Doctor looks surprised. Manyikas are good and clever people, the best people. But maybe others . . . Basutos, Shangaans, Zulus . . . Fingo, Xosa . . . maybe they are also good."

297

I had discussed tribal rivalries with John before. I had repeatedly tried to show him how necessary it was to submerge petty differences among the tribes in a unanimous effort to better their common lot. We talked about the policy in the mines of separating the workers into compounds according to tribe.

"Is it good or bad," John had asked me a few weeks ago, "this separation?"

Bad, very bad, I said — because it exaggerated tribal differences, perpetuated strife.

John had made no comment. He seemed merely to have wanted my opinion, perhaps to help him make up his own mind. Apparently my teachings on racial tolerance were beginning to bear fruit.

"I heard about this fight," John was saying, "from plenty of my patients from Vandi location. You know, Doctor, I go there, even though it's thirty miles. I have patients from everywhere now. This Vandi fight was going to be a real war — like the one between the Germans and the English — only this one is between Basutos and Shangaans. It began like this. A Basuto woman was found murdered, raped. Everybody knew it was a Shangaan who did it — because Shangaans are very bad people. And things were not so good already between the Basutos and the Shangaans. You see, at the last war dance, the Basutos danced very badly, and they say it was because the Shangaan witch doctors — they're very powerful, you know — bewitched the young Basutos. And the Basutos afterwards were the laughing-stock of all Vandi location."

He didn't care, John said, about this bewitching business and the war dances. What he wanted to do was to stop the fight that was coming. A war in the location would only help the whites, give them an excuse to clamp down on the Africans, and a lot of innocent people would suffer. Everybody knew that the police, instead of trying to prevent bloodshed, were actually doing everything to keep feeling high. Every day the dreaded pick-up van came, trapping beermakers and people who hadn't paid their poll tax. Everybody in Vandi was afraid all the time. The people had done all they could. The Vandi Native Advisory Committee had gone to the police and written to the Central Native Affairs Department about the situation. But who ever listens to black men in South Africa?

And so every day more and more Basuto warriors would come all the way to Blacktown to get luck-medicine from John against the great day. And then he had hit upon his great idea, to use his profession to prevent the coming bloodshed.

"It was hard getting into Vandi," John said, "but my friends managed to get me in. When word got around that I was there, many patients came. But I purposely refused to see anyone but young Basutos. Those, I asked for their dreams, Doctor, like you — and threw the bones and the horns. And I could see how much they wanted to fight. What I did was tell them, all of them, that their luck was against them, they'd better not fight. I told them the dead people were asking them to wait a little, their enemies are too strong now."

But in his anxiety to prevent the war, John overplayed his cards. The Basutos found they had all been given identical interpretations, noted that none of them had been charged the customary high fee. They became suspicious, and it was not long before they discovered John's motive. This medicine man from Blacktown was not even a Basuto, they said among themselves; he was a foreigner, and how could a foreigner understand the deep injury the Shangaans

299

had done them? Maybe he was a Shangaan spy! If he were, that meant the Shangaans were afraid. Then this was the very time to attack them!

John, though able through some of his devoted patients to prove his good will to the Basutos, could do no more with the warriors. He had, temporarily, to admit failure and go back home.

Back in Johannesburg he sought the counsel of some of the more able and educated of his friends. They gave him no help. Indeed they even ridiculed the whole project. What, they argued, did a single tribal fight matter in the over-all picture of black suffering?

"But they will kill each other!" John protested. "There'll be broken bones, blood will flow." He was determined to do what he could to stop it.

I interrupted John's story at this point to ask him why he had not come to me with his problem. He had not wanted to implicate me, he explained. My suspicion, however, was that he was afraid I would stop him from carrying out his purpose.

John finally found his solution — in a dream.

"Many women, half naked," he described it to me, "were dancing in a big, open space. Many Vandi women — the ones the mineworkers sleep with for money — were dancing and dancing, wildly, like in war dances. Then suddenly they disappeared, and there were other girls dancing. They looked like the same girls I've seen when I was with you, Doctor, at the Nazarenes', near Durban, doing religious dances. The girls in my dream kneeled down, and a man dressed in white with a long stick like the pictures in the Bible stood in front of them."

John, doing his own interpreting, said the Biblical figure was his father, who in the dream changed the bad Vandi

300

women into good ones. And it was these girls who should help him in his mission.

So, that same morning, John said, he again went to Vandi, this time to plead with the prostitutes there to induce the men who came to them not to fight. But they laughed at him. Sure, lots of men would die, they knew that. But there were always plenty of others. Besides, they liked a fight. It was exciting.

But John would not give up. The living had failed him; he would appeal to his dead, his *midzimu*. In the afternoon he would sacrifice the snow-white goat ready in his back yard. Let blood flow from its veins instead of from the veins of the men of Vandi.

John got up and went out to the back yard. I followed. I watched as he began to wash the goat, anoint it with a variety of colorful and malodorous concoctions. Helping him were two of the young disciples who were in training with him for the profession of *nganga*. None but *ngangas* were traditionally allowed to be present at the rites. John rationalized my presence by recognizing me as a medicine man, also; and my white skin, he added, would in any case safeguard me against the evil forces released from the goat in the course of the rites.

The goat was ready. Now arose the whisper of John's *mrem-mrem* intercourse with his *midzimu*. Ten minutes passed. Then from its long sheath of hide John drew the hereditary ritual knife, a rusty iron blade sharpened to a deadly point. While his assistants held the goat's head firm, John thrust the knife into the exact midpoint of the white throat, so dextrously that not a drop of blood was lost.

Now, while the blood drained into the vessel standing ready to receive it, there would be nothing for me to watch. I left, going into the house. There, deep in discussion, I found N'Komo, Tshakada and Dhlamini. The talk was all of the war, of course. I agreed that the news was not good but remarked that we would not lose because we could not afford to. But Dhlamini differed with me. He had heard the Germans would soon be in South Africa, that they were going to free the country from the Jews and the Indians and give their shops to the blacks.

"And you fools," interjected Tshakada furiously, "believe that rot? So — our local Nazis have suddenly discovered black Aryans? But don't worry, Doctor," he said, turning to me, "the white man always gives us what we don't want. We ask for food, beer. They give us pass laws. We seek freedom, brotherhood. They give us hatred."

Dhlamini had nothing to say. Tshakada was a fluent speaker, commanding an exceptional flow of language. His speech was calculated and well-reasoned. I always liked to listen to him.

2

"YOU ask me, Doctor, what are the African attitudes to the war and white people?" Tshakada went on. "Here is how an African writer, Dhomo, has put it. The tribal African is ignorant. He still is nationalistic and militaristic, in a certain way. He accepted defeat in his battle with the white man and regards the white man's dictatorship as a result of this defeat. But deep down there still glows in him the hope that someday, somehow, he will again try his strength against the European, and that a new Lobengula, a new Dingaan, will arise. An unconscious, childish wish, of course.

"The tribal African leads a Jekyll-and-Hyde existence.

302

In town he is a beggarly laborer, docile, foolish. He obeys with a childish smile his master, salutes him 'baas' or 'nkosi'; in short he is the beloved 'unspoiled nigger.' In his kraal, he is the dignified patriarch. Here he composes his songs, maintains his tribal traditions, and prays to his gods.

"Then there is the 'neither-nor' African, the one who is neither wholly African nor fully Europeanized. He is not sure of himself, not proud of his ancestry, his national institutions, his deities. He has lost his tribal communism. He tries to be individualistic and Christian. He follows the European blindly: the liberals, the missionaries, the philanthropists — good masters and benevolent administrators. Socialistic ideas, trade-unions, he dreads — like his masters. It's people like that who fall easy prey to the kind of Nazi propaganda we've just heard from Dhlamini. Any white man's word may become gospel.

"Then there is the new African. And I'm not ashamed to call myself such. We are a small group but our numbers are growing. If you want to know us, go to police headquarters — we're all in their files. We are organized workers and we try to understand the issues at stake, here and in the rest of the world. We want to create leaders, organize masses, establish contact with other colored people in Africa and in America.

"I know what I belong to and what belongs to me. The African worker strikes — the organized passive resistance — mass defiance of injustice — all of these are not incidents, but straws in the wind. What we want is simple enough — to take part in the destiny, in the shaping of our sunny South Africa. We're anti-nobody. We're not racialists. And we're ready to give every racial white minority full rights in South Africa. We are against violence and anarchy, but unfortunately our aims are deliberately misunderstood and misinterpreted."

Tshakada spoke with deep pain; the emotion with which he had expressed his feelings seemed to have exhausted him. Apologizing to me for monopolizing the conversation, he asked me what Europeans thought of Africans.

John, who had come in a few moments before, interrupted laughingly, "Doctor doesn't talk too much. He always listens, listens. You know, Tshakada, for months and months I would talk to him lying on the sofa and he would just say 'Yes' . . . 'Very interesting' . . . 'Tell me more . . . 'What do *you* think of it?' . . . It would make me so angry, so angry! I wanted to leave him so many times and never come back, so angry he made me with his silence. And I will tell you now," he went on, not realizing that he was defeating his own purpose of making me talk, "*I* will tell you what the white people say about us. They say we're no good, our brains will never be as good as theirs. We're babies. We just enjoy ourselves. 'Can't you see how happy they are?' the white people say of us. 'They even sing and dance.' Sometimes we get naughty. Then the white men spank us. We cry, they spank us more. Then we become bad children — dirty, unreliable. Am I right, Doctor? We are children to you white people, aren't we? Children you never want to see grow up."

3

MEANWHILE, the room had filled up. Now Maggie, bringing in a grass mat, darted away again to finish the preparations for the ceremony. On the open fire, the sacrificial blood was being slowly cooked. It would then

304

be cooled until it had congealed, then the ritual feast would begin.

When everything was ready, Maggie and the other women left with the children. Only men could participate in the ceremonies. To each of us was handed a metal tumbler of beer — I had prevailed upon John to omit the highly intoxicating *skokiaan* — and there were placed in the center of the circle of men sitting cross-legged on the ceremonial grass mat two large metal vessels. I watched as the others took from one vessel a lump of hard-cooked mealie-meal and, dipping it into the vessel of congealed blood, brought it up to their lips. I went through the motions but one taste of the noxious mess was enough. John understandingly excused me from further participation and I remained as a spectator while the tempo rose in a steady crescendo of religious ecstasy.

I cannot remember at what point I became aware of music being played somewhere near. But shortly after, John raised the curtain that hung before the bed-alcove and brought out a slim youngster of about seventeen or eighteen who was doing extraordinary things to a jazz melody on a tiny mouth-organ. Everyone seemed to know him. Cries of "Sunshine! Sunshine!" greeted him. Obviously he was a great favorite.

Sunshine made a remarkable impression on me. He was tall and slim, his shoulders square and broad. The eyes were black, large in his scarred face. I noticed particularly the long, slim-fingered hands of extraordinary grace.

The jazz melody died away in a delicate nuance of minor chords, and the sad, monotonous native music of the kraal filled the little room. I realized I was listening to a consummate artist. But the next moment Sunshine had put down the instrument and was enthralling his audience with a series of pantomimes and monologues. He was a group of Blacktown small fry shooting dice, he was a mob of gangsters, he was an enthusiastic young blood from the kraal setting out for the white man's city to win his fortune only to land in the inevitable jail. And then he was dancing, as good tap-dancing as any I had seen on the European or American stage.

It was a memorable afternoon for John and his friends. But in that same hour, while they were seeking to avert disaster for the people of Vandi, terrible bloodshed was already taking place in that location. It began, as John had feared, between the Basutos and the Shangaans, but it ended with a slaughter of both by the police. Just a cold-blooded slaughter.

306

III

AFTER the failure of his Vandi mission, John began to manifest increasing hostility, hostility directed not only against the outside world but against himself.

"I am so angry," he would reiterate continuously. "I was no good. No good. I should have been able to do something."

John's hostility manifested itself most strongly in his dreams. He dreamed incessantly during this period. It was understandable that he should. His emotional tension was unendurably high. He could not consciously lay the blame for his failure on me, on Tshakada, on his *midzimu*. So the bottled turbulence of hate and aggression found outlet in his dreams.

In one, John found himself on top of a big house. "I touched the grass roof with my burning cigarette. The house began to burn. I was on the roof. And all the people in the house burned to death. I tried to bring water in a big basin" (the usual concession to conscience), "but it did no good."

And, a few days later, "I dreamed I was in Blacktown, and all around was smoke. I didn't see anybody and I didn't know where I was going. I saw plenty of white goats, more than a hundred goats. And I went away with them. Then a white man came to buy the goats. But he took them away

307

without giving me any money. So I made the goats follow me back."

John gave a number of interesting associations, coming to the conclusion that the killing of the goat had been of no avail because it had been spoiled by the white influences; in the kraal, there might have been a chance. He neither accepted nor rejected my suggestion that he really meant the influence of my presence had spoiled it.

Another time he dreamed that Johannesburg was under water, all its buildings demolished. "People ran away," John related. "Only I was left." Here was the universal megalomaniac fantasy of the whole cosmos perishing save the "I."

"I came to my room," John went on, "and found Maggie and the children. I told Maggie I must go and look for the Doctor. I'm very worried about him. I went back to Johannesburg. All the buildings were there again, just as they always were, and I found you in your consulting room."

John, associating freely after narrating this dream, said, "The water . . . white stuff, a lot, coming out from me because I haven't slept with a woman for a long time. Broken buildings . . . big war . . . will kill everyone. Everybody ran away . . . terrible times are ahead."

Here again his sexual potency served as an expression of his aggressive strength to be used against the white world. His ambivalent feelings of love and hate toward me were clear in the fantasy of having first overwhelmed me along with the other whites, then of finding me safe again on his return to the city. Through me, too, he made restitution to the white world by finding the city restored.

Finally, he came out with a dream which pointed to an anxiety more concrete than the diffused aggression of his other dreams.

308

"I was in a kraal — not my own. There was a dead man who spoke to me saying he had a big boy in Blacktown. There was no woman there. He was drinking beer, but he told me I should not drink because I am from Johannesburg where nothing was pure. Then I met a man, Jacob, a white man, rich, who has a grocery store." ("Jacob" later proved to represent me.) "Then we were both riding motorcycles through very low grass until we reached two huts. There were no women there, only men. And the men took all the machinery out of my bicycle and burned the body of it in a fire. I took water and put the fire out. I felt lost and didn't know what to do. I begged them to give the machinery back. They said they didn't know where it was. But then they brought it back. Only it was no good. It didn't fit my bicycle. I woke up in fright."

Associating, John said, "The dead man's boy is Sunshine. His father died in 1933. Sunshine's real name is Jefferet. His mother is dead too."

He and Maggie, said John, loved Sunshine. They took him into their house and treated him like their own son. But Sunshine was spoiled, he wouldn't listen to them, he ran around with girls. He would get the sickness! And he coughed all the time; maybe his lungs were bad.

"I threw the bones and the shells for him. They showed he has a sickness in the chest. Also that Sunshine is not a good boy. Maybe he's been stealing. Something is very bad with Sunshine. Doctor, can you help him?" John appealed to me. "Do you like Sunshine?"

Of course I liked Sunshine, I told John. Sunshine was indeed a rare personality, an artist of infinite promise. Under other circumstances, he could have developed his rare gifts. I was pleased that John took this interest in the boy, not only for Sunshine's sake but because this constructive, positive activity was the best antidote for his sense of failure and the depression it produced.

John and Maggie followed with devoted care my instructions about Sunshine's health, making sure he took the vitamins and other medication I supplied them. John now began to initiate Sunshine into the mysteries of medicine. Sunshine·learned quickly, soon becoming a combination entertainer-disciple. And then he joined me and John in a study of the workings of the African mind. John and Sunshine submitted to their numerous patients a questionnaire I had devised investigating their attitudes towards death, God, hell, and heaven, sexual relationships such as masturbation, frequency, strength of libido, fidelity, perversions.

John interrogated the female patients himself. Sunshine dealt mostly with elderly men. On many occasions I was present myself, especially during the first few months of the study, for it was most important to make sure that the answers were not influenced. The work went on for six months, during which we investigated sixty subjects. The results were illuminating. The African apparently has no conception of heaven and hell. Prayers and churchgoing are to them abnormal; many of them thought of Christ as God's secretary. Their fear of death is less intense than the white man's. Sexually, the picture bears little resemblance to the popular conception of the potent, lustful black. Actually the endless taboos frustrate desire. Most of the women we questioned were frigid, and foreplay was almost unknown to the urbanized blacks.

At the same time I was seeing Sunshine privately, trying to help him with his own conflicts as well as his money difficulties. What I failed to do, however, was give sufficient attention to his serious physical state. True, I prob-

310

ably could have done nothing to delay the widespread tuberculous process. A few months before Sunshine's death, I disclosed to John how gravely ill the boy was. But John refused to accept the inevitable. Though acquainted now with the true nature of such diseases as tuberculosis, John reverted to his old belief in poison and attempted to combat the evil with his own magic. For two months John, and Maggie too, fought bravely for Sunshine's life. The urbanized African witnessing death and illness every day becomes inured to them. Moreover, having to fight inch by inch for his own existence, he seldom has enough energy to spare for others. Knowing this, it was an impressive experience to see John fighting for the youngster. For John to engage in a struggle for another individual showed how far his education in civilized human relationship had progressed.

This fight, though John did not of course realize it, was a step forward along the road he thought he had left after his failure in Vandi. When, soon after Sunshine died, John was faced with another battle, he was ready.

2

IN the first few years of the war, all the unemployed — black and white — were swallowed up by the army and the war industries, and there began an exodus from the kraal and Native Reserves of countless Africans seeking the fabulous new prosperity rumored to be awaiting them in the cities. They came, they found work, they earned wages, but there was nowhere to put their heads, no shelter for their children and their few miserable possessions. The Locations were already overcrowded beyond all possibility of absorbing any newcomers. The factories

311

had no compounds, as did the gold mines, where they could live. The government made no move to house the tremendous new population, much as it needed the labor. They let it go at hoping that somehow, somewhere, these thousands would squeeze themselves into the elastic limbo of the locations. Blacktown, soon overwhelmed by the influx, could hold no more. And government regulations, which had always forbidden blacks to build homes for themselves, were not relaxed even in the face of this emergency.

The need of the homeless was too great, too urgent. They could not wait until the ponderous machinery of government would begin to move, but took things into their own hands. Overnight, a mushroom growth of beaverboard, straw, packing cases and canvas shelters sprang up in the empty fields bordering on Blacktown. This was what came to be known as Shantytown.

How he came to be involved in the birth of Shantytown was something John was never able to explain to me. As usual, it was from his patients that he got wind of the goings-on. The idea that fellow blacks were about to take something and take it without fighting appealed tremendously to John. As he put it, "It is like getting what I want without a fight, without hurting anybody. The land was empty. The people got the things to build the houses out of from nothing." He was sorry he knew nothing about building, himself. At least, however, he could give them his blessing and good luck.

And so he went to a special place to dig *umdhlavini* roots, certain to bring luck to new settlers. It was of first importance, he said, to cover the hole after the roots were dug up, otherwise the foundations of the houses would collapse. He dreamed continuously about cities springing up overnight. This wish-fulfillment he interpreted as a sign from his *midzimu* that they approved.

In his zeal, John almost abandoned his family, leaving Maggie to deal with domestic problems at home while he busied himself with the graver issues of Shantytown. Disease flourished like a weed in the primitive conditions that prevailed there. There was no sanitation, no water, no lights. There was no protection against wind and cold and rain.

John was endlessly busy, sending to me daily messengers for supplies of cough medicines, laxatives, aspirin. But Maggie had little understanding of the political and social significance of Shantytown to John. She knew only that again he had abandoned her and the children. And then it was rumored that a girl named Liza, one of John's old sweethearts, was being seen with him all the time. I explained to Maggie that John's absorption in the fate of Shantytown was the best thing that could have happened now that he had lost Sunshine. At the mention of the dead boy's name, tears came to Maggie's eyes. She left the room and came back with a soiled envelope. On it I saw, written in Sunshine's hand, "To Doctor, from Jefferet." She had found it among his few belongings only a few days ago.

It was a pathetic little document. In it Sunshine had tried to tell what he had been too ashamed, while he was alive, to relate to me and John about his life. First he told about his childhood, how he had lost both his parents, how he had craved education.

At last came the incident he had kept hidden from us. It was at the beginning of the war that he was arrested on the accusation of having a perverted relationship with his white master. This man (whom I as well as the whole

European community knew to have made a practice of seducing the young black boys he liked to employ), it is true, had approached him, but he had refused to comply with his demands. Soon afterwards, when the white man was arrested and the young boys in his employ were haled in as witnesses, Sunshine told the police his story. But the white man was powerful, and had in the meanwhile succeeded in having the case quashed, then left the continent. Immediately pressure was put on Sunshine to withdraw his complaint, but he stubbornly refused. The white men prated about Justice. All right, he wanted Justice too. So that what happened then was something he would never understand. He obeyed the white man's law. He told the truth. But it seemed that they did not want the truth. Because when he insisted on telling it, they used every means to make him withdraw his statement, even beating him. Then they sent him away to a prison farm, where every day there were blows and bitter work and more blows. Finally he fell ill of pneumonia. And though, after he recovered, he managed to escape, he had never been well after that. He had come to Blacktown, living precariously as a fugitive, until John finally found him.

Poor Sunshine. Such an experience as his was unique, even for South Africa. Only now did his peculiar behavior in the months I knew him become understandable. He would never come to my house, as I so often had asked him, to entertain. Nothing John or I said could move him from his stubborn refusal to go into the hospital, even for X-rays of his chest. I explained it to myself at the time as some twist of his artist's personality, a neurotic phobia or obsession. John's explanation was that all Africans hated the hospital, that "death trap where patients were packed in like in the death house" (he meant the mortuary we had

314

once visited together), only, he added, the dead were allotted more space than the living.

But now I saw what very good and objective reasons Sunshine had had for keeping away from white men and their institutions.

Maggie, when I told her the contents of Sunshine's pathetic last testament, was baffled. She could not understand the perversion of Sunshine's white master that had been the cause of the tragedy. Nor could she understand why Sunshine should have insisted, at such cost to himself, on telling the police the truth.

"If the white man wants lies, why not tell him lies?" she queried. And she fell to accusing John and me.

"Jefferet," she cried, saying Sunshine's name in her soft Zulu speech, "shouldn't have died. He was sick with a white man's sickness. Only the doctors could have helped him. Doctor is no good lately. My heart is bad, and you don't bring me any medicine. My heart is not poisoned by *abathakathi*. Jefferet's lungs weren't poisoned either. The white man gave the disease to me and to him, and the white man must cure. White people will kill us all one day!"

I did not argue. Indirectly, Maggie might have been right.

To distract her, I suggested that we go to Shantytown to see John. She was delighted. We had no difficulty finding John there. Everybody seemed to know the *nganga* preacher, as they called him. John was glad to see us, genuinely glad. But he did not say much to Maggie, so eager was he to consult me about the problems that faced him here.

"What's happening to our people? Please explain, Doctor. They are fighting each other again. Not properly, but with words, at the meetings. They shout at each other. It is because we have no proper chief. In the kraal, too, when the chief is away, the people are also fighting. Now they have broken up into two camps, the Sofasonke Party and the Vigilance Committee. Each wants to be in charge. And now the City Council and the Blacktown Advisory Council threaten to close us down. They refuse to talk to any of the committees.

"But how can we run a town without a council? I called for Tshakada. He came — a few days ago. He is a great friend of Ngubana, the founder of Shantytown. Tshakada is so clever, Doctor. He called all the people together, and after he explained everything properly, they agreed to stop quarreling. We made a new committee with four people from each part, and Ngubana as chairman. Some stupid people even shouted that the *nganga* preacher should be on the committee. I wish I could be like Tshakada.

"For two weeks everything was okay. We opened a little shop and some white people brought us goods. You know there are many white people who are good to us now. We built better houses, arranged a little school. More *ngangas* came. I gave the people that were really sick your medicines. But then other people started to come from Blacktown, to make trouble. The police began to arrest our best people here. That's why Tshakada never slept a single night in Shantytown, saying that Dhlamini — you remember, he spoke for the Germans that day in my house — was doing dirty work. What does it mean, Doctor, 'dirty work'?"

I explained what it meant, adding that traitors were found everywhere.

John was worried now. Should he stay here or give up what was surely a lost cause? I explained to him that much more was at stake than he realized in this spontaneous attempt of his people to fight constructively for their rights.

316

I advised John to remain in Shantytown as long as he was needed.

But we reckoned without Maggie. While we were talking, she had been doing some sleuthing on the subject of Liza, whom rumor reported to be one reason for John's staying in Shantytown. And now, as we finished our discussion, she came in, her chin stubborn, her eyes determined. John must come back to Blacktown, and immediately. She would not stir from the spot, she said, until he and his belongings were back at home in Blacktown. John was not as upset as he would once have been.

Almost humorously, he turned to me saying, "What shall I do with that woman?" But he ended by doing as she demanded. He reassured me, in an aside, that he would be coming back in a few days.

The Africans have a saying, "Only the *midzimu* know what tomorrow brings." There are other possible reasons why they refuse to make plans for the morrow. This attitude can be traced psychologically to the native method of child-rearing. But chiefly, it develops because the African is too much at the mercy of the white man's caprice to make any kind of planning for the future of value.

From the very Sunday of his return to Blacktown, John could not, dared not, leave his house, let alone Blacktown.

3

JOHANNESBURG'S white community was suddenly swept by mass hysteria, provoked by a recent crime wave. Every kind of crime, whether against property or life, petty or serious, was laid at the door of the blacks. It was true that more criminal acts were committed by black than by white offenders. But that was only to be expected in a population where blacks made up 80 per cent of the total. Obviously, since they also made up the most impoverished and depressed stratum and suffered more from the dislocations brought on by the war, they would provide a greater proportion of lawbreakers. Actually, however, the average black is a law-abiding citizen.

As Tshakada once pointed out to John, "If the whites were herded together the way we are in these slums, and had, like us, to watch half of all the children born die of starvation and disease, there would have been blood flowing in revolution long ago, let alone a few cases of stealing."

In the frenzy that had seized the Johannesburgers, every African was looked upon as a criminal. How else explain the enormity of arresting — as they did — ten thousand African men and women in one day, their only crime, in most cases, black skin? Letters to the editors of the newspapers recommended lynching. Especially savage were the remarks about returned black soldiers (who had, incidentally, volunteered), accused of "spoiling" their fellow men. Race riots broke out sporadically all over the city.

It was especially important now for every black to have his papers in order, his taxes paid. John had always been slow to pay his taxes; now he refused, altogether.

"Why should I pay my poll tax?" he demanded of me. "Where does the money I pay go? For us? No! For the police, for the prisons, for the magistrates! I heard that our country uses more money for prisons and less for schools than any other country in the world. We are foolish. We should all stay at home — not fighting, not being cheeky — but just not work and not pay taxes as long as they go on arresting us and beating us up."

It was no time for me to argue. I merely pointed out to

318

John that at the moment his people needed him desperately; he would do them no good shut away in prison, no matter how righteous his cause. I paid his tax arrears myself and, for his protection, registered him officially as my servant. I warned him to stay inside the house as much as possible, never to be out at night, and to ring me daily that I might know he was safe. Luckily he escaped the madness unscathed.

But as the days passed, John became more and more depressed. He began to talk about going back to his home in Manyikaland, where, he said, black people fared better. As it happened, his people wanted him to return home. He remembered now that a Manyika recently arrived in Johannesburg had brought him the news that his sister Junia was very sick with eye trouble, that Amos was in a hospital in Salisbury — they said his brain was no good — and Patrick, his eldest brother, was having a lot of trouble with his second wife. Charlie, the man had said, was so old that he could not see patients any more. But his cousin Nathan was very lucky with his family, his money, and his school; he was only teaching now, having dropped altogether the profession of *nganga*.

True, mused John, they didn't pay as good wages in Rhodesia as in Johannesburg, and there was a drought in Manyikaland; but at least one's life was safe there. In his enthusiasm, John saw everything as wonderful in Manyikaland. The white man was kinder now to the blacks since the war. Why, the English in London had even sent money to help the Manyikas! They had opened new schools; perhaps now every child would soon be able to go to school.

"Why," asked John of no one in particular, "did I stay here all these years, wasting my time and health? When I think about it, it makes my heart sore. It's all Maggie's

319

fault. When I wanted to go and live in my own country, she wouldn't. She said she was afraid to go to a strange country where maybe my people would dislike her and make her — with her lame leg and bad heart — work in the fields."

Here he was in daily danger, he continued. His *midzimu* had warned him of it, as evidenced by the dreams he was having.

"I was walking with other men. I had an ax, a chopper. Then three white people came up to us. They were looking for a black man that was eating a white in the street. While I was talking to them I saw myself undressed. I wanted to go back home but I lost my way. Then there were four horses, a saddle on each horse, but no riders. I ran away, then a very big dog chased me. When I finally came home, I found there three men dressed in white. They came to arrest us all."

The associations John had with this dream revealed clearly that he suffered from a great sense of failure. Finding himself naked was a typical failure-dream. The ax he carried symbolized anger and aggression, but this was frustrated by his sense of inferiority to the white men. The horses he associated with the Four Horses of the Apocalypse.

John was now a deeply disappointed man who had lost faith in himself and others. The Vandi failure, the death of Sunshine, the failure of Shantytown, Dhlamini's betrayal, and now the mass arrests — all these were certainly sufficient to break a stronger spirit than John's. I did not discourage him from returning to Manyikaland. And so he began to plan for his final return to his ancestral home. But, like so many of John's plans, this one too came to nothing.

For something of great significance was brewing among

320

the blacks in Johannesburg. Nothing concrete had emerged yet, but the beginnings were there and John was daily becoming more and more aware of them. At first there were minor stirrings.

One day John would see a procession of ragged Africans straggling down Eloff Street singing a song of defiance against the pass laws. Or he would read in the newspapers of strikes breaking out among African workers in various parts of the country in spite of the hated Emergency Regulation 145 forbidding Africans to strike. He guessed that the strikes were minor, but they won the natives at least a slight increase in wages or a decrease in hours. But what chiefly captured John's imagination was the steadily gaining momentum of a passive resistance movement. Feeling was running so high that it made him think, he told me once, of the Manyika mountain freshets coursing down in the spring, swelling with the seasonal rains until an angry flood overwhelmed the land.

John came to me to talk again and again about what was going on. This idea of passive resistance was not new to him, he said, but what made it so exciting now was that he was seeing it actually put into practice by his own people.

"You see, Doctor," he said, "everything is very simple. Whenever the white man demands of us what we cannot possibly do, we won't say anything; we'll just do as little as we can. We won't spoil their machines or anything like that, the way some foolish people say we should do. No. We'll come to work but do as little as possible."

The idea of fooling the white man seemed to appeal to John as much as any actual benefit that might be derived from these tactics.

"What about going back home, John?" I asked him.

"That can wait. Better times are coming here now. Is it

321

true, Doctor, I heard the Germans are finished? People say it will be much better for the blacks, too, now. My friend Simon told me, when we passed by the big hospital on the main road built for the soldiers, it will be given to us Africans now."

And so John would go on, fantasying the glorious possibilities the future held here in the city, just as only a short while ago he had been fantasying the prosperity and happiness that awaited him in Rhodesia.

When rumors began to crop up that a big bus boycott was about to begin in Nandi township, John decided to go there and be on the scene when things began to happen, just as he had not long before gone to Shantytown.

Nandi township was the largest of the locations around Johannesburg. About twenty thousand of its inhabitants — roughly a fourth of the population — made the fifteen-mile trip into Johannesburg daily by bus to get in to their work. The municipal buses did not service Nandi township, since it was outside the city limits. The bus concession was held by a private company, which charged the blacks a penny more than the fare paid by whites. So miserable was the income of the average black who made this daily round trip that the fare represented fifteen per cent of his total earnings.

But in the last winter of the war, the bus company, on the pretext of increased expenses, raised the fare on the Nandi bus line still another penny, on holidays twopence. In the weeks before this change went into effect, the people of the township warned the company officials that they would refuse to pay the additional fare; they threatened to boycott the bus line and walk to Johannesburg if they had to, rather than submit to such an outrage. The distance was fifteen miles; the owners thought it inconceivable that the

Nandi women would make that trip with clothesbaskets on their heads, that the men, after working ten long hours at their factory benches, would walk that distance home. But it was no empty threat. For this is exactly what the people of Nandi did, day after day, for five weeks — walk the fifteen miles to Johannesburg and, at the end of a hard day's work, fifteen miles back. They had to get up at three o'clock in the morning to arrive at work on time. They did not get back home before nine or ten in the evening. But to the last man they persisted until the company had to admit defeat and restore the previous fare.

But in this ordeal, the people of Nandi needed all the support of their fellow men. And among them no one gave more generously and sincerely than John. He was no more merely a *nganga* to give them what inspiration they could derive from his shells and bones and herbs. John by now had become an effective propagandist. He addressed small groups (assemblies of more than ten natives were forbidden by the authorities throughout South Africa), pointing out the dangers of violence, which would lose them the sympathy of the many whites who for once stood solidly behind them. He was vigilant in his watch against such fifth columnists as Dhlamini had proved to be in the Shantytown episode. And when victory was finally won, the first in John's experience, he felt it as his own personal achievement.

4

ALTHOUGH this victory did little to lighten the black man's burden as a whole, still John felt that the picture for the future held some promise of better things to come. And when I came, in August 1945, to say good-by to him before leaving for a visit to America, he was not despondent at my departure as he had been when once before I left Africa. He merely asked me to tell the people in the United States, especially the Negroes, how it was with his people in Africa, how alone, how isolated they were in their misery, with no one in the world to appeal to.

We sat in the familiar little room of John's house in Blacktown, neglected and poverty-stricken, Maggie ill in bed, the children sad-eyed. But John did not see these things; he was looking beyond to a new vision — a bond with his people in America.

I understood how important this new hope was to John, and I promised I would do what I could to realize it.

And thus it was that this story, which was to have been about John, the subject of a psychoanalytic study, to be read by a limited number of scientists, became the story of John the man, written to be read by everyone.